AMERICAN CATHOLIC HORIZONS

AMERICAN CATHOLIC HORIZONS

Edited by Eugene K. Culhane, S.J.

1966

Doubleday & Company, Inc., Garden City, New York

Nihil obstat: John A. Goodwine, J.C.D.
            Censor Librorum

Imprimatur: ✠ Terence J. Cooke, D.D., V.G.
            Archdiocese of New York
            January 6, 1966

CONTENTS

INTRODUCTION

The editors of *America* are pleased to offer in book form these articles chosen from the pages of *America*. The articles have been selected as representing the best and most typical of what appeared in the four-year span, 1961–1965.

Those years saw great happenings in the history of the United States and even more epoch-making events in the history of the Church. The three productive years of President Kennedy's Administration and the opening of that of President Johnson found the country grappling with a hundred new moods, problems, and challenges—in its domestic policies and foreign affairs, in education, philosophy, social welfare, and, increasingly, interracial relations. Similarly the twilight of Pope John's reign and the dawn of the age of Pope Paul brought—with the first three sessions of Vatican Council II—unforeseeably sweeping changes in the quality of Catholic thought and worship.

Obviously any selection will pass over articles that certain readers may recall as especially significant. "How could they possibly not have included such and such?" they will ask. We are aware that any choice is, in the most literal sense, arbitrary. Our hope is that, after reading the collection, our friends will recognize in it something really representative of the spirit of those years.

EUGENE K. CULHANE, S.J.
Managing Editor, *America*

SECTION I

GOD, MAN AND THINGS

THOMAS E. CLARKE
The World Is Already Christic

¶Christian secularity finds positive values outside the institutional
Church

Ecumenical Councils tend to survive in popular history in some
word or phrase that encapsules their contribution to the ongoing
life of the Church. The mention of Nicaea evokes the famous
homoousios; Florence, reconciliation; Trent, justification; Vatican
I, papal infallibility. As Vatican II approaches its final session,
many will be inclined to speculate on future history's image of it.
Will the word be *ecumenism?* Or *collegiality? Religious freedom?
The people of God?* Or the triad of *self-realization, self-reform,
dialogue,* with which the two Popes of the Council designated its
goals? I would venture the guess that, important as all these aspects
are, Vatican II may well live in history as the Council in which
the Church inaugurated the age of *Christian secularity.*

The very suggestion may be startling to some. Apart from communism, has not secularism been the chief target of Popes and
bishops during the past several decades? Are we not confronted
today, particularly in the United States, with a progressive and
almost systematic effort to exclude religion from significant influence on our national life, specifically in the area of education?

Yet pure error without at least a dash of profound truth is rare,
and it has frequently happened in the Church that a period of
rejection of heresy is quickly followed by the gradual assimilation
of the truth embedded in the error. May we not interpret the
warnings against secularism of earlier years as a necessary preparation for the eventual endorsement of Christian secularity?

At this point the reader may quite legitimately be asking for a
distinction between secularism and secularity. Later in this article
I hope to oblige (at least to some degree). But for an initial
image of Christian secularity and its opposite, I would propose
the following rather oversimplified example. Over a decade ago,

like countless visitors in Rome, I was startled by the sign *"Banco di Spirito Santo."* My first reaction was one of amusement: "Isn't this just like the Italians?" There quickly followed, as I recall, a feeling of approval: "Finding God in all things," "a thoroughly Christian atmosphere in the whole of life," were a few of the comments that came to mind. Today, however, the memory of the sign and of my reaction to it somewhat embarrasses and chagrins me. Today I feel: A bank is a bank is a bank. It is not a church. It is a place for money and finance, not for devotion. There are surely enough churches in Rome whose names may honor the Holy Spirit.

However homely and even trivial, the example may serve to raise the issue: Is my present attitude secularistic? Or does it represent a legitimate Christian secularity? And if banks are to be stripped of Christian labels, why not political parties and (to be trivial again and closer to America) breads and wines and hotels and aspirins and cough medicines? But then—what of hospitals and welfare organizations? More delicately still, what of schools and learning? Should we not also say: A poem is a poem is a poem; or, an atom is an atom is an atom, and leave the non-religious aspects of education and scholarship unembarrassed by religious preoccupations?

One of the most deeply rooted attitudes of modern man is his refusal to see his cherished human values captured or manipulated by forces and institutions he considers extraneous, whether it be by party-line communism or party-line Christianity. To what extent should the Church accommodate herself to this tenacious mentality? And to what extent is it a matter not merely of pragmatic accommodation (which frequently breeds even deeper resentment), but of a real exigency of the gospel, that human institutions be permitted a larger autonomy in Christian thought and action than they have enjoyed in the past?

The dilemma confronting Christian man today may be expressed as follows: He is, on the one hand, deeply convinced that the Incarnation profoundly touches human (and cosmic) life in all its aspects; for him it is inconceivable that any area of human endeavor should be unaffected by the gospel. On the other hand, he knows from history and perhaps from his own life that a too facile or imperialistic "baptizing" of human values ultimately serves neither these values nor Christianity. Is there not some way that the world can be fully Christ's world without violence being done to its very *Weltlichkeit?*

It is curious and doubtless providential that two movements of modern Christian thought, at first glance contradictory, are today coming into vital confrontation in our effort to adopt a new Christian posture before the world and its values. For the sake of a name, we may identify these currents with the labels of *immanence* and *secularity*.

The first movement, reaching back to Maurice Blondel at the turn of the century, was a reaction against a certain dichotomy between natural and supernatural, between the human and the Christian. For over half a century now, through the sometimes risky and always tentative gropings of such thinkers as De Lubac, Von Balthasar and Karl Rahner, the insistence has been on the *unity* (rather than the distinction) of natural and supernatural orders, the *immanence* of the Christian in the human (rather than its transcendence of the human). The openness of nature to grace, a certain exigency in existential man for the gift of grace, a radical orientation of all men to the vision of God—such are the key affirmations of this current of ideas. It has more than a merely technical theological importance. For, in a most profound way, it strikes at the very roots of secularism, by maintaining the orientation of all human values not merely to God but to the Christian supernatural. It is one of the principal reasons why the Christian of tomorrow will find it impossible to think of his Christianity as a glossy finish sprayed on the natural surface of human life. *Nil humanum alienum* and *ta panta en to Christo*—will be inseparable from his vision of Christ.

But the movement of immanence, if it answered a real need, also ran a real risk—the risk of a regression to a certain Augustinianism, which would so enclose natural and temporal structures within the Christian destiny of man as to deprive them of their inherent autonomy and consistency. The danger was perceived by many, and has been met by a movement of quite a different tenor, which still needs to be better integrated with the movement of immanence. This is the movement of Christian secularity. It has been gaining momentum in the last few decades.

Secularity is by no means new in modern Christian thought. Three decades ago, Jacques Maritain gave it powerful and distinctive expression in his remarkable *True Humanism*. He held up for the coming age the ideal of a Christendom (a term that today is expendable) that would not represent, as did the Middle Ages, a *consecration* of the temporal order and its *instrumentalization* for spiritual goals, but would rather aim at a refraction of the gospel in the world that would be secular in character, i.e., that would leave to the created and the temporal a certain status of autonomy that they lacked in the Middle Ages.

Much of what Maritain said may need revision today, but the basic insights were truly prophetic and are now finding many echoes in Christian thought. It is noteworthy that Karl Rahner, whose conception of the "supernatural existential" is the most prominent contemporary formulation of the movement of immanence stemming from Blondel, has also been in the forefront of those calling upon the Church to recognize that her medieval stance toward the world is no longer possible. He and many others have pointed out, for example, that it was Christianity that denuminized the forum and the market place, so that men might pursue their human tasks without being haunted by intruders from the upper world. His insistence on the "diaspora" situation of Christians today is too well known to need elaboration here.

Other Catholic thinkers have been writing in this vein. The Dominican Père Chenu has recently asked whether and in what sense the phrase *consecratio mundi*, despite its occurrence in modern papal documents, is an appropriate one to describe the layman's function with respect to the world. Another prominent Dominican, Fr. E. Schillebeeckx, in his essay "The Church and Mankind" (in the volume of the same name in the Paulist *Concilium* series), moves in a similar direction. On one specific aspect of the Church-world confrontation, that of religious freedom and Church-State relationships, it has been the effect of the contribution of Fr. John Courtney Murray to show that we are *not* reduced to choosing between a sacralistic and a secularistic solution.

Among Protestants a very influential movement, which stems from the writings of Dietrich Bonhoeffer (executed by the Nazis in 1945) and finds its chief popularizer in Bishop John Robinson, whose *Honest to God* and other publications currently have English Christians excited, has called for a secular version of Christianity in tones that have shocked many people. More recently, Paul Van Buren's *The Secular Meaning of the Gospel* and Harvey Cox's *The Secular City* show that the movement is by no means confined to the other side of the Atlantic. One of the tantalizing things about evaluating such writings is the difficulty of discerning where pastoral and apologetic adaptation stop and doctrinal innovation begins.

But enough of mere description of current theological trends. What is being proposed here under the rubric of Christian secularity? And how does it differ from secularism? Let me say at once that the following remarks are not intended as a definition of secularity. Probably we are in need of a few more decades of experience of it in actual life before we can adequately define it. Nevertheless, a few points of a descriptive nature may render the idea less vague.

First, Christian secularity excludes *instrumentalization*. The goodness of the creature (and not merely its non-evilness), of the world, of time and temporal institutions, is a central conviction of Christian secularity. Any *purely* instrumental approach to the world —that is, any attitude that would see in it merely a tool for Christian evangelization, that would neglect its innate values, its own immanent dynamisms and finalities—is incompatible with Christian secularity. The world is to be taken seriously. As Fr. Robert Johann has put it: "Whatever ultimate meaning life may have . . . life is a call to share in the world's making" (AM, 2/27, p. 287).

Secondly, Christian secularity excludes *sacralization*. This must not be misunderstood. The distinction between the *sacred* and the *secular* is beyond question. There is an area of man's life that is necessarily withdrawn (though not isolated) from his temporal concerns. In heaven the distinction will cease; God will be all in all, and the tension between man's commitments to the world and to God will have ceased. But as long as he is in this life, Christian man will need to express and confirm his transcendence of the temporal and the worldly by creating a realm of the sacred. Liturgy, or, to use Josef Pieper's term, celebration, is the heart of this realm of the sacred.

But it is one thing to affirm the distinction of the sacred and the secular, and something else again to deny all Christian and salvific value to the non-sacral areas of human life, or to approach the secular with the attitude that unless it is sacralized it is somehow lost or at least irrelevant to the Christian destiny of man. It is here

that modern theology gives us an immense advantage over the man
of the Middle Ages. For him, it was only the presence of the
institutional and sacramental Church that rescued the world from
its sinful condition, or at least brought the world, conceived as a
neutral reality, within the sphere of the holy. For Francis Xavier,
the ancestors of the pagans he evangelized were lost, because only
the presence of the baptizing Church made salvation possible. More
broadly, only the formal consecration (not to speak of exorcism)
of the temporal gave it salvific status.

Today, we realize that the theology underlying such convictions, though correct in its insistence on the universal necessity of
Christ and the Church for salvation, was not correct in some of the
inferences it drew. Today, while we still realize that there is no
salvation *apart from* Christ and the Church in the full scope of
their presence and activity, we are aware that there is salvation for
men and institutions *outside* the institutional, sacramental Church.
We realize, too, that the world, as set over against the Church, is
not necessarily to be conceived as a hostile or merely neutral force.
By the Incarnation, by the cross and resurrection, the world is
already Christic and ecclesial in its dynamic orientation. Its Christianity is, in Rahner's now famous term, *anonymous*, but it is real.
To quote Fr. Schillebeeckx: "In the plan of salvation, the concrete
world, by definition, is an *implicit Christianity;* it is an objective,
non-sacral but saintly and sanctified expression of mankind's communion with the living God; whereas the Church, *qua* institution
of salvation, with her explicit creed, her worship and sacraments,
is the direct and sacral expression of that identical communion"
(*The Church and Mankind*, p. 84).

Even from this sketchy presentation, one may see the implications
of such a theology for the Christian's attitude toward the world—
and toward the Church. The world is not so much to be consecrated, captured, given meaning and salvific relevance. Rather it is
to be recognized, endorsed, brought to fulfillment. Also, if the
world is, in a true sense, the undisclosed Church, the Church in
her turn is the world fulfilled and manifested. In St. Augustine's
beautiful phrase: "The Church *is* the world reconciled." She is
not only the sign of Christ but the sign of the world—*sacramentum
mundi*.

From all this it may be seen that Christian secularity is not
merely to be distinguished from secularism; it is at the opposite

pole from it. Where secularism maintains that religion and Christianity are irrelevant for the world, Christian secularity insists that the world itself, even prior to its contact with institutional Christianity, is inescapably religious and Christian. Indeed, Christian secularity may run a greater risk of being a neo-sacralism than of being secularistic. The balance between these two extremes is a most delicate one. Even in such a champion of the world as Teilhard de Chardin there are passages (such as the one in which he says that the only reason he came to China was that he might preach the "great Christ" in Paris) that could appear to succumb to instrumentalism and sacralization.

Of the many possible ramifications of this view of the Church and the world, only one may be touched on here: the role of the laity in an era of Christian secularity. Among many others, Maritain, Rahner and, in a more pragmatic way, John Cogley, have warned against conceiving the lay apostolate as merely the secular arm of the institutional Church. Certainly there is in the Church a variety of instrumental roles—from parish catechist to member of a secular institute—for those of the laity who wish to participate in the hierarchy's task of formal evangelization. But the layman's primary role as Christian and therefore as apostle must be simply his active, Christian, witnessing presence in and to the world through his performance of the tasks of the world.

A host of other questions are raised by this idea of Christian secularity: Does it throw a theoretical light on the current debates over Catholic schools and over the presence of the Church on secular campuses? Will it reduce our emphasis across the board on Catholic organizations in favor of greater participation by Catholics in the secular counterparts of these organizations? One thinks, for example, of some recent differences of opinion regarding the Peace Corps as compared with Catholic lay missionary organizations. What of the nature and role of religious men and women in a Church characterized by secularity? Should religious (who, as religious, are not members of the clergy) reinterpret their embracing of the evangelical counsels in such a way that, while still to be distinguished from the members of secular institutes, they are less removed from the world and the secular quest? Or, on the contrary, in an era in which the Christian role of the laity and of the secular institutes in the world will be stressed, should religious withdraw from some of the active roles they have assumed in the modern Church?

It would be a mistake, I feel, to seek a solution to such questions merely in terms of theology. Actual Christian experience in the years ahead will help to disclose what is possible and valuable, and what is not. But, in turn, this experience needs to be guided and stimulated by the fruits of theological reflection. More concretely, it is now to the closing session of Vatican II that we look, with the well-founded hope that Schema 13, in its final form, will provide us with our primary guidelines for the coming era of Christian secularity.

EUNICE DE SOUZA
Christian India

¶Past and present show how missionaries can adapt to native culture patterns

Christianity in India is as old as Christianity itself. Firm tradition holds that, as far back as 52 A.D., the Apostle Thomas came to South India, motivated possibly by knowledge of the Jewish communities established there. Not much is known of his early activity; he was apparently quite successful, however, for many of his converts were men of position in Hindu society. This group, which adopted the rites of the Syrian Christians, was a vital one, and it was constantly reinforced by waves of colonists from the churches of Persia and Mesopotamia, until it grew into a flourishing community. For more than a thousand years the Church in South India continued undisturbed by changes from outside.

In 1498 came the Portuguese, searching, as Vasco da Gama is supposed to have said, for "pepper and souls." In the wake of the merchants came missionaries—full of zeal, but with neither an understanding of the people they met nor imagination enough to see any need of understanding. Failing to understand the Eastern rites of the Thomas-Christians, and suspecting them of being influenced by the Nestorian heresy, the Portuguese decided to impose the Latin rite. Accordingly, the Chaldean Patriarch was discharged and a Portuguese bishop installed in his place. Very naturally, the Indian Christians protested against this infringement of their identity. They felt, moreover, that their traditional rites and services were far more suitable to the Indian mind than the more formal Roman ritual. When their protestations were ignored, the Thomas-Christians turned in despair to schism.

Unfortunate, too, was the Portuguese method of handling converts from Hinduism. The missionaries felt that if the new Christians were to achieve lasting results, they should make a complete break with their past, and a plan of systematic Europeanization was put into effect. Henceforth, converts were required to imitate their foreign masters in their style of dress, the food they ate, and their general way of life. Family names were changed. All this had the advantage of enabling the Christians to move easily in two cultures, but the plan also had major detrimental repercussions. The Brahmins, members of the highest level of the Hindu socio-religious system and traditionally the guardians of Indian culture, began to despise the Christians; the latter, by eating beef and intermarrying with the Portuguese, had violated the code of physical and spiritual purity central to the philosophy of caste. No orthodox Hindu could run the risk of losing his caste by association with either the missionaries or the Christian converts. Christianity, moreover, came to be regarded as something European and alien; as the centuries passed by, it was associated with colonialism. In the last analysis, Christianity seemed incompatible with Indian culture.

St. Francis Xavier's coming to Goa in 1542 marked a new era in the evangelical activity of Catholic missionaries. This disciple of Ignatius of Loyola was at once sensitive, sensible, courageous and concerned. His willingness to respect new ideas and customs was a welcome change from the arrogance of earlier missionaries, who had dismissed the Hindu deities as repulsive, the mythology as ridiculous, and the ritual as unpardonably superstitious. Determined to use only love and tolerance, he presented a striking contrast to his predecessors, who in pursuing their objectives had not hesitated to use threats and force.

His methods were immediately successful. Those who had formerly been alienated now felt they were accepted on a footing of reciprocal tolerance. Everywhere along the southwest coast of

India, people received him with joy, and many thousands requested baptism.

St. Francis Xavier was followed, in 1606, by another Jesuit missionary, Robert de Nobili, who was equally brilliant and farsighted. It soon became apparent to him that the overwhelming majority of the converts belonged to the lower castes, and he made it his life's work to win back from the Brahmins and other high-caste Hindus that respect for Christianity which had been lost through the dubious tactics of the Portuguese pioneers.

With the approval of his superiors, De Nobili learned the local Southern languages as well as Sanskrit, the language of the Hindu sacred books, or Vedas. He then proceeded to Madurai, a great center of Hindu culture, and began to live as a Hindu *sannyasi*, a holy man who fasted and prayed and taught. His food was the simplest: rice, herbs, milk. With extraordinary perceptiveness, he explained the concepts of Christianity in terms of the Vedic teachings, and many Brahmins were attracted to Christ.

De Nobili and the group of young Jesuits who joined him were vigorously criticized for their progressive methods. He certainly was far in advance of his times, and missionaries can learn from him today. After 19 centuries of evangelical activity, the Catholic population of India amounts to only one per cent. If they are to advance the cause of Christ in India, it is to De Nobili, to his disciple John de Britto, and to St. Francis Xavier that they must turn.

One would be wrong, of course, to judge the impact of Christianity in India merely by its numerical strength: the Christian influence has been more effective than the mere numbers would indicate. Nevertheless, if the Church wishes to prosper, her missionaries must learn how to adapt and accommodate themselves more effectively to the milieu in which they are placed. The trend of Indian thought makes this the only feasible approach.

From time immemorial in India, the search for God has been the essence of the traditional way of life. The impact of industrialization, however, has raised the question of the adaptability of Hindu concepts to changing patterns of thought and society, and indeed of their very validity for modern man. Forward-looking Indians are now concerned with constructing a broad-based society built on free choice and not on birth, its structure uninfluenced by social and political ideas deriving from religion, caste or tradition. Now is the opportunity for missionaries to show that Christianity is compatible with Indian concepts and Indian aspirations. Now is the time to show that the catholicity of the Church is not something merely theoretical, but a living reality that has meaning for the Indian people.

A beginning has been made. Catholics in India—priests, religious and laymen—have responded to the need for adaptation to rapidly changing circumstances. Already they are making adjustments in terms of philosophy, art and liturgy so that Christianity in India may become a composite expression of Indian and Christian life.

Most significant of all is the question of intellectual adaptation. Hindu philosophy, which is known as Vedanta, is profoundly occupied with the Supreme Being; at the same time, and perhaps for this very reason, it denies the substantial reality of the world. In very ancient times, Hinduism gave mankind one of the most penetrating of all definitions of God: Absolute Being, Intelligence, Bliss (*Sat-Chit-Ananda*). Though the "nondualist" school of philosophy failed to attribute personality and holiness—in the sense of perfection in righteousness and divine love—to the Supreme Being, these attributes, so important in the Greco-Judeo-Christian vision, were stressed by other philosophical schools and by the dualistic sects in Hinduism, which some scholars believe were strongly influenced by Christianity.

But though its most characteristic philosophy failed to attribute personality and holiness to God, personal sanctity as a means of achieving communion with God holds a fascination for the Hindu that is almost impossible to describe. According to the *Bhagavad Gita*, one of the most important sacred books of the Hindus, it is achieved mainly through the practice of two all-embracing virtues: nonattachment and love. The chapter of this scripture entitled the "Yoga of Meditation" expresses the first of these means in a cogent and beautiful way: "He who does the work he ought to do and does not seek its fruit—he is a *sannyasi* and a *yogi*. . . . For a sage who wants to attain *yoga* (union), action is said to be the means; but when he has attained *yoga*, serenity is said to be the means. When a man has no attachment to the objects of the senses or to works, and when he has wholly renounced his will, he is said to have attained *yoga*."

And the chapter "The Way to Liberation Through Renunciation" expresses the second no less beautifully: "Fix your heart on Me (Krishna), give your love to Me, worship Me, bow down before Me; so shall you come to Me. This is My pledge to you, for you are dear to Me. Abandon all duties and come to Me alone for shelter. I will deliver you from all sins . . ." (*The Bhagavad Gita*, trans. Swami Nikhilananda. Ramakrishna-Vivekananda Center).

Certainly, the themes of subjugation of the ego and of the senses, and the "holy indifference" of St. Francis de Sales, are familiar ones in Christian thought. Indian Christians would like to see these ideals embodied not only in the lives of those especially consecrated to a life of meditation, but also in the forms of devotion used by the generality of Christians.

Fr. Thomas Ohm, in his book *Asia Looks at Western Christianity* (Herder and Herder), explains the Indian approach to God: "The eager outward activity inherent in Western forms of devotion bewilders many Asians. Some of our Christian services strike many Hindus, who see in God only tranquillity and immutability, as far too restless and disturbing. They demand a religious service which does not, with its ceaseless flow of words and chant, preclude the true silence for which they long. During the services in Gandhi's *Ashram*, silence played a dominant part. . . . Men like the fakirs are praised who are capable of excluding . . . thoughts and emotions. This emptiness is regarded as a value and an advantage. The Oriental wants to immerse himself in the well of nothingness and to escape from time."

This "nothingness" does not connote, however, a complete negation. It is the negation, as far as is possible, of all that is not-God, so that God may flood the waiting devotee with His own being and presence.

A few years ago, a concrete attempt was made to integrate the ideas of Christian contemplation with the ancient monastic tradition of India. Two French priests, Dom Henri Le Saux, O.S.B., and Fr. J. Monchanin, S.A.M., established the Saccidananda Hermitage in South India. The inspiration for this was the methods of De Nobili and St. John de Britto. The aims are similar, too: to show that Christianity is not something alien and merely Western, but all-embracing in its scope and meaning. Further work along these lines is being done at the present time by Dom Bede Griffiths, O.S.B., in the state of Kerala.

Of great significance, too, is the question of artistic adaptation. Here the efforts of Angelo da Fonseca and Angela Trinidade have won world-wide recognition. Christ, in the paintings of both artists, wears the symbols associated with the Indian sage. Mary epitomizes the qualities of Eastern beauty, especially in the emphasis on the eyes, traditionally the mirror of the soul. In the representation of the Mother of God in her various roles, such as Comforter of the Afflicted, the painters show her using the Indian gestural language of *mudras*, which consists of diverse expressions of such principal moods as compassion, love, serenity. These adaptations may perhaps appear superficial, but for those whose education has not geared them to move easily in the cultures of both Orient and Occident, pictures like these have deep significance.

Classical Indian dance, the essential meaning of which has always been spiritual, is rich in potential for interpretation of Christian themes. *Bharat Natyam*, one of the principal schools, was inspired by the idea of devotion to a personal God and love as a means of salvation; *Kathakali* centers on the interpretation of the traditional stories of the triumph of good over evil; *Manipuri* is in praise of Lord Krishna, one of the Hindu manifestations or *Avataras* of God. In using these as a vehicle for Christian teaching, careful selection is necessary so that the end product is not one of confused religious significances.

In the main, however, the Christian versions follow the traditional structural arrangement. This consists of, first, an invocation, which is suitable for the opening of Christian recitals; then passages of complicated foot-work, called *jethiswaram*, to express feelings of peace, energy, joy; then *shabdam* and *varnam*, which involve the use of sensitive facial expression and strong rhythmical movement of the legs. (All the movements embodied in these can be used to depict Christian themes and ideas; for example, vigorous movements can be used to depict the might of God, and there are gentle dances more suitable to our Lady.) The last part of the sequence consists of a dance composed according to the meaning of some song, for example, the Magnificat.

Finally, the liturgy and Christian religious life in India would gain immensely by adopting Hindu rites and regional festivals, which are full of symbolism that can be interpreted as Christian once they are removed from their specific Hindu context. Such an adaptation would also have a salutary effect on new converts. It is hard for those who have been born Catholic to realize the void created in the religious psyche of the convert when the Church does not substitute for his ancient forms of devotion others that seem to be manifestly analogous. It is a great temptation to apostasy. Some changes have already been made. In many of the churches, devotees enter barefoot and make always a double genuflection. In churches where the vernacular is used for communal prayer, the form used is that of the *mantras* or sacred chants of the Hindus. Hymns in the vernaculars have been composed that employ pure Indian rhythms.

This growing consciousness of past and present may lead in time to a more fruitful future—a future in which will be fulfilled the desire and the efforts to create a Church strongly indigenous and at the same time vitally universal. Such a Church would understand that, in relation to God, there is no East and no West, but only one mankind united by one common longing that has found expression again and again, as in the millenniums-old prayer of the *Brihadaranyaka Upanishad:*

> From the unreal lead me to the Real,
> From darkness lead me to the Light,
> From death lead me to Immortality.

WALTER CISZEK
Return From Russia

My plane landed at Idlewild International Airport, at 6:55 A.M., in the gray dawn of October 12, 1963. All during the long flight from Moscow, I had wondered what it would be like to see the United States again after 24 years in the Soviet Union, mostly in Siberia. Yet, as we taxied to the terminal, I forgot all about that; I could think only of my sisters and of the fellow Jesuits I saw waiting to meet me. My throat seemed somehow to grow suddenly tighter; I felt a nervous happiness in the expectancy of that first meeting. I hardly remember much about Idlewild, therefore, except flashing lights in the early dawn, the crowd of reporters and that feeling of joy at being home. It was a long while before I could even begin to sift out my impressions of things here.

Cars, of course. Everybody asks about that, and it's true. You notice them immediately. Moscow streets are busy, but here the streets are crammed with cars—north, south, east and west—cars coming, cars going, and block after block of cars standing along the curbs. Not just in the cities, but along the country roads and in small towns, the main streets and the side streets and the alleys seem almost carpeted with cars.

And what cars! For five years I was a mechanic at ATK-50, the government garage in Abakan, working on the city's fleet of taxis. Those are really about the only cars there are, for few people can afford their own. The average workingman's salary is 90 rubles (roughly $90) a month; a really good salary is 150 rubles a month. But the little four-cylinder *Moskvicz* costs almost 3,000 rubles (nearly three years' salary!), and the bigger, six-cylinder *Volga* costs about 6,000. Those were the cars I worked with, and practically every American car I have seen looks like a battleship compared to them—especially after they had spent a month on the roads around Abakan.

Two other things connected with American cars amazed me. One was the very low cost of a secondhand car; even a dilapidated, rebuilt refugee from ATK-50 would cost a minimum of 2,000 rubles in Abakan. The other was the sight of a nun driving a car. When I stop to think about it, I suppose nuns are no better—or worse—drivers than anyone else, since most young people here seem to grow up behind the wheel. But I hadn't seen a nun in a religious habit for almost twenty-five years; the sight of one behind the wheel of a car struck me as incredible—and funny.

Housing, of course, impressed me tremendously. I don't mean the skyscraper skyline of New York and the block on block of soaring glass, steel and aluminum towers that loom over you as you walk through the city. Everyone expects that of New York. What struck me, however, was the mile after mile of neat, well-painted and well-kept houses: the big, comfortable farmhouses in the countryside, the trim, sharp rows of "modern" brick and glass homes in every suburb, the solid, sturdy brick houses with their frame front porches in every little town.

Sometimes I still feel uneasy when I visit these homes. The idea that one family should occupy six, seven or eight rooms! I can't shake the feeling that something is wrong. And every room has carpets, pictures, mirrors, lamps, chairs, even a radio. A house that had four rooms was a luxury in Siberia, and even then the "spare" room was generally rented out. I lived in such spare rooms all through my stay in Abakan, sleeping on a little iron bed with boards in place of springs. Frankly, you couldn't have fitted some of the "standard" American beds—with their oversized frames and mattresses a foot thick—into the room I had for the last two years in Abakan.

I can't get used to the notion, either, that hot water is available all day and all night, or that you can take a bath any time you want. In Siberia, houses that had hot water had it only twice a week, at best, during the winter. Central heating where I lived meant that the corners of the big, brick kitchen stove stuck into all four rooms of the house. Here even the poorest homes have central heating, and stoves are gas or electric, with the kitchens full of electric toasters, electric mixers, electric frying pans, electric roasters—electric everything, including can-openers. Everybody has a vacuum cleaner; I even saw teen-agers walking around with portable hair-dryers. When people here buy a washing machine (and everybody does), they can choose between a dozen makes, all with special features and most of them with matching dryers. In Russia, there is only one type, the *Bielka*, with a hand wringer, no dryer—and you put the water in by hand! When you can get one, it costs 90 rubles, just about a man's whole wages for a month.

You don't just walk into the *Magazin* (department store) and buy a washing machine; you order one, and you put your name at the bottom of the list of those who have ordered before you. Then you go back every week and put a check beside your name to show that you still want and need that machine. If you fail to check your name for two weeks in a row, or if you miss about three times all told, your name drops off the list. There may be 500 or more names on the list, but only 35 or 40 machines will be delivered to the *Magazin* each month; so a wait of more than a year is not unusual. The same thing is true of rugs and refrigerators; it seemed incredible to see a kitchen with *two* refrigerators back home in Shenandoah, Pa.

The food in those refrigerators, or in the stores! You can't imagine what it means to see fruit in the middle of winter. Apples, melons and grapes were about the only fruit we had in Abakan, and then only during harvest time. If you saw someone with an apple, even a stranger, you'd go right up to him and ask where he got it—then go there right away. We did buy oranges a few times while I was there, but they were little Chinese oranges, and of course you never see them now. We never saw grapefruit, or such things as peaches, pears, plums, cherries and pineapples. Bananas were so rare that some people honestly and literally didn't know what to do with them; they couldn't be sure whether they were fruit or vegetable, whether they should be cooked or eaten as they were. But here, store windows are full of every kind of fruit all winter long—and the people pass by without looking.

Here you can go into any store on any street and buy meat, milk, butter and every kind of vegetable, fresh, frozen or canned. My sisters began to think the years in Siberia had affected my mind, when I went wandering for hours through a supermarket, staring wide-eyed and unbelieving at so much food. All the stores are that way. You never have to stand in line for anything, except the time it takes the girl to check out the baskets of food each person buys. In Abakan, you stood in line for everything; when there was a line in a store it meant they finally had something to sell. Before you went to work, on your way home from work, if you saw a line you automatically got into it. Whatever they were selling, it would be something you needed.

It isn't only the food in the stores that amazes me, it's the food an average family puts on the table for an average meal. The first few times I went to visit friends in Shenandoah, I felt guilty because they were going to such an expense for me. Several times I asked them how they could afford it. They'd look at me as if they didn't understand, then smile at me and wink at one another. In Abakan, I used to cook myself a pot of soup from cabbage, onions and potatoes, with perhaps some beef or lamb bones I had saved—or a piece of meat if I could get it—and that would be my breakfast and my supper for the next three days. A handful of lard added to the soup, so that it would be covered with a layer of grease as thick as your little finger, was the way I added fats to my diet. A chunk of chewy, dark rye bread completed the meal.

I seldom had meat, except now and again a piece of boloney with another piece of bread for lunch. Otherwise, my lunch at the garage consisted of a piece of bread and an onion, or perhaps a piece of bread and fat. Here in America, I've watched mothers in the kitchen after a meal throw away more food, and better food, than I might eat in Russia in half a week. The dogs here eat more meat in a week than I did in a month. And I simply can't help staring when people leave their plates half full, as they do so often in restaurants.

The waste of paper here! Everything comes wrapped in paper, boxed in paper, rolled in paper, packaged in paper. And if it isn't paper, it's plastic. Each piece of fruit is individually wrapped, vegetables are bagged in cellophane, and everything is boxed in brightly printed, attractive cartons. Then all this is thrown away or burned! In Siberia, on the other hand, you bring your own wrapping paper to the store. Most people found the best solution was to buy a newspaper; it gave you something to do during those endless waits in line, too.

When I say things like this, of course, I am only recounting my impressions, not offering criticisms. Somewhat like a Siberian Rip Van Winkle, I can't help being struck by things in my own country that seem strange and new to me. After all, as Wladimir Martinovich I lived the life of the people in Siberia, conformed to all the regulations, got used to all the customs and came to take for granted all the hardships. Abakan, Krasnoyarsk, Norilsk—the Siberian cities where I was allowed to live as a free man after my release from the camps—are not Moscow, Leningrad, Kiev or Odessa. As a released "political" prisoner who had been accused of "spying for the Vatican," I was not allowed to live in any of those major, or "regime," cities. Neither am I a sociologist; so I don't pretend to judge life in the Soviet Union as compared to life in the United States, or vice versa. I am only recording my surface impressions, the things that struck me when I first returned and continue to startle me from time to time in many little ways.

Just a few weeks ago, for instance, I was struck by the sight of a crucifix on the classroom wall as I talked to the children in St. Ladislaus parish school in Philadelphia. You never see that in Russia. Somehow I suddenly felt strange; I almost felt out of place. I could see in the children's eyes an eagerness and a respect for what I was (not who I was), a priest whom they called "Father." I thought of the Russian children who used to come to me for help with their English lessons. How cautious I had to be with them never to mention God! Here in this classroom, beneath the

crucifix, I could tell these children anything, speak to them of
anything. In Abakan I felt restricted, and I had to be careful not
to startle the children.

I remember a day I forgot and made some reference to God; I
could see the surprise and the near-horror in their eyes. "Wladimir
Martinovich," said one little girl, "is it possible that you believe in
God, a smart man like you? How can you still let yourself be
influenced by unscientific stories about God and religion?" She
was perhaps in the seventh grade. I didn't want them to go away
without an answer, so I told them they would come across the idea
of God wherever they went; it was a serious problem that troubled
many people, and they would make a serious mistake if they didn't
consider it carefully and try to solve it for themselves. Under the
circumstances, that was the best I could do. I had just been warned
again by the KGB not to "agitate" the people about religion. If I
had tried to tell these children about God, or to instruct them,
it would have been considered "proselytizing immature minds."
That's how it is in Russia.

Article 124 of the Constitution of the USSR states that "in order
to ensure the citizen's freedom of conscience, the church in the
USSR is separated from the state, and the school from the church.
Freedom of religious worship and freedom of antireligious propaganda are recognized for all citizens." What that means in effect
is that the right to propagate religion ends at the church door or
at a mother's knee. In the churches that are open (generally only
the Orthodox churches, except in the big cities like Moscow),
services are held and people are free to attend—as long as they
are not Party members or do not hold responsible jobs or positions
they would hesitate to lose. That is "freedom of worship." But
you cannot proselytize or talk about religion or try to make converts; whereas with the "freedom of antireligious propaganda" exercised by the schools, the Party, the labor unions, the press,
radio and television, atheism is actively and continuously preached.

Religion in Russia, therefore, is not suppressed or persecuted,
as people here understand the words. Instead, it is talked about as
something that retards the movement toward communism and impedes the education of the "new communistic man." In special
courses, seminars and lectures, Party members, school teachers,
komsomols (members of the official youth organizations) and labor
union members get a thorough grounding in atheism in order to

help fight religion—not by government legislation, but by word of mouth and by example. In school, everything is "scientifically" explained to the children; ideas of God and of religion are treated as holdovers from the unscientific past. Children are told to humor their elders who still believe in such things and have never had the scientific and technical training that would show them how incompatible such notions are with modern science. The method can be devastatingly effective, up to a point.

Older people, however, still believe in God, and their influence is still noticeable in family life. As a result, the young people hear talks against religion in school but still can see examples of religious practices at home. It confuses them. Publicly, they do not believe; they will argue with anyone who suggests they should believe. Privately, however, they are not sure.

I have had young married komsomols come to me to have their children baptized. When I asked about the possibility of religious education for the child, and why they wanted him baptized, they would tell me simply they had heard all sorts of things about God and against God, in school and in the Party organizations, but they were not convinced. They wanted to do for their children what their parents had done for them—just in case. When I asked, then, if they would teach their children what their parents had taught them, they were eager to agree. It was a strange and sad and yet, somehow, hopeful experience. The more I see here in America, the stranger it seems in a way. For the contrast between that hidden faith, fluttering as if it were always about to go out and yet somehow remaining alight, and the open, free and almost proud profession of faith in this country is simply staggering.

Yet when I walked through St. Patrick's Cathedral in New York, do you know what impressed me most? The few people, out of all the crowds streaming by, who came in through those open doors to make a visit. I understand that my impression was not fair, that at noontime on a working day the church is jammed with office workers who take time out from their lunch hour to go to Mass and to Communion. At first glance religion here seems almost a formality, an obligation that can be dispensed with if you have been out late the night before.

In Siberia, when I said Mass, people risked arrest to come; here, they risk nothing, neither do they always come. In Krasnoyarsk and Norilsk, when people learned a priest was in town or was saying Mass at such and such a place, they came for miles, bringing their children to be baptized, going to confession before Mass and then Communion during Mass, asking to have their marriages blessed after Mass, begging me to come and bless their homes or sing the *panikida* (a requiem service) for members of the family who had died. They came to huts, to barracks rooms, to private homes, and they risked their jobs, their union membership, their chance for an apartment or an education for their children. Having ministered to such faith, therefore, it was incredible to me to think that people here could look on Sunday Mass as an obligation, or the supporting of their parish and their school as a burden.

I should repeat again that these were my first reactions, my impressions, and are not meant in any way as criticisms. I am only reporting what struck me when I first looked at America again. As a priest who had worked very hard to help people who were so eager just to be able to go to Mass, I could not help being struck, thunderstruck, at this initial impression of indifference to religion in a country where there was nothing to restrain its open practice.

There is one topic about which people always ask me: the race question. Quite frankly, I was amazed to see Negroes eating in restaurants, working alongside white people (even in the government in Washington!), sitting beside them on trains and buses, talking with them freely and openly. I couldn't believe my eyes at first. I had read of riots in America, of Negroes being beaten. I had heard they couldn't go to school to get an education or eat with whites, and that they weren't allowed to hold certain jobs. I had seen pictures on television of several Black Muslim speakers in Harlem calling for a separate section of the country as their own, where they could be free and independent of the whites.

I tried to tell the Russians who asked me about this that such stories must be exaggerated. But what could I say about the TV pictures and the news photos, or the statements by prominent American leaders, both Negro and white, that were quoted so frequently in the Soviet press? What could I think? I had left America to study theology in Rome in 1934; I had no way of knowing what things were like in America after 30 years. I could say the news was exaggerated, but was I sure? You can imagine, then, how stunned I was to see Negroes walking freely everywhere, accepted by everyone. Again, this was my first impression, my spontaneous reaction in view of what I had been led to believe.

I have begun to learn what problems still remain and how much is still to be done; but perhaps my impression will show how much the average Russian knows about America.

I am an American, happy to be home; but in many ways I am almost a stranger, as you can tell by these initial reactions to America. It may take me a while to feel at home, but I am happy to be back. What sort of picture, though, must others have of us who have no way of finding out the truth?

WALTER E. O'DONNELL, M.D.

The Good Physician

¶An American doctor makes a plea for more well-rounded general practitioners

Pope Pius XII once said: "Before everything else, a doctor has to consider the entire man in the unity of his person, that is, not only his physical condition but also his psychology, his moral and spiritual ideals and his place in society."

Patients come to their doctors with an astonishing variety of problems. Many of these people are not really sick; their difficulties have nothing to do with the science of medicine. A similar number are actually ailing, but their complaints of nervousness, fatigue, depression, are no more than surface manifestations of a maelstrom of emotional currents and crosscurrents.

As I sit in my office or make my rounds day after day, I am constantly struck by how many of the emotional, personal and even medical problems I am called upon to handle involve major spiritual or moral issues. Here are a few situations I have encountered in recent months:

A 17-year-old high school girl complains of nausea and fatigue, and is found to be three months pregnant. The news has to be broken to her mother and father. Then follow questions: Should she marry the boy? Should she keep the baby? Can't something be done about this pregnancy?

A husband and wife both have many physical complaints for

which they are consuming bottles of pills. The real cause of their symptoms is their mentally retarded adolescent son, who is becoming a problem. They clash violently over whether he should be "put away" or remain at home.

A couple in their thirties seek advice regarding their being overweight and always tired. Their real problem emerges only after careful questioning. It is their barren ten-year marriage. They feel like outsiders and strangers to their friends, whose lives center around their children.

A 30-year-old mother of five, overwhelmed by repeated estrangements from her irresponsible husband and appalled by the bleak prospect of going it alone, attempts suicide with sleeping-pills.

An 18-year-old single working girl comes in with a venereal disease that she has contracted from a married man.

A 52-year-old father of six children, ranging in age from 10 to 25 years, has incurable cancer. Two children are in college and one is scheduled to enter next year. He has many financial obligations and his business partner keeps inquiring how things are, asking whether they should go ahead with their expansion program. The patient's wife is vehemently opposed to her husband's knowing the truth and insists on carrying out an elaborate pretense. The patient wonders why he is not gaining faster.

These are but a few samples of what passes through a doctor's office. To them could be appended an almost endless list of problems brought on by controversies over birth control, working mothers, straying fathers, personality conflicts at work—and so on.

In trying to cope with problems such as these, the doctor may use various techniques.

One method is to concern himself only with appearances and approach everything as a strictly medical problem. Here the case of gonorrhea is treated with penicillin as merely another infectious disease, the childless couple is put on a diet and given some pep pills, and the attempted suicide has her stomach washed out, is allowed to sleep off her overdosage and is then discharged with pills for her nerves.

Another method is to regard these troublesome problems as nonmedical or at least as someone else's responsibility. Here the unwed mother is considered just another maternity case and is given routine prenatal care or turned over to an obstetrical clinic and a social worker, and the couple with the retarded child is referred to a psychiatrist. (Priests, ministers and rabbis are also favorite targets for this type of referral.)

Still another method allows the doctor to appear to deal with the problem without coming to grips with it at all. Early in his career, this type of man develops a standard set of solutions for what he regards as a standard set of problems. Here the patient with incurable cancer is *always* told the truth (and usually the whole truth and nothing but the truth), or the patient is never let in on the secret (even when pretense becomes a mockery).

These are easy ways out—and some doctors take them. To follow any other course is often frustrating, emotionally exhausting and time-consuming. What is more, the doctor's efforts are frequently unappreciated and often resented.

The good physician, however, is mindful of medicine's long tradition of helpfulness in these areas. Dedicated to his calling, and untainted by modern medicine's fragmentation of the human personality and body, he interprets his role in a very broad manner. Whatever makes his patient feel sick—physically or emotionally —is his concern. He is not afraid of "getting involved." Professional detachment and objectivity are necessary to him, no doubt, but they have not become his hallmark.

But there is not a little risk involved in this sort of responsibility. A doctor spends most of his time being asked for and giving advice. And amazingly enough, people listen to his advice and usually follow it. Decisions one would think would have required months or years of thoughtful, prayerful, patient consideration are made almost in an instant in a doctor's office. People change jobs, leave home, divorce their husbands or wives, sell their homes or businesses, move across the country and effect dozens of other epochal changes in their lives simply on the doctor's say-so. Under these circumstances, certain doctors succumb to the temptation to "play God."

When the instincts of these medical autocrats are good, and they pay due heed to the moral and spiritual aspects of the patient's life, their influence can be a beneficent one. They can provide courage and a sense of direction and purpose. But when strong, authoritarian, father-image physicians base the edicts they hand to their unquestioning patients on materialistic, utilitarian or pragmatic grounds, trouble begins. Because the advice they give is "medical," patients feel it is not subject to critical review or appeal, regardless of spiritual or moral considerations.

I often wonder how the nonspiritual, amoral and irreligious doctor handles the great times of crisis in people's lives. What can the agnostic or atheist say to the 12-year-old boy who suddenly finds himself the man of the house? Or to the middle-aged woman who has just found her husband dead in the bedroom? Where can the materialist find words of sympathy-without-pity for the 45-year-old woman irreversibly crippled with arthritis? How can a physician who is a moral relativist himself, or who denies the concept of personal responsibility, help to bolster a crumbling marriage, rehabilitate an alcoholic or provide any rule of conduct or spiritual guidepost for his patients?

Obviously, such a man cannot give the help that patients and their families need and expect. A dispassionate recitation of the medical, physical and biological reasons as to how illness came and what it did is never enough. Pope Pius XII put it succinctly: "The doctor, whether he wishes to or not, must take a stand on human destiny." Though doctors cannot preach sermons, their words of understanding, comfort and counsel carry far more weight when they are inspired by a spiritual point of view. There is nothing new about this aspect of the doctor-patient relationship. It simply has been lost sight of, obscured by the more spectacular facets of modern medicine: dazzling technological advances, incredible surgical accomplishments and awesome research breakthroughs.

How do today's physicians handle their unique and vital responsibility? All things considered, I believe that most of them still acquit themselves very commendably. Usually they understand patients' problems surprisingly well and manage to give reasonable and workable advice that duly respects the over-all spiritual and moral considerations as well as the patients' particular beliefs. There are exceptions, but the balance, I believe, is clearly on the credit side.

The pendulum, however, is swinging in the opposite direction —toward the pure "science" of medicine and away from the "art." Symptomatic of this trend is the fact that "bedside manner" (one of the most potent therapeutic agents known to man) has become a term of opprobrium. On the other hand, status has now been conferred on many of the qualities and attitudes associated with the art of medicine by giving them "scientific" names. Many an older physician is amused by the revelation that he has spent a good

many years practicing successful psychotherapy without even
knowing it.

But now that we have at our disposal the tremendous resources
of psychiatric research, should we not turn there for a solution?
Do not all the facts we have been considering simply show that we
need more psychiatrists to handle the nonphysical aspects of medicine? Two considerations suggest an answer in the negative.

First, the overwhelming majority of mental and emotional—not
to mention moral and spiritual—problems are now being handled,
and during our lifetime must continue to be handled, by others
than psychiatrists. There are only twelve to fifteen thousand
psychiatrists in the United States today, and only a thousand new
ones are added yearly to this number. These men are heavily
concentrated in a relatively few cities in a few large States. The
number of patients they can take care of is thus not large. It
should also be remembered that many patients cannot undertake
prolonged psychiatric treatment because of the crushing financial
burden it can impose. The community mental health program recently enacted by Congress is expected to be of help; but for many
years psychiatric consultation will be available only to a minority.

Secondly, and very important, the spiritual, moral and religious
aspects of a man's character and problems are for the most part
not viewed with much sympathy, and are therefore not covered,
by psychiatry as it is presently constituted and practiced in most
areas. There are only 400 Catholic psychiatrists for a nation of
almost 45 million Catholics. This is not to suggest that all non-
Catholic psychiatrists maintain a non-Christian or even anti-Chris-
tian point of view. But a substantial percentage do, and the patient
has no way of determining this until he is well along in the course
of diagnosis and treatment.

Psychiatry and psychiatrists are not the answer. It is clear that if
help is to come, it must come from the physician—probably a non-
Catholic—doing family practice in the community. He will have to
utilize psychiatric knowledge and techniques, of course, but most
important will be his personal code of spiritual, moral and religious
values and how he uses it in practice.

There are, however, several factors—each directly or indirectly
tending to play down man's spiritual aspect—that complicate the
present medical scene. Until these are countered, physicians will be
unable to master their patients' spiritual and moral problems.

Recently, AMERICA wondered editorially "whether modern American medicine is getting too technological and too impersonal for anybody's good." The answer is decidedly yes. There has been, in recent years, a marked tendency to exalt science and technology over humanity. Along with this goes an overemphasis on super-specialists, clinics and hospitals, at the expense of the general physician, the private office and the home. As a result, there is widespread confusion as to what a doctor should be. Medical schools have been turning out an increasing proportion of scientists, researchers, clinical investigators and specialists.

All these factors do much to distort your physicians' perspective on their calling. These men, after years of exposure to once-in-a-lifetime patients, tend to a greater extent than ever before to devote their interest to the rare, the unlikely, the obscure disease. Yet when they go into practice, they are confronted with the common, the likely, the simple. Many of them, failing to make the necessary adjustment, spend much of their time brushing aside the mass of patients in search of the one with a problem worthy of their talents and training. Such men can be vitally important as consultants, but they fail to make reliable physicians.

I am not suggesting a return to the "good old days," horse-and-buggy doctors, or unscientific medicine. The medical centers and the super-specialists who work in them have provided the fuel and the thrust for our great surge of recent medical progress. But a sense of proportion is called for. The surpassing need in the United States today is for well-rounded and well-grounded physicians who will practice general medicine as general practitioners, internists or pediatricians. The individual's needs are still best served in his own community by physicians who know him well and regard him as a person rather than a case.

Equally significant, as a complicating factor, has been the almost complete failure of medical schools to take into account man's moral and spiritual aspects—and particularly the doctor's role in understanding them. A few schools manage to consider these in courses on medical ethics or the history and philosophy of medicine; and in psychiatric studies they loom up too large to be ignored. But the subject is hardly treated sympathetically or in proper perspective. The physician must rely on his premedical training, or on what he picks up elsewhere, to fill this important void when he goes out to take care of the public.

Carl G. Jung has written in his well-known book *Psychology and Religion: West and East* (Pantheon): "Among all my patients in the second half of life—that is to say, over 35—there has not been one whose problem in the last resort was not that of finding a religious outlook on life." His remark applied, obviously, to a particular type of patient, and cannot be accepted as true of all the patients an American doctor must treat. Nevertheless, he seems to have come close to the truth about a large proportion of those who seek medical help today.

The National Federation of Catholic Physicians' Guilds, through meetings of its local units and its official journal, *The Linacre Quarterly*, has long concerned itself with this aspect of medicine. In recent years there have been stirrings in other quarters, which suggest an awakening to this curious void in the medical spectrum. In 1954 the National Academy of Religious and Mental Health was founded. This organization draws its 4,000 members from the ranks of psychiatry, psychology, sociology and other behavioral sciences as well as from the clergy. In 1961, the American Medical Association announced the formation of a Department of Religion and Mental Health, designed to explore the relationships between religious and mental, spiritual and physical, health. Medical educators, too, are well aware of some of the unhealthy tendencies of modern medicine and are considering means to remedy them—or at least soften their impact. Loyola of Chicago's new medical center, for example, will include an Institute of Medicine and Morals designed to "explore the partnership between medical science and religion."

There is thus some basis for hoping that medical schools will restore proper emphasis to the production of ordinary physicians with an appreciation of the spiritual, moral and religious factors in his patients.

All this reorientation of training will avail nothing, however, unless medicine can attract the right kind of young man. This is a problem that is proving to be more and more difficult. In my view, medicine is man's noblest profession. It is not so, however, because it is the most challenging branch of science or offers the greatest opportunities for research, teaching or prestige. It is so because it offers an unparalleled opportunity for service to one's fellow men.

Medicine has need, certainly, of scientists; but medical practitioners who will ply their art in office, home or hospital must be drawn from idealistic young men—men for whom service to mankind is a sufficient reward and goal.

If the new generation of physicians—Catholic and non-Catholic alike—is to inspire confidence in their patients and fulfill their deepest needs, they must give evidence that they actually have an appreciation of the spiritual and moral aspects of human life. This is not, of course, a requirement in any sense peculiar to our own age. It was John Wesley who wrote, in 1747, in his famous *Primitive Physic:* "In complicated cases or where life is in immediate danger, let everyone apply without delay to a physician that fears God."

MOIRA WALSH

Making Mature Movie Viewers

¶Straight-from-the-shoulder talk about films and the people who watch them

Like Topsy, films "just growed" in the space of a few years from Edison's casual invention of the magic lantern into a multi-million-dollar industry, run largely by men whose sole affinity for the film form was the recognition that it was a lucrative business and whose only guiding principle was to give the public what it wanted.

The public, for its part, was uncritically mesmerized in the early days by anything and everything shown on the screen, ludicrous though most of it would seem today. This, too, is understandable when we consider that mass entertainment as we know it today did not exist before this century. The great bulk of the population existed under conditions of boredom and drudgery and were starved for a touch of color and vicarious excitement in their lives.

Students today are stunned to learn that John Donne's congregation used to urge him to turn his hourglass timer over and go on preaching for a second hour. This was not religious zeal on the part of the listeners. It was that the sermons were the closest thing to drama that entered their intolerably dull lives. The appeal of oratorical windbags like William Jennings Bryan can be explained in much the same way.

The two earliest notions about films, then, were the movie industry's assumption that they were a business and the public's assumption that they were a highly welcome diversion. The third group to take cognizance of films and to take a more or less official position on them was what might roughly be described as the opinion-makers—civic and religious leaders and government agencies of one sort or another.

These people took the view that movies were, in certain circumstances, a threat to public morality. Their judgment in this matter was founded in large part on the assumption that the general public was semi-illiterate, debased in inclinations, totally uninformed about everything in the world lying beyond the range of its narrow personal experience, and weak in both the knowledge and practice of those religious and patriotic truths which the authorities deemed it to be their duty to maintain. It was assumed, in other words, that exposure to any new and/or erroneous ideas would constitute a temptation to which the public would almost inevitably succumb.

Most of the early efforts to regulate films reflected these age-old assumptions and were directed toward eliminating dangerous ideas and keeping movies as innocuous as possible. It should be remembered, incidentally, that most of the efforts to control films in the early days took the form of civil censorship rather than action by religious groups. It seems to me, however, that there are two crucial factors about films which have been given insufficient consideration by all the various forces attempting to regulate them. The first is that films came into being at the beginning of a period of technological and social change virtually unique in the history of the world and that, furthermore, films were themselves one of the major influences in effecting this change.

Suddenly, in the 20th century, the average man broke out of the mold he had occupied since time immemorial. Education, industrialization and increasingly rapid and easy transportation changed him in two generations from an uninformed, religiously and socially inhibited citizen of a region or a village into a relatively knowledge-

able member of the world community. Movies, despite their
esthetic and moral inadequacy, were another important factor in informing the average citizen about people and events all over the
world.

I am not suggesting that the moral characters of Americans have
improved radically in the last sixty years or that all the changes in
the composition of our national life have been for the better. I am
saying that we now have a genuinely pluralistic society in which
"dangerous" ideas are commonplace and differences in religious and
ethical beliefs are taken for granted as a fact rather than a threat.

For better or for worse, the kind of society in which a citizen
could be protected willy-nilly from evil influences by social and religious pressures and government decrees is gone forever. Our
churches, schools, communities and nations must rise to the new
challenge of informing and inspiring their citizens to choose wisely
for themselves.

The second area in which groups concerned with the effects of
films are open to criticism is in their failure to study and understand
movies before passing judgment. The estimate of opinion-makers
that films were a threat to public morality was true enough as far as
it went. They also regarded them as a frivolous and essentially artificial diversion—and that was their mistake. It was a perfectly natural mistake to make at most periods in the development of the
screen. It was also a misapprehension shared by most of the best
people, including movie executives, the public and the Supreme
Court, whose 1916 opinion—which stood until partially superseded
by the *Miracle* decision in 1952—denied films the protection of the
First Amendment on the grounds that they were a diversion, not a
medium of communication.

Yet despite the general consensus of contrary opinion, motion
pictures turned out to be an art form. They are the only new art
form devised since ancient times, the only art form that worked its
way up from very disreputable beginnings at the bottom of the
social ladder, and an art form that is frequently put to disreputable
use even today. Nevertheless, an art form they are, and as such they
have, by their nature, a particular way of communicating with
audiences. They also have their own esthetic-philosophic rationale,
and they must be judged according to this rather than by a few
moral dicta hastily concocted to keep the public from burning its
fingers on the new toy.

The objection usually interposed at this point is that, by the kindest estimate, eighty per cent of all the films ever made are not art, and that, therefore, to insist that they are an art form is high-brow and basically unrealistic estheticism. The objectors, it seems to me, miss the more fundamental point that, regardless of their quality, it is as an art form that movies exercise their impact on the audience. The camera, the film, the script, the performers, the sound, the sets, the light and shadow, the music, etc., are tools with which the cinema creator works to convey an implicit, over-all statement on life. What gets across to the audience, to a great extent without their knowing it, is not the subject matter of the film, but rather what the creator thinks about the subject matter.

In actual practice, what a shockingly large proportion of films communicate subliminally to audiences is a superficially pleasurable but stultifying collection of myths, illusions and wishful thinking. This, in a sense, is the most pressing moral problem presented by the mass media of communication, yet it has never been adequately faced up to by the guardians of film morality. Because they did not understand that movies were an art form, they did not challenge on philosophical grounds the fallacious principle that underlies and corrupts most of today's mass-media entertainment—namely, that pleasure is, in itself, the legitimate end of film viewing.

Again, this probably sounds like a quibble, because, obviously, if people did not derive pleasure from movies, they would not go to them. Yet there is a world of difference between pleasure as an end in itself and pleasure as a legitimate and inevitable side-effect. If pleasure is not the proper end of filmgoing, what is? Pius XI, in his encyclical *Vigilanti Cura*, wrote: "The essential purpose of art, its *raison d'être*, is to assist in the perfecting of the moral personality, which is man." How does art bring about this perfecting of man's moral personality? By increasing his knowledge of self, especially in relationship to God and his neighbor.

But the acquisition of knowledge from art presupposes that the artist is living up to his obligation, which is to convey the truth. The artist's ability to convey the truth, in turn, rests on the supposition, first, that he is in possession of at least some kernel of it that is worth communicating, and, second, that he has sufficient mastery of the creative tools of his medium so that what he means to say actually gets across.

Lest the reader be by this time envisioning truthful films in terms of cracked washbasins, prostitution and general gloom, I should perhaps make it clear that this is not what I mean. A film need not be at all serious to be truthful. It need only sustain a decently plausible connection between its premises and its conclusion. For example, I would consider Walt Disney's highly diverting and popular *The Absent-Minded Professor* a truthful film and a modestly effective social satire on its own fantastic terms.

At most individual periods in the history of the screen, the number of artists then working in the field could be counted, by generous estimate, on the fingers of two hands. There are probably more men with integrity, vision and skill making movies today than ever before. They are outnumbered, however, and always have been, by the commercial operators, who are interested, not in truth, but only in popularity and profits. Because of the unique nature of the film form, these commercial-minded non-artists have been extraordinarily successful over the years in selling the public wooden nickels and making it like them.

Films, as Pius XI pointed out, are readily accessible both physically and intellectually to all levels of people. They can exert their impact on a passive audience that, unlike the reader of a book, for example, need make no effort nor possess any special skill in order to respond and be entertained. A child can understand them, and it is as children, if not in age at least in the quality of our reactions, that we first see them. Unfortunately, this primary level of response is so natural and satisfying that moviegoers, regardless of their capacity, tend to get "frozen" there. As a result, countless people, even otherwise sophisticated, intelligent, knowledgeable ones, go through a lifetime of moviegoing without getting beyond what Edward Fischer, in *The Screen Arts*, called the "I liked it. It was good. I didn't like it. It was no good" level of film appreciation.

If you ask a typical teen-ager why *That Touch of Mink* was cute, she might respond that Cary Grant was cute, Doris Day was cute and the situations were cute, but otherwise she would be unable to answer your question. If you asked the same question of the women in an average parish society (and make no mistake about it, this film, the biggest box-office hit of the current year, was seen and enjoyed by a fair number of Catholics as well as other Americans), they would probably substitute the adjective "delightful" for "cute" and add that they liked Doris Day's *haute couture* wardrobe (which, incidentally, she wore in the role of an unemployed stenographer), but otherwise their answers would be just as unilluminating.

The people who made the film, however, know exactly why it is popular. They know that the average moviegoer's uncritical and rather childish quest for pleasure can best be satisfied by subconsciously imparting to him the message he wants to hear—in other words, by distorting reality to give the spectator a delusive sense of his own importance. *That Touch of Mink* is popular precisely because it is not art and does not tell the truth. It deals with a valid contemporary situation—a girl's dilemma about whether or not to surrender her virtue when a particularly attractive proposition from a millionaire comes her way. At every turn, however, it substitutes wishful-thinking fantasy for any semblance of reality, so that the audience can happily imagine that a girl can say "yes" to the proposition and yet wind up, virtue intact, at the altar with the propositioner. The viewers can also conclude that millionaires on the make are just charming overgrown boys like Cary Grant, who obviously did not mean any harm in the first place.

Now it happens that *That Touch of Mink* is a film to which the Legion of Decency did object. Unfortunately, the kind of false, stultifying assumptions about life that it conveys are frequently present in "unobjectionable" movies. A pleasant story about family life can actually be putting a tacit stamp of approval on a perniciously bad outlook on child-rearing and other family relationships. A comedy about a working-class "everyman" can be imparting the message that stupidity is a virtue and that anybody with money or a position of authority is, ipso facto, venal and corrupt. A poorly made religious film is not only "inartistic." It also conveys a trashy, inadequate, superficial and sometimes downright false idea of religion—and, therefore, can be literally immoral.

What audiences have needed, and never gotten, is a little instruction in how to look at films like rational human beings. Left to their own devices, they have erroneously assumed that "good" films are bland and comforting, like soothing syrup or a hot water bottle. As a natural corollary to this, they have tended to reject anything that was unpleasant, shocking or disturbing. Granted there have been sordid films that trafficked in sensationalism for its own sake. What audiences are subconsciously rejecting are not so much the real or imagined excesses of any given unpleasant film, but the fact that it is conveying a little bit of harsh truth—and with it a challenge to the spectator's conscience.

Up to this point I have deliberately refrained from discussing the Legion of Decency, though some of my criticisms of the viewpoint of movie guardians in general apply to them. People who do not approve of the Legion tend to see it as a monstrous and unique threat to freedom. I have tried to show that, on the contrary, it is a small manifestation of a widespread and long-established outlook. If the Legion's influence on films had really been destructive, then its primary victims would have been the people who supported it, with the result that Catholics would be demonstrably more ignorant about movies than other groups. This is not so. The tragedy is that, after nearly thirty years of hard work and sincerity of moral purpose, Catholic audiences are not any brighter than other groups.

My own judgment about the Legion of Decency is that it originated as a stop-gap expedient to cope with the admittedly deplorable condition of movie morals at the time. With a great deal of grass-roots support from many religious bodies, the Legion at first succeeded, at least pragmatically, beyond anyone's wildest expectations. In the face of an economic boycott, the movie executives, notoriously lacking in the courage of their convictions (largely because they did not have any convictions except financial ones to be courageous about), collapsed and started to make pictures like *A Tale of Two Cities* instead of *Ten Nights in a Boudoir*. Because nobody quits a poker game when he is ahead, the Legion's hastily improvised working rules were frozen into a permanent policy.

In retrospect, it seems ironic that the Legion of Decency, whose outlook was based on the traditional, rather than the modern, method of influencing public opinion, was founded in 1933, the year in which Franklin D. Roosevelt's inauguration gave fresh impetus to the social revolution that was transforming the country. As a matter of fact, Catholics were changing during this period even more noticeably than their neighbors, because they were evolving from a persecuted, underprivileged minority into full-fledged, secure members of the community. If the Legion had been founded only a few years later, it would almost certainly have been given a different title. Similar organizations in other countries have dignified, neutral titles such as the Swiss Catholic "Film Commission," etc.

Not many years elapsed before the Legion began to realize that asking people to select their movies by blind reliance on a list was not the best method of turning them into discerning filmgoers, and also that some of their rules for judging movies were based on an unrealistic estimate of the public's needs and susceptibilities. Finally, in 1957, the Legion did adopt a definite change in policy.

The immediate inspiration for it was the appearance of the encyclical *Miranda Prorsus*, Pius XII's wise, constructive and humanistic discussion of the function and responsibilities of the communication arts. This remarkable document contains, for example, the following analysis of the problem in film viewing which I have already indicated I consider crucial:

In order, then, that shows of this kind may be able to achieve their proper purpose, it is essential that the minds and inclinations of the spectators be rightly trained and educated, so that they may not only understand the form proper to each of the arts, but especially that they may be guided in this matter by a right conscience.

Thus they will be enabled to weigh and pass mature judgment on the various items which the film or television or radio puts before them; and not, as frequently happens, be lured and arbitrarily swept away by their power and attractiveness.

If there is lacking this mental training and formation, enlightened by Christian teaching, then neither reasonable pleasures, which everyone readily admits are necessary for all who are involved in the business and troubles of life, nor the progress of mental development can be kept safe.

In the spirit of this document, in 1957, the Legion introduced a new category, A-III (unobjectionable for adults), and made the old category A-II "suitable for adults and adolescents." At the same time, it placed emphasis on rating films according to a sensible appraisal of the facts of contemporary life coupled with the conviction that movies cannot be expected to protect people from influences which they encounter, as a matter of course, in day-to-day life. It also began actively to encourage serious discussion of films both in the Catholic press and in the schools.

Unfortunately, this new and enlightened policy has not, up to now, had its desired effect. The people who disapproved of the

Legion in earlier days apparently have not recognized that its operating principles are now soundly based, as *Miranda Prorsus* said they should be, on an understanding of both the film art and the artist. On the other hand, those of the Legion's erstwhile supporters who had held to the visceral opinion that only tranquilizing movies are moral movies, and who had been confirmed in their judgment by the standard ratings of the "old" Legion, are now outraged by the frank and disquieting words and actions sometimes emanating from the screen with the Legion's tacit approval or, at least, its non-objection.

This confusion of unpleasantness with immorality is by no means an exclusively Catholic phenomenon. I would guess that, of all the editorials and statements from secular and non-Catholic sources viewing current movies with alarm, 90 per cent of them lump together indiscriminately the valid and responsible social documents and the irresponsible sensationalism. Furthermore, these viewerswith-alarm seem blissfully unaware that the alternative (a screen which would not reflect the unpleasant aspects of contemporary life along with the pleasant) would be a sure menace to our welfare as a free nation.

There is one other irony about dependence on the Legion's classification as a guide to film-viewing. Fifteen years after its formation the movies were supplanted as the number-one mass media entertainment by television, which is not only broader in circulation and more easily accessible, but also virtually impossible to regulate by classification. Two highly publicized programs presented recently on CBS-TV demonstrated clearly the confused state of Catholic opinion.

1. When Graham Greene's *The Power and the Glory* was televised, the network was inundated by protesting letters and phone calls from Catholics. They were indignant over the portrayal of a priest as a drunkard who had fathered an illegitimate child. This shock, in turn, rendered them incapable of seeing that the play was saying 1) that the priest was a hero in spite of his human weaknesses, and 2) that the priesthood is a holy and imperishable institution that transcends the individual failings of its members.

A reasonable case might be made that it was imprudent to present the play for such a wide and varied audience. I don't agree with this viewpoint, since I believe that "safe" programing is never on the side of the angels and that this particular risk was worth running.

Besides, simply on a practical level, treacly and inept "pro-Catholic" programing, such as the TV *Going My Way*, gives ten times more aid and comfort to those with an anti-Catholic bias than *The Power and the Glory* ever could. In any event, prudence was not, for the most part, the consideration on which the protests were based.

2. Several months later, along came the episode in "The Defenders" series called *The Benefactor*, which, incredible though it might seem, was built around the portrayal of an abortionist as a crusading altruist and which was, both dramatically and intellectually, an outrageously specious plea for the liberalization of abortion laws. Understandably, the network braced itself for another tidal wave of protests. But only a trickle came. The explanation would seem to be that the play took the form of a nice, familiar, soothing courtroom drama in which the defense lawyer, like all good TV heroes, ran circles around the district attorney to protect his client, and the audience never took a good look at the ideas that were being slipped over to them under the surface.

Obviously, I would not have compiled this lengthy and melancholy estimate of the present condition of American Catholics vis-à-vis films and TV if I did not propose to offer a suggested cure. The proposal simply is that Bishop Scully's call for the formation of film-study clubs, made in AMERICA ("The Movies: A Positive Plan," 3/30/57), be implemented on a large scale. Like most good cures, this one will not work any revolutionary changes overnight. Also, there are booby traps in such a program that must be avoided. For example, it is essential that the people selected to conduct the discussions understand the movies. Furthermore, their purpose must be to stimulate and develop the participants' own critical faculties, not to impose their own esthetic prejudices on unformed minds. I have seen enough of the already existing, good study clubs in action to know how readily and rapidly they succeed in turning young people into discerning filmgoers, when all the casual movie attendance in the world cannot accomplish this.

Perhaps an anecdote I heard last summer can best illustrate the change in outlook which study clubs can bring about. At the end of a ten-week session which included such standard study-club items as *The Informer*, *All the King's Men* and *La Strada*, a high school senior came up to the priest-moderator and with the refreshing directness of youth asked:

"Father, what were we supposed to get out of this program?"

Being a good teacher the priest prodded the youth to answer his own question.

"Gee," he said after a moment, "I don't know. But I'll tell you one thing. I'll never be able to look at *Surfside 6* again."

Take this one youngster who, having realized for himself how he was being cheated by the adolescent drivel cluttering up the mass media, would never again be satisfied with anything but the best. If we can develop a million like him, it will, in time, revolutionize the movie and TV industries.

C. J. McNASPY
Several Ways to Spoil a Museum

¶A few rules of thumb can make your visit more profitable and more pleasant

Twenty-five years ago, as statistics prove, relatively few Americans visited art museums, and of those, even fewer were willing to admit it. Today (again I am leaning on statistics to bolster observation) most museums are thronged. When the Rembrandt painting of "Aristotle Contemplating the Bust of Homer" went on exhibit recently for three days in New York's Parke-Bernet Galleries before its spectacular auction, some 20,000 viewers pressed by to get a glimpse of the treasure. The price of $2,300,000 for which it was bought has already lured additional tens of thousands to the Metropolitan, over and above the millions who visit that museum annually. Today the snob has to assure everyone that he has *not* seen "Aristotle," or he is no true snob. Sheer numbers have quite spoiled many a museum for him.

Next to not going at all, the most effective way to get nothing out of a museum is to go under coercion. Have someone force you to go. This way you can dash through, mutter epithets as you go, and spread ruin about you. I remember spoiling the Pitti gallery in Florence by pressing a medievalist friend into visiting it with me. He was determined not to like anything after 1300, and his spleen was vented particularly on people like Raphael. It took me years before I could work up courage to revisit the Pitti and recover its treasures.

Nor should you enter a museum when you want quick thrills—even of the more exalted sort provided by opera, symphony or drama. Even painting and visual arts generally require some contemplation in time; the temporal arts (music, poetry, etc.) simply force you to sit still as they unfold their message, but to works of art that exist in space *you* have to give time yourself. Speed-reading doubtless has its place, as have other devices of instant information. A blitz tour of a gallery, on the other hand, invites disaster. It is really wiser and more restful to sit outside the Louvre, enjoy the garden, and check it off your "must" list. This way, your memory will be pleasant and clean.

More subtly vulgar, but almost as unfruitful, is the get-your-money's-worth approach to a great museum. In America or Britain, where most museums are free of charge, one may be less inclined to be miserly. The pittance charged in Continental museums, however, may lead you astray. Try to see everything in the Prado during one visit, and you will surely perish of esthetic satiety. Better yet, insist on a glimpse of every one of the 364,000 *objets d'art* in New York's Metropolitan or the endless treasury of the British Museum, and you will be cured of the museum habit for life—if you survive the test at all.

Seriously, though, the problem is not unlike that of approaching a smörgåsbord. You *must* choose. But how? Most museums offer guided tours, and if you can bear being herded about, this may be the answer. Better, if you have a really knowledgeable friend—not just someone who can rattle off the current clichés—and can get a personal tour, you are fortunate. Some museums, like the Washington National Gallery, now have electronic guides—earphones which are easy to turn on and off without discourtesy.

Even better, try to have some preparation before you go. Here, as well as elsewhere, "the more you bring, the more you take away." Try to spend at least a few hours with an introduction to art. There are several excellent paperbacks on sale, my favorite for this purpose being Eric Newton's *European Painting and Sculpture* (the first two chapters are especially enlightening). Among larger works, Newton's *The Arts of Man* (New York Graphic Society. 1960. $5.95) is an excellent value; so are the standard histories of art by Helen Gardner (especially the new Crosby edition) and by E.

H. Gombrich. From a more introductory viewpoint, you can do no better than spend time with John Canaday's *Metropolitan Seminars in Art*, particularly Portfolio No. 1, *What Is a Painting?*

Apart from this general equipment, it is a good idea to know something of the contents of the museum about to be invaded. If you are in a foreign country, don't be above purchasing a printed guide. Even before leaving America, you may want to examine a new *Guide Bleu*, or the revised Baedeker, or, on a more modest scale, the delightfully written *Holiday* series on various nations. (Of these latter, I found the introduction to the Prado contained in the volume on Spain most perceptive.) A compact, pocket-size volume that you may want to carry along with you—it gives the history of art and what to see in the most important art museums in Europe and America—is Howard Daniel's *Adventures in Art* (Abelard-Schuman. 1960. $5). For museums in the United States, we are fortunate to have *American Art Museums and Galleries*, by that sensitive and informed critic, Eloise Spaeth (Harper. 1960. $5.95). It gives you everything you need for an intelligent first visit to museums, from Seattle to Sarasota, great and small.

But books are not the only aids readily available. If your time or energy are limited (when are they not?), swallow all pride and ask someone at the entrance: "What room is the 'Mona Lisa' in? Or Botticelli's 'Spring'? Or the 'Night Watch'? Or the 'Third of May'?" If you happen to be in quest of a particular painter or school or period, simply ask, in all humility: "Where are your Veroneses, or your cubists, or your Flemish primitives?" If your humility is overwhelming—a good state of mind for all learning—you may even ask: "What would you suggest that I see? This is my first visit and I don't know very much."

A completely different approach, which is rewarding, especially when you have lots of time and are in the right museum, is simply to browse. This is, I believe, the thing to do in small, perfect galleries like the Frick (Fifth Avenue at 70th St., New York City), or the utterly fantastic ones, like Fenway Court (the Isabella Stewart Gardner Museum) in Boston, where just about everything is close to top-drawer. Both these museums are excellent antidotes to their colossal neighbors (the Metropolitan and the Museum of Fine Arts), where one risks being crushed by sheer bulk.

Again, a skillful way to spoil even the finest museum is to go in a state of exhaustion. The largest collections are particularly vulnerable, and none rivals the Louvre in this regard. Time after time, I tried that uneven palace of beauty and ugliness, before discovering that the problem was not the unevenness so much as my physical state of being—I was worn out before I started. If you are touring Europe, I strongly suggest that you "do" your museums in the morning, when you are fresh, saving less exhausting things for the afternoon. When you are physically or mentally weary, your esthetic metabolism is low and you had better rest or play golf. Otherwise you may find reason to join with someone overheard in the Prado: "Yes, dear, I know it's a masterpiece, and that's a masterpiece, and they're all masterpieces! But my feet hurt."

Akin to this is the matter of mental and emotional fatigue. Even the most toughened museum trotter needs variety in order to survive, and variety involves timing and spacing. Never "do" two museums—or two anything, for that matter—on the same day. By judicious planning, you may succeed in enjoying a museum (or part of one) in the morning, a cathedral in the afternoon, the mood of the city toward evening.

There is a form of snobbery that spoils many fine museums. It is the notion that in order for anything to be really great, it must be far away. True, if you live in the Dakotas, Mississippi or Alabama, you are probably accustomed to travel, and are willing to go as far as Minneapolis, New Orleans or Atlanta for a view of one of the masters. However, surpassingly great as are the Hague Mauritshuis, the Amsterdam Rijksmuseum, the Florence Uffizi, the Barcelona Palacio Nacional, the Venice Accademia, the London National Gallery, and a few other favorite European museums, we are foolish to forget that at least ten of the world's finest are here in the United States. The geographical distribution of the art works they contain may not be as wide as we should like, but there are good collections available in every population center of the country, and among the very greatest anywhere are the Art Institute (Chicago), the Cleveland Art Institute and the Museum of Art (Philadelphia).

Moreover, our American museums are, as a rule, well planned and balanced, entrance is free and many (e.g., the National Gallery, the Frick and the Museum of Modern Art) are air-conditioned. It is true, we have no collection of Velasquez, El Greco or Goya to match the Prado (but no museum has), nor of Raphael to match the Pitti or the Uffizi, nor of Tintoretto to match the Accademia, nor of Michelangelo to match the Sistine, nor of Giotto to match the Scrovegni Chapel (Padua), nor of Romanesque art to match the Barcelona Palacio Nacional, nor of Turner to match the Tate (London). But think of the treasures we do have: the Vermeers in the National Gallery and the Frick; the impressionists in Chicago and Boston, not to mention the Barnes collection in Philadelphia; the 41 Picassos in the Museum of Modern Art and those in the National Gallery. One could go on and on, not forgetting that unique treasury of all medieval arts, New York's Cloisters.

A caution for you who plan your first trip to Europe next summer: much of the greatest art is not and never was planned to be in museums. Byzantine mosaics, Romanesque statuary and stained glass, Gothic tapestries and reredoses, and the summits of Renaissance painting were most commonly destined for churches—long before museums were dreamed of. And, appropriately, it is in church that they still perform their function most fully. Only in relatively recent times, with the secularization of European art, has the private gallery or public museum become the Sanctuary of Art (cynics would say: the Sepulchre of Art), all too unrelated to a meaningful social function. This partial unreality makes for the misery of museums—though, in default of anything better, we gratefully grant their edge of glory.

One last word. Do the obvious. See the famous things; they are likely to be the best. And don't be embarrassed about being thought a tourist. You wouldn't want to be taken for an expert, would you?

CYRIL B. EGAN

Subway Stations of the Cross

¶We can pray in the spirit of the season even when using public transportation

As a church, the subway is not much. In a pinch, a subway might pass for a church basement, maybe. But in general, not the place where you would expect to find God. Of course, you could make a smashing punch line out of such an upstairs in the downstairs. Just imagine: *I found God in the subway*. Sensational. But just a little bit absurd—or is it absurd?

I have seen a number of people reading prayer books in the subway. I have seen a priest reading his office in the subway. I have
several times seen an old woman—at other times, a young woman
—thumbing her rosary. And I am sure there are people who pray
here or who devoutly meditate here without so much as moving
their hands or their lips.

Prayer is the lifting of the mind and heart to God. God knows,
a rider needs a lift in the subway. True, you can do crossword
puzzles or read the ads, count beards and beatniks or the number
of people who smile. But maybe what a man needs in the subway
is to get away from people—to take off, imaginatively at least, in a
flight to God.

But this is not religion. Religion must begin with people. These
are the stubborn facts. Soulless as they appear, all these people have
souls. I must face them—empathize, sympathize with my neighbor.

Who is my neighbor? My neighbor is an Irishman, an Irish-
American. He is German, German-American. He is Negro, Puerto-
Rican, Swedish, Chinese. My neighbor is the drunk across the aisle,
the man who has squeezed into the half-foot of space between me
and the next sitter. He is the swivel-hipped kid who is frazzling
my ears with his transistor. Certainly I don't have to like these people; but I must love them.

If that's the case, I've got my task cut out for me here. All the
sad, bored faces. The alien faces. Oh, to be back in the subway I
first rode in 1904! Such a nice clean car, and so few people, and
those mostly Irish-American and German-American. Today, if I
saw an Italian in the subway, I, of Irish descent, would shout *Hur-
ray, here's one of us!*

Why do I feel such a repulsion to these people? Do I dislike them
because they are poor? Do I dislike them because they are bored?
Because they do not smile? Because they are but cracked and dirty
mirrors of exemplary me?

Who is my neighbor? "A certain Samaritan went down from
Jerusalem to Jericho." Maybe he's only going from City Hall, at
one end of town, to Fordham Road, at the other; but even a
Samaritan moves warily here, worried lest the victim repudiate the
rescue, or, acceptant of the rescuer, snarl him in a web of litigious
trouble.

I remember, after the lonely city streets of World War II, seeing
at 34th and Broadway my first crowd of postwar people pouring

into the subway. I felt overwhelmed. Some evil force seemed to be pelting people at me. I sighed with relief when I had moved off to the lonely end of the subway platform.

There is little physical aloneness, however, in this subway car where I now damply sit. . . . Enter through the center doors a man with a sign in bright heaven-blue letters: LOVE YOUR NEIGHBOR. JESUS DIED FOR YOU AND ME. . . . Isn't that ridiculous? In the middle of the subway! It's as if Christ walked in—in the rush hour—staggering under the weight of His cross. Would some Simon the Cyrenian help Him carry it? Would this Simon later get off with him to give him a hand? What an explanation Simon would have to make when he got home to his wife! Can you imagine the curtain lecture Simon's wife would give him?

"You're late. What's the reason? . . . You had to help someone out? A blonde? . . . Oh, a man. Did you *have* to help him? . . . An officer called on you to help him? Couldn't you have told him no? . . . Well, you sure were a sucker to carry a cross all that way. What did *you* get out of it? . . . He said he was God? You really *are* crazy, aren't you? . . . So you want some liniment for your shoulder? Well, don't ask me to go get it for you. It's a long time since you went out of your way to carry anything for *me*."

On Good Friday I have seen at least one subway rider reading the Passion from the New Testament. Glancing over his shoulder at the page and the purple ribbon, I suddenly asked myself: Why not the Subway Stations of the Cross?

They're putting jazz in the liturgy, aren't they? I don't see why we can't put the Stations of the Cross in the subway. Maybe not *put* them, just *say* them. Does that sound blasphemous? Sometimes blasphemy and piety are separated by a hair's breadth. After all, I'm not taking God for a subway ride. God is everywhere, even in the dank air of the tomb, even in the subway, for that matter—as He was in the catacombs. The fact that I can conceive of His presence here as blasphemous indicates a certain unhealthiness in my own spiritual outlook.

Why *shouldn't* I make the Stations of the Cross in the subway? Why *shouldn't* I say: First Station, 14th Street?

The air is stale and stinking and a little sickening with pomade and cheap perfumes and scent of tired bubble gum. The doors open to admit a surge of sticky, pushing people. Last man on has a bandaged head smelling of liniment. . . . "Hey, you, quit your shoving." "Get off my feet." . . . First Station, 14th Street: *Jesus is condemned to death.*

Identify, identify, identify. Well, if you can't identify, at least relate. Give me a rousing crisis, a big event, and I'll rise to it, finding not too much difficulty and not a little drama in relating to the sufferings of Christ. But the prosaic little difficulties that lie at the grass-roots level—at the subway level—are something else again.

What has my neighbor's kick in the shins—*my* shins—to do with the Passion of Christ? What have these sweating, stinking, aggressively scented, staring, glaring people to do with the Mystical Body? Who in this fifteen-cent hell is my neighbor? Maybe I can answer who *is* my neighbor—but not who *are* my neighbors, when there are seven and a half million of them, hundreds of whom have been packed hip to hip, sometimes almost eyeball to eyeball, in this mobile sardine can. How can I say: *Here Jesus is condemned to death*—where death has degenerated to a creeping claustrophobia for creatures whose life is already a part-time entombment?

We adore Thee, O Christ, and we bless Thee, because by Thy holy cross Thou hast redeemed the world.

Second Station, 42nd Street. . . . At Times Square, five or six blocks west, my thoughts might readily escalate to the neighborhood aboveground—to the wantonness rampant on newsstand and movie billboard. That neighborhood bears a kind of cross. But here underground, at the drabber crossroads of 42nd Street and Lexington Avenue—how can I say, even under my breath, *Jesus is made to bear His cross?* Isn't it a bit melodramatic to call the hot, stale air a cross—the swastikas and sex symbols scrawled here a cross? How can I dignify as crosses the smell of dirty feet and oversweet perfume and humid humanity? Irritants, true. But what have they to do with God, or with me and religion?

We adore Thee, O Christ, and we bless Thee, because by Thy holy cross Thou hast redeemed the world. But to tell the truth, Lord, I find it pretty hard to relate these perspiring, prosaic experiences to myself and the Passion of Christ. You understand, Lord, don't You?

I think I have set myself too tough an exercise. I could of course make the Stations and ignore the people. But somehow this seems wrong. Somehow the people must come into this picture. But how? By stumbling over my feet? But I can't identify this sprawling somebody with the Saviour.

Jesus falls the first time, the second time, the third time; meets
His mother, Veronica, the women of Jerusalem; is stripped of His
garments, dies on the cross, is taken down and ensepulchered. . . .
Where does any of this fit in the subway, unless it's the last stop at
Woodlawn Cemetery? I know—that sounds like a ghastly joke. But
it's no more than the honest hysteria of an overwhelmed imagination. Anyway, you can be sure there will be someone stopping off
at Woodlawn, widow or widower, orphan or child-bereft, with the
hope, if not of resurrection, at least of reunion in an eternal future
—undistracted by frenetic subway noise.

A girl across the way opens a pocketbook. The title reads *The
Agony and the Ecstasy*. Very little ecstasy here in the subway.
Change to the agony and the ugliness, and you have something
more like it. A kind of small-time crucifixion. Creep, crawl, jolt,
lurch.

Some people treasure the crucifix. Others hold it monstrous. Both
are right. The crucifixion was monstrous, bloody and ugly. What
could such a defacing be but ugly? But to the inner vision, the
crucifix is God's love suffering and transforming ugliness—a bitterness that is but the prelude to beauty.

The train screeches to a halt. The motors stop; only the fans go
whirling overhead, churning the stale air. Now the man standing to
the right of my seat is arranging the pages of his newspaper so page
one comes foremost. GANG LORD GETS CHAIR, reads the headline.
Nineteen hundred and thirty years backward and forward, this
could be—could have been—JESUS GETS THE CHAIR. And *Ecce
Homo* could have been *Take a good look at this guy*. . . . Is this
too crude for you to stomach? So was the cross and the aching
I.N.R.I. they tacked over the head of the Christ.

It looks, it feels, as if this subway will never run again. We are a
carload of lost gaspers—a welter of suspended animation sidetracked
in a corridor of eternity. Only the subway crusader, the holy guy
with the inspirational signs, shows any evidence of being on the go.
He has come back to our car and is passing through it with a new
sign, which he has flipped over the old one.

WILL YOU NOT, says the sign, WATCH AND PRAY AN HOUR WITH ME?
. . . The woman sitting on my right sees the signbearer not. A
luncheon tippler, she has been boozily dozing since she took her
seat in the train. The passengers standing in front of me look be-

yond the signbearer to the door. They are wondering if this car called claustrophobia is ever going to move again. "Watch and pray!" snorts the man on my left. He nudges me in the side. "Where the hell did that creep come from?"

"From the rear car," say I. "He was in this car a few minutes ago—with another sign. And I am beginning to think he may be the one sane man in the train. Maybe you and I are nuts."

Luckily, the sound of the motor stirring and the wheels rolling into action drown out my last sentence. In a minute we are moving into the streaming sunlight of the overground, on to my last station. Not to my last Station of the Cross (metaphor cannot stand so much strain), but to the end of my meditation—and a wheel-grinding *Amen.*

SECTION II

YOUTH ASKS QUESTIONS

ANDREW M. GREELEY
A New Breed

¶There aren't very many of them as yet, but they are important just the same

There has risen up a New Breed that was all but invisible five years ago. There are not very many of them; they might not show up in any sample; the majority of their classmates in the colleges, the seminaries, the juniorates of the country continue to be listless and indifferent. But the New Breed is making so much noise that one hardly has time to notice the majority. Almost any college president or seminary rector will admit their existence and will confess puzzlement about what they want.

All I can report about the New Breed are my own impressions, and the impressions are often confused. There are many things about the New Breed that I like, but many things that baffle me.

First of all, they are greatly concerned about things like honesty, integrity and authenticity. They must know the reason why. They do not refuse to obey, but before they obey they want to sit down and discuss the reasons for orders; they are confused when those in authority feel threatened by this desire for discussion. As a Jesuit college administrator observed: "For four hundred years we have been in the apostolate of Christian education, and now we suddenly find that our seminarians are demanding that we justify this apostolate." And a confrere added: "Jesuit seminarians are the most radical people in the American church—bar none." Neither of the two was opposed to the New Breed, just puzzled by them.

With this concern for integrity and honesty there comes an inability to be devious or opportunist—or even diplomatic. One generation of Catholic radicals (at least of the variety I know in Chicago) accomplished their modest goals by infinite tact, patience and political skill. The New Breed will have none of this. All issues, minor or major, must be brought into the open and discussed. Truth must be spoken even if speaking it does no good and may even cause harm. To do less would be to debase one's honesty, to compromise one's authenticity. It is hard to negotiate with them, because they seem to feel that the mere repetition of what they take to be true will eventually carry the day; they seem so eager to make almost any question a matter of principle that one is tempted to feel that they are looking for a fight—though perhaps they are only looking for a cause.

With some exceptions, however, they are not intentionally disobedient or disrespectful of authority. They are appalled when their honesty is taken as disrespect and their desire to discuss is understood as disobedience; they can't see how such an interpretation can be put on their intentions. They think that they are being much more open with their superiors than those who comply with an external show of docility and then complain bitterly about authority when authority's back is turned. They contend that their desire for understanding is much to be preferred to a literal obedience that deliberately sabotages the goals of authority. They argue that superiors are much better off with the consent of free men than the compliance of automatons. They cannot understand why many superiors do not seem to agree with them.

They are greatly worried about "fulfillment." Their predecessors saw a job that had to be done and did not ask whether the job was going to fulfill the needs of the people who did it. But the fierce personalism of the New Breed will not tolerate such a "nonhuman" approach. They feel that they can help others only if they can relate as persons and that they cannot relate unless there is a possibility of "fulfillment" in the relationship. They are not attracted by a task that seems to rule out the possibility of an "I-Thou" dyad.

They are anxious about loving and being loved—or more precisely, with whether they are able to love. It is not at all unusual for young people to be concerned with love; but it is surely new for youth to question its own ability to love, especially when to the outside observer it often seems that those who are the most able to love are the most likely to doubt their powers of love. They do not identify love with sexual romance, and indeed this latter aspect of love is much less a source of worry to them than friendship, encounter, relationship. They have no doubt that they can be sexually stimulated, but they are not sure that they can be "friends," that they can "encounter" a sexual partner or anyone else.

As a result their "radicalism" is not likely to have anything to do with "causes"; they are more interested in people than in ideas. Their predecessors on the picket lines of the 1930's were quite unconcerned with whether they were "liked" or not; there were enemies to be fought, principles to be defended, wars to be won. The New Breed wants to help people and wants to be loved by them. Hence they are not political ideologues; they are not "radicals" in the traditional sense of the word, since they are almost completely without a coherent political philosophy. While they work for civil rights, and may periodically throw up picket lines (sometimes, one thinks, for the sheer hell of it), they are not very active in the militant civil rights organizations or in the peace movement and studiously ignore the ideological overtones of these movements. Neither do they find much but amusement in the radical conservatives who are shouting so loudly. The New Breed is not, by any means, uninterested in politics; they are fascinated by the political game, may be active at the precinct level, and are tempted by governmental careers. But, like their heroes of the Irish Maffia, they are pragmatic rather than ideological in their approach.

Unlike the "Strangers in the House" of whom I wrote five years ago, the New Breed does more than talk about human suffering. It is from the ranks of the New Breed that volunteers are recruited for the Peace Corps, Pavla, the Extension home missions, and especially the various inner-city student programs that are spreading across the country like a prairie fire. Such work is with people; it is non-ideological and "fulfilling." One hears the volunteers observe: "We're getting more out of it than the people are we are supposed to be helping."

While such statements may not be true, they furnish a very revealing insight into the New Breed. But whatever their views as to the nature of the work, make no mistake about it, they are proceeding with a cool and nonchalant competence that is often quite disconcerting. The Northern Student Movement and related tutoring programs are anything but amateur. The New Breed knows how to work with committees, write brochures, give speeches, raise money, utilize community resources and issue press releases. CALM (Chicago Area Lay Movement), the inner-city movement I am most familiar with, was a going concern almost before those of us who were watching it closely were conscious that it had even started moving. Indeed, it managed to get stories into the newspapers about its work *before it had begun to work*—which is surely the height of something or other. This competence should not be too surprising, since the New Breed is composed of the young people who have been student leaders through high school and college and know all about organizations. As one full-time worker put it: "After running things for eight years, it would be terribly dull just to sit in a classroom and teach school." Nor does the New Breed seem inclined to view its involvement in the inner-city as a passing phenomenon. Grace Ann Carroll, the cofounder of CALM, spoke for most of the New Breed when she said: "Before we're finished, we're going to think up a lot more things to do, so that everyone who wants, no matter what their age or responsibilities, can get involved."

We may be witnessing a major social change as the future members of the upper middle class return to the inner-city from which their parents fled.

The non-ideological coolness of the New Breed does not make them easy to deal with. Those who have positions of authority and responsibility over them surely deserve sympathy. The New Breed are frequently groping and inarticulate about precisely what they want, but they know that they want change. Often they seem almost to be hoping that their superiors will refuse their requests so that there may be a clear issue about which to fight, a definite change around which they can rally. They want *freedom now*— whatever that may mean.

The "radical" Catholic youth of the past never expected to win. They did not think that in their lifetime they would see the ideals of the social or liturgical teachings of the Church become a reality. They were resigned to being a despised minority fighting for a lost cause. But the New Breed is not going to play the game that way. They have tasted enough change in the last few years to want much more. They are quite confident that they are going to win and that they will live to bury those who stand in their way.

The New Breed is not flexible, it is not gradualist. It wants a Church that is relevant to its own needs and the needs it sees in the world, and it wants it now, not next week. Unfortunately, it is not able to say exactly what that relevance involves, and at this stage of the game neither is anyone else. Thus the New Breed is a trial to its elders; we cannot understand them and they can't really understand themselves. They are the product of a revolution of expanding expectations, and in the midst of such transitional situations, friction (and occasionally very serious friction) is inevitable. As much as we are annoyed by the inconsistencies and irrationality that the New Breed often seem to display, we must not overlook what they are trying to tell us; they are trying to say that you cannot have a half-souled *aggiornamento*, that if you open the window you are not going to be able to close it again and that the wind that blows in is likely to bring all sorts of strange things with it.

I have a hunch that the New Breed is basically gradualist; if it sees progress being made it will be content with a moderate pace of change and not demand everything all at once. Their present resistance to the gradualist approach may be merely an objection to a pace of change that is so slow as to be almost imperceptible. They may oppose a gradualist *aggiornamento* because many of them feel that almost no change has filtered down to their level. As the pace of reform and renewal accelerates at the grass roots, they may be much easier to deal with. This view however, could be the wishful thinking of a member of the older generation, hoping that in a few years the New Breed will start acting like them.

Yet it would be a terrible mistake to think that they are going to leave the Church, either by apostasy or alienation. It is their Church and it would be difficult even to drive them out of it. They have been told that they are the Church so often that they now believe it, and while they may dislike many of the things they see in the Church today, they are sophisticated enough to know that these things can be changed and young enough to think that they are going to help change them. They are restless with the Church, but they are restless with it as the fair bride that they love. Nor are they anticlerical, even though they may object to many of the policies they take to be "clerical." Indeed, anticlericalism may well decline among the New Breed since its lay and clerical members share so many common problems and hopes. It often seems that the most "anticlerical" of the New Breed are those who are seminarians; and while a very few of the ex-seminarians have, temporarily at least, left the Church, the majority of the "ex's" simply become leaders of the New Breed laity (as do the "ex-postulants" and "ex-novices"). No, the New Breed is not going to leave, nor is it going to be quiet. We are going to have to put up with it for a long time.

How has the New Breed come to be? How can we explain it?

The answers are not easy. The New Breed has known neither war nor depression, but only cold war and prosperity. It lives in the midst of a psychological age when even the Sunday magazines talk about existentialism. It has read the philosophy and literature of the day, with its heavy emphasis on significance and personalism. It hears of the *aggiornamento* in the Church and can follow in detail the progress of reform in journals of the Catholic Establishment. Its prophet is Fr. Teilhard (in one New Breed college apartment I saw a shrine to Teilhard), and it has found its patron saint in John Kennedy, who, with his youthfulness, his pragmatism, his restlessness, his desire for challenge and service, his vision of a new freedom, reflected in so many ways what the New Breed wants to be. Perhaps there are other explanations too. It is too early to say whence the New Breed has come; we will have to wait until they can explain themselves.

What will come of them? We have said that few will leave the Church. Some will become cynical and alienated. Others will bow to pressures of family and friends and settle for the good life; yet others will dissipate their energies in romantic dreams or confused and futile love affairs. Not a few of them will marry people who are not of the New Breed and endure lives of agony or frustration. Some will mellow with age. But it is a fair bet that enough of them will remain. They will mature with time, but we will be kidding ourselves if we think they will mature in our patterns. They are different now and they will be different twenty-five years from now.

They are a paradoxical bunch, supremely self-confident, yet anxious and restless; they are organizationally efficient and yet often diplomatically tactless; they are eager to engage in dialogue and yet frequently inarticulate in what they want to say; they are without ideology and yet insistent on freedom; they are generous with the poor and suffering and terribly harsh in their judgments of their elders and superiors; they are ecumenical to the core and yet astonishingly parochial in their tastes and fashions; they want desperately to love but are not sure that they know how to love. They want to scale the heights yet are mired in the foothills. I am sure there is a resolution of these paradoxes, that the New Breed has some principle of inner consistency, but because I am not one of them I cannot discover this principle.

It should be clear that I am ambivalent about the New Breed. I

am fascinated by them and I admire their courage; yet they frighten
me. In another quarter of a century they will be taking over the
American Church. They will be the bishops, the mothers general,
the rectors, the pastors, the provincials, the superiors, the scholars,
the politicians, the organizers, the editors, the leaders of lay organizations. I don't know quite what their Church will look like and
I wonder how much room there will be in it for someone like me.
The New Breed has reason to be confident. Everything is on their
side—their youth, time, the wave of history, and, one suspects, the
Holy Spirit.

ANDREW M. GREELEY
The Temptation of the New Breed

¶A critical second look at the young people originally identified
and labeled by this writer as the New Breed

Not long ago in AMERICA I tried to tie together some impressions
about modern youth under the label of "A New Breed." I must
confess I was overwhelmed by the reaction. All sorts of people announced—some of them validly—that they were members of this
New Breed and happily proclaimed that at long last there was someone who understood them. (Alas, it is not true; I do not understand
them.) On the other hand, many of those who had identified in the
New Breed a dangerous enemy blamed me for the New Breed
phenomenon—on the same principle, I suppose, that ancient kings
invoked in executing messengers who brought bad news: he who
announces bad news is the one responsible for its coming to be.

Not having learned my lesson from this experience, I am now
venturing back into the land where the New Breed dwell, with
some new impressions. I have not changed my mind about the New
Breed. I still like them; I am still sympathetic, puzzled and hopeful.
But I think now I understand more clearly what their problems are
and what is the crucial temptation they face. My friends in the
New Breed must excuse me for sounding more critical in this article

than in the previous one; but a year ago I was talking *about* the
New Breed, and at this point I am talking *to* them. If I may borrow
a tactic from their own approach to life, I would say that honesty
compels me to write the things that I am writing here.

First of all, I feel that the New Breed are increasingly handicapped by a lack of ideology. What I mean by ideology is something rather different from what the New Breed mean by it. I mean
a coherent and specific set of goals, a consistent series of norms according to which society is to be remade.

We ask the New Breed what they want of us, or what they want
of society, and they say: "We want you to love us, we want you to
permit us to make something of the world where you have failed."
But then if we ask: "How have we failed, and how do you want
us to love you?" their words become vague. They tell us simply
that we have failed because there is not enough love or freedom
in the world.

"Freedom," "self-fulfillment" and "love" are for them the only
ideology necessary. These are ends sufficient in themselves, and
they need not be specified any further. When you ask them:
"Freedom for what?" "Self-fulfillment toward what goals?" "Love
in what systematic fashion?" they look at you as though you were
a relic of another era.

Secondly, the lack of ideology interferes in many instances with
the critical social analysis and the systematic commitment to work
that is necessary to accomplish a change. The "radicalism" of the
New Breed is too often a kind of free-floating social concern.
There are all sorts of things wrong with society, and the New
Breed are going to do something about these things; but they
are not very specific about what is wrong with society—or what
must be done about it—aside from saying that they do not feel
free in it to be themselves. As one very honest member of the
New Breed put it: "It's not just that we don't know the answers
to what is wrong with the world; we don't even know the proper
words to phrase the question."

It is relatively easy to throw up a picket line, or to tutor a
culturally deprived child in the inner city, or even to join the
Peace Corps or go to Mississippi. But these actions, while they
demonstrate concern and, in some instances even heroism, deal
generally with the symptoms of social problems and not with the

roots. All the picket lines in the world will not resolve the difficulties of segregated education in the large urban centers unless the tax structures and the revenue codes under which these giant cities must operate are drastically reformed.

Young people ask me what organization they should join if they wish to accomplish social change in the Chicago metropolitan area. They wonder if it ought to be CORE, or SNCC, or the Catholic Interracial Council. When I reply that they ought to consider becoming precinct captains or assistant precinct captains in the Cook County Regular Democratic Organization, they look at me as though I were insane. The New Breed seem to have little taste for acquiring the knowledge and the skills necessary to deal with the causes of social problems. They have no taste at all for the complicated details of revenue codes or the grubby day-to-day work of a political organization.

Thirdly, the New Breed, for all the skill they can display when they finally commit themselves to organizational work, are basically suspicious and distrustful of organization of any kind. They just want to love, and they think that love and interpersonal relationship more or less by themselves are enough to solve the problems of society. Organizations cramp the style of the human spirit: they restrict the spontaneity and creative love of the individual person. The New Breed want no part of this. They find it hard to believe there was a time in the not too distant past when young people could enthusiastically dedicate themselves to an organization—whether the Young Peoples' Socialist League in the 1930's or the Young Christian Students immediately after World War II.

It seems to me, however, that in the absence of carefully planned organizations, human love will, in the final analysis, become weak and ineffective. Even the most elemental kind of human love only becomes really effective when it is put into the organized structure we call the family. To be able to love at all effectively, the New Breed will have to overcome their distrust of organizations. They must learn to distinguish between those organizations that stifle the human spirit and those that create a situation where the human personality can flower much more fully than it could if left to itself. Unless they do so, they will pass from the scene without having accomplished much besides stirring up quite a bit of noise and excitement.

Here, then, is the crucial temptation facing the New Breed: either they acquire at least a provisional and concrete ideology and the ability to commit themselves to organizational work, or they expose themselves to becoming disenchanted and disillusioned idealists.

One hears that some of the young people coming back from the Peace Corps, or from PAVLA, or from Mississippi, are disappointed in their experience. They have left the comfort of their homes to help others, to love them, and they have found that many people don't seem to want their love, won't co-operate with them, won't accept the values that these young Americans bring. Those who were to be helped will not "relate" in a satisfactory fashion and will not behave like upper-middle-class white Americans. Love is just not enough; to re-evaluate everything that has been done in the past does not furnish automatic answers as to what must be done in the future. Our social problems are more complicated than they thought.

Feeling rejected, discouraged, disillusioned, the member of the New Breed is strongly tempted to give up, to retreat, to find some comfortable ivory tower where he can "relate" to a small group of like-minded people. Thus, the disillusioned New Breeder often thinks he will find in the academic life the love and freedom he is seeking. (Yet, in a year or two, he will undergo the even worse disillusionment of discovering that the academic life is the last sanctuary of the inner-directed man—the last of the "jungles" to be found in the Western world.)

The alternative for the New Breeder is to drastically change his style—to become concerned with the technical, the political, the organizational; to acquire the competencies and the skills necessary for the complicated grubby work that must be done if the social structure of the world is to be even slightly modified. For whether the problems are in South America, or Mississippi, or the inner city of Chicago, solutions cannot be discovered without profound understanding of law, government methods and the economics and social organization of modern life. The New Breeder, too, must fashion for himself a highly specific set of goals and norms; without these, any human effort is likely to flounder in the sea of well-meaning but ineffective good intentions. If he is to manage to keep alive the bright enthusiasm of his early days in the New Breed, he must abandon the cheap clichés and slogans of the books of existentialist philosophy and become hard-nosed and practical. As yet few have attempted this.

The problem of disillusionment is aggravated by the fact that the New Breed seem to have their own built-in variety of mental disturbance in the "identity crisis" syndrome. There isn't much doubt to any of us who have tried to work with the New Breed that they go through tremendous mental anguish in the process of growing up. The basic problem is that the very best young people we have simply are not sure *who* they are, *where* they are going, or *what* they want out of life. Erik Erikson's phrase "identity crisis" serves only to give a name to an experience that especially torments the members of the New Breed.

As Erikson has pointed out, it is essential to the weathering of this phase in the struggle for maturity that the young person be able to fashion an ideology that will guide the rest of his life. Part of the New Breed's problem arises because they do not know what they want, because they have no ideology. But part of the problem, too, comes from the "honesty" and self-consciousness of the New Breed. Young people today have discovered, to a greater extent than any of their predecessors, that they have an unconscious. They feel compelled to question and examine constantly their motives and their emotional states. As one fairly cynical New Breeder put it: "The trouble with us is that we must make a great big hairy deal out of all our problems." The difficulties that previous generations might have dismissed as minor take on major importance with the New Breed. This is especially true of "problems of faith." Religious doubts are not new, but the seriousness with which they are pondered seems to be much more intense with the New Breed.

The result of this intense emotionalism is that psychological ups and downs are greatly magnified. New Breeders seem to be manic-depressives. This is why it is so difficult to work with them. For all their organizational skills, one can never be quite sure that, when the chips are down, the young person may not find himself in a paralyzing emotional crisis. One finds oneself in the position of saying: "Follow me. We are going to storm the barricades!" and then looking around and finding one's followers sitting down and pondering the latest phase of their identity crisis. Again, their moods force them into taking extreme positions. Many of them leave college or seminary because, as they say, "I will be destroyed if I stay here any longer." Perhaps, indeed, they *will* be destroyed, though one wonders if the problem may be, more simply, that they lack the emotional fortitude to stick out a difficult situation.

I cannot help feeling that, for all their rejection of "phoniness," the New Breed's emotionalism has just a bit of phony about it, too. The problems they have can be solved with intelligent effort; it is possible for the New Breed to take counsel, to put their life in order. What I find almost inexcusable is the tendency of so many of them to drift. It seems to me that in their lives there are, indeed, just too many "great big hairy deals."

Surely I am too harsh in judging the moods and identity crises of the New Breed. For New Breeders have grown up in a very different world, a world that I do not know and cannot really understand. No doubt I have permitted myself to become embittered because I have seen so many of their efforts collapse under strain. I know such a great number of young people going through these intense emotional crises. I wish there was something I could do to assist them, but having failed so many times, I fear there is nothing I can do. Sometimes I am tempted to believe that all that any of us from the older generation can do is leave them alone and let them work things out by themselves.

Thus, the final element in the temptation of the New Breed is the almost total misunderstanding between them and their predecessors, a misunderstanding perhaps more acute than has ever before separated an older and a younger generation. The older generation interprets the constant questioning of established traditions, the incessant demand for explanation, the persistent and often apparently unreasonable criticism as being signs of revolt. But this revolt is one that can neither describe what it opposes nor make clear what it wants to substitute for the present order of the Church and of society. Superiors, parents, teachers, advisors—all of us find it exceedingly difficult to communicate with these young people. The New Breed will have to excuse us of the older generation if, in the absence of a more articulate description of their goals, we say that we simply do not understand them. We would like to enter into dialogue, but there seems to exist an almost insuperable barrier to communication. Even those of us who admire them, who are sympathetic to them, who want to help them, find the languages we speak, the cultures from which we come, discouragingly different.

And so the New Breed feel, in the words of one member of the Free Speech Movement, that "you really can't trust anyone who is over thirty." The New Breed want to start all over again; they want to remake the world into a place of love and freedom. This desire of theirs to remake the world is a laudable one, indeed, but it seems to me that they will never accomplish their goal unless they can re-establish communication with those who have gone before them. In the absence of communication, we cannot help them and they cannot help us—and I think that they're going to need our help if the temptation to disillusionment and discouragement is not to overwhelm them. Nor do I think they can resolve their problems of identity unless they find at least some of the older generation who can, in some vague fashion, understand what they are trying to say.

These are dark days for the New Breed. They are going through a particularly unpleasant form of hell—a hell that they have made for themselves but that results also from the misunderstanding of those who are older. For the New Breed, the future still looks bright. They shall overcome—someday. The older generation, we Old Breeds and Half-Breeds, are no problem in the long run. But the crucial question is: can the New Breed overcome themselves, their own inarticulateness, their own confusion, their own uncertainty? At times, I confess, I have my doubts. But I am certainly not prepared to bet against the New Breed. Everything is still on their side.

JAMES B. KELLEY
We're Bigger Than They Are!

¶Many adults "view with alarm" the teen-age world, but they forget who made it

"Why should the children run the world? We're bigger than they are."

There is only one trouble with this query. From the way we grown-ups act a good part of the time, it appears as if the difference in bigness is limited to our physical dimensions. It is rather hopeless to try to "run the world" if our behavior cannot command respect. The youngster who said to me recently, in resigned disgust: "Adults act like a bunch of jerks!" was only saying what any person of normal intelligence is bound to say after a quick perusal of the morning newspapers or even a glance at the headlines on the newsstand. If this be adult behavior, then deliver us from the "immature"!

Adults may as well face up to the fact that the phrase "survival of the fittest" applies to more than the evolution of animal forms. It applies to human evolution, too. The child begins his fight to rule his environment almost at birth. We have all seen the prekindergarten youngster who twists his parents around his little finger in public places, as he blackmails his way to the top. Not only have parents been blackmailed and browbeaten, but the entire adult population seems to have been willing to submit to a prolonged brainwashing—until we have now convinced ourselves that *we* are really the victors, and the children are doing exactly what we want them to do.

While this new approach to child-rearing is in its heyday, various adult groups are showing concern about the older children. They view with alarm the plight of our youngsters and the neglect that *other* segments of the adult community exhibit toward the "teenage problem." The home blames the Church and the school; the school blames the home and the Church, and the Church blames the home and the school. Actually the fault lies with *all* adults.

After all, this is an adult world. It is run by adults; it was designed by adults; the profit from it accrues to adults. The mistakes of one adult generation are usually paid for dearly by the upcoming generation of youngsters. Though we have allowed our children excessive freedom, by no stretch of the imagination can this world ever be made into a child's world. We cannot even give it to the children, because by its very nature it belongs to us. Yet in our worship of the bland, we have developed a cream cheese approach to all problems. We are "understanding."

The youngster quoted above was no hood, no revolutionary. He was a bright boy who saw in the adult world the worship of the cheap and the shoddy, the tawdry, the vulgar. He could read that there was hardly a community in the United States without its police scandals; that officials, business leaders, public figures, could all be bought or sold if the price was right; marriage, the home, children, were all secondary to a transient desire or whim. He could read about public figures who alibied their transgressions by whining: "We needed the money." Who is not in need of money? But suddenly, in the 20th century in America, the need for money is an excuse for stealing, for betrayal of trust, for degrading high office. As the youngster added: "Adults act like this was a jungle and they were all wild animals, but we kids are supposed to have all the morals and all the principles they never heard of."

From time to time, we read in the press or we hear it proclaimed from public platforms that what we need in our schools is more physical force, more muscle. "Let the kids know who's boss." It may come as a surprise to those who feel this way, but the youngsters already know who's boss, or at least who *should* be boss. Youngsters expect adults to be the bosses *and* the leaders.

The case of a young limb of Satan comes to mind. It was a Sunday morning at 10 A.M. Mass. From the minute he hit the church door he was off and running. Mama was there, but as far as her little doll was concerned, Mama was not even an unneccessary encumbrance—except to be told, occasionally, to "shut up." Finally Mass ended—it was about seven hours long—and on the way out of church, Mama finally delivered the *coup de grâce*. She said firmly and with great self-assurance: "Wait till next year. You're going to a Catholic school, and the nuns will teach you manners."

Or do you prefer the story of the mother who sent her daughter to a Catholic high school and then complained: "I can't understand why the nuns let the girls wear their hair the way they do." She didn't like the way her daughter was doing her hair—but after all, was that her responsibility now that the daughter was in a Catholic high school?

A major league baseball umpire of long experience and high reputation was being interviewed on TV one evening after a game. The interviewer, a former player, after a series of half-joking, half-needling questions, said: "Let's be serious for a minute. What makes a good umpire?"

Without a second's hesitation the answer came back: "Respect. If the players don't respect you, you'd better quit. To gain respect you have to know what you're doing, you have to do it to the best of your ability, and you have to let them know that your job as an umpire is to keep the game moving. If you start out by having their respect, you'll wind up with their admiration, no matter what they tell you during a game. I've never worried about being popular; I've only worried about being right."

That advice holds for every parent and every adult who works with youngsters. How long would baseball players respect the authority of the umpire, if every little while an umpire was being dragged off to jail for taking bribes? Even the good and honest umpires would be suspect. Can we have public officials, even judges, being dismissed and prosecuted for dishonesty in office and then demand of children that they respect adult authority? Never mind the excuses about human weakness. If a man in such a position feels that the pressures for a fast dollar will be too great to bear, then he should quit. The same is true of the parent who holds forth on integrity and then brags about cheating on income tax, about lying to get a day off to go fishing or play golf, who talks of honesty and then brings home hundreds of dollars in office supplies or tools *stolen* from his firm. And let's not forget the mother who tells the youngsters: "Don't tell your father." Father had objected to an expenditure or a date or this or that. But mother feels she is more understanding, so she connives with the children to circumvent him. Does this promote respect, family unity, filial love? Yet how often do all these things happen in homes! What a bad example the growing child sees in the adults around him!

A pastor in a suburban parish found it necessary to mount the pulpit at every Mass one summer Sunday to lecture parents on the way the teen-age girls were dressed on the street. Afterwards he said: "Of course, when I thought more about it, I knew I was really wrong. In nearly every case where I saw an immodestly dressed teen-ager, her mother was dressed worse." Another pastor said he was abandoning retreats for first communicants in favor of retreats for the parents of the first communicants.

If children are dating too early, if steady company keeping is rampant in our land, why haven't parents stopped it? It is easy enough to do, and most youngsters would prefer to have it stopped. But first we have to do something about the mothers *and* the fathers who want to have "popular" sons and daughters.

As the Indians on TV are wont to say: "White man speak with forked tongue." We can't bemoan dating, steady company keeping, early marriages, the rising rate of teen-age pregnancies, and at the same time be pushing for social popularity among the same teen-agers and preteen-agers.

Not long ago a nun friend who was then teaching in the eighth grade told this story. The first year she was in the school, she arranged a party for the graduating class. This party took the form of an all-day picnic, complete with all sorts of races, games and general fun. The youngsters had a wonderful time, and during the following year a number of them stopped by to tell her that picnic was one of the highlights of the year.

As spring approached and plans for another picnic were in the air, a group of mothers visited the nun to explain that they thought a picnic was a little childish, and that children "these days" were a little more sophisticated. (The "these days" was made to sound as though the nun were approaching her hundredth birthday, when in fact she was younger than any of the mothers.) A dance was what the children would really like, and the mothers would be happy to take responsibility for the children's social life out of the nun's hands. So a dance they had. All the boys sat on one side of the room, and all the girls sat on the other side of the room, and they stared at each other, while the socially adjusted mothers almost went frantic trying to get their sophisticated children together. On Monday, when the graduates returned for their last good-byes, a group of them came up to the nun and said: "Sister, why are you mad at us?" The nun was puzzled.

"I'm not mad at you. What makes you think I am?"

"But you must be, Sister, or you would have let us have a picnic like last year's class."

What could she say? She knew what she would like to say—but what could she say?

"We thought you might like to have a dance for a change," she finally managed.

"But, Sister, a picnic is more fun."

Why do adults want children to grow up too soon? Youth cannot be recaptured, despite the strenuous efforts groups of forty-year-olds make at parties, on the beaches, in picnic grounds and elsewhere. There is fun to be had when you are a teen-ager—fun, the like of which you may never have again. But this fun is not trying to act like an adult or live an adult life. Social adjustment is far more than dating or dancing or steady company keeping. Social adjustment includes learning how to speak correctly, learning good manners, reading, athletics (particularly what I call the "social athletics," such as swimming, tennis, golf, ice skating and the like), learning how to dress—in other words, learning how to be the complete man or woman.

One part of the whole picture, and by no means the most important part, is socializing with members of the opposite sex. Some of the most socially maladjusted adults I know were steady company keepers from their early teens (many of the problems of modern youth have been with us for years; they are merely more widespread today). There is no one path guaranteed to lead to social adjustment. Man is too complex a being for that. And certainly social adjustment can never be achieved, even to the slightest degree, if there is not first an intellectual and emotional adjustment. Without these life is a series of frustrations.

When we adults complain, as we often do, about the financial demands our children make on us, we might remember that it is expensive to be a youngster these days. In our area, once a youngster reaches the age of twelve, he must pay adult prices at the movies. This can amount to as much as $1.25 for a Sunday *afternoon* movie—particularly if the movie is one aimed at the teen-age audience. Prices invariably are increased for those pictures especially suited to children or teen-agers. So the next time you complain about the money demands placed on you, remember who is ringing the cash register at the other end of the line: it's an adult every time.

If clothing styles for teen-agers change too often, if teen-age clothing appears to wear out too quickly, remember that the teen-age world is manipulated by adults—for an adult profit. Adults not only create teen-age styles; they dictate to the teen-age world—what the teen-ager will wear, will read, will see, will hear, will eat, almost what he will breathe.

The truth of the matter is that the world of the youngster is made and will continue to be made by adults, whether these adults are parents or preachers, married or single, whether they are high or low in the councils of the world. This is an adult world and always will be. It is time, and past time, that parents got a little steel into their spines—and stopped crying for someone else to lay the hickory across youngsters' backs.

JAMES J. GALLAGHER
The Other Side of Obedience

¶Leaders, too, have obligations and responsibilities toward their followers

If the lay apostolate is ever to fulfill its partnership with the hierarchy in the divine mission of the Church, it needs a clear understanding of the principle of authority. Yet how many lay leaders actually know in what respects the layman stands under obligation to his pastor or his bishop? Perhaps more important, how many can clearly determine the layman's obligation to the leaders of his own Catholic Action organizations?

No one, of course, denies that the group must be united if it is to achieve its specific apostolic goals. The necessity for clear-cut lines of authority is as readily admitted as is the need for obedience. But, unfortunately, whenever the subject of obedience or authority is discussed, the emphasis is almost always placed upon only two aspects—one negative, the other only half-true.

The negative aspect is easily recognized in the constant repetition of questions concerning the limitations of authority: Under what conditions may the bishop ask for my compliance in campaigns on aid-to-education laws? What are the limits of my obligation to support parish building funds? By what right does the prefect of my Sodality ask me to participate in antismut campaigns (and perhaps expose myself to public ridicule for so doing)?

Answers to such questions too often turn into half-true harangues that "thou shalt" and "thou shalt not." The inspiring principle of obedience in the Church of Christ is too often explained only in terms of its obligations upon those who obey. Seldom, if ever, is the other side of the question considered: namely, the responsibilities of those in authority who issue the orders which others must follow. What will be discussed here, then, is a more responsible attitude on the part of leaders in Catholic Action projects.

In a discussion of this sort it is important, first of all, to recognize that a leader imposes upon himself a weighty obligation when he assumes the function of leadership. Besides knowing when his followers must obey, the leader must also be sure he is giving the kind of orders which can be obeyed. And above all, he must realize that it is his responsibility to develop his followers in such a way that they become both able and willing to render him their obedience.

Experience shows that good leaders give good orders. Good orders are the kind that can—and will—be obeyed. Followers revolt, dissent and become uncooperative when the person ranking over them misuses his authority.

Take as a basic premise the fact, obvious in our current society, that old standards of respect for authority are weakening. We read articles about hoodlums beating policemen, about labor unions usurping the historical functions of management, about corruption in high places in public life and industry. These conditions cannot but show us how anti-authoritarian is today's social climate.

Now it would be wishful thinking to suppose that the social climate of our civilization has no effect on the members of the Church living in it. And therefore, today more than ever before, Catholic Action leaders must understand the necessity of conscious and conscientious application of the responsibilities of leadership in the work of the Church.

Today's social conditions underscore the point (it has always been true) that one of the most important functions of a leader is to develop those under his command. The leader must develop his followers to the point where they are psychologically capable of accepting and following his orders. He must motivate them so that they respond enthusiastically when an order is issued—and even achieve heights of accomplishment that were not required in the original order. Leaders of men, inside the Church and out, have demonstrated these abilities from the time of Moses to the years of Churchill.

When such constructive leadership is lacking, are failures of the group to be blamed only on the followers? Whose fault is it, for example, when a whole class of students rebels against an unjust teacher; when a whole nation rises against an oppressive ruler; or when an appeal for apostolic action in a Catholic Action group is met with total apathy?

The task of the leader, then, is to be responsible for his followers;

responsible for their obedience and responsible for their enthusiasm. It might be expressed in the simple slogan: A leader makes sure that he never gives an order which won't be carried out.

This principle is not the property of any ruling class. It is sheer common sense. It has its place, for example, in the basic training of soldiers. The cadre sergeant does not march his trainees on ten-mile hikes during the first week of training. He builds them up physically. They do push-ups, run around parade fields, rise at early hours and learn to respond instantaneously to simple commands. Such things condition the recruits for their later efforts, so that by the time such efforts are commanded, they have been made into soldiers capable of following orders.

A parent, more benignly and almost instinctively, appreciates this principle in training his children. It would be futile for a father to order his one-year-old child to repeat the Hail Mary before going to bed. But lovingly he teaches the child first to speak, then to pray, and then to appreciate the daily obligation of homage to God.

Faced with precisely the same challenge of our modern social climate—the breakdown in respect for authority—thoughtful business executives have recognized their obligation to do more than simply supply the tools for a man's work, his quotas for production and his paycheck at the end of the week. Business leaders have re-examined their own proficiency at leadership and developed some sound principles for the operation of modern enterprises. Here, for example, are the tests of a capable manager as proposed by Frederick R. Kappel, president of the American Telephone & Telegraph Co.: "He is able to state a goal and reach it. . . . He reaches these goals by organizing and inspiring the efforts of other people. He is able to lead others in such a way that they find their pursuit of the goals a satisfying experience. Demonstrating his own industry and devotion helps a lot, naturally; people want not only a boss but a man they can admire. . . . His judgment is respected by those whose co-operation is needed. The structure of business is a chain of command, but most people outside of business do not realize how little command is used."

Such is the attitude of a business leader evaluating his own performance with a view to developing loyalty and performance in his workers. Contrast it with the attitude of a man who has not grown into his authority: "Give me results. Never mind how you get the job done!" Yet just such an attitude, we sadly submit, is too often expressed in Church organizations. Whether spoken or implied, it says in effect: "Do it because I represent the authority of Christ—and because I am telling you to do it." One questions whether such representation is worthy of such authority.

And yet there is ample evidence that Christ Himself operated on the principle of responsible leadership, and intended that His Church should operate in the same way through the ages. And for the type of organizations under discussion—lay apostolate groups that aim to carry on His mission—such a consideration of the way Christ operated is highly appropriate.

Look for a moment at the manner in which Christ first structured the organization that endures some twenty centuries later, still carrying out the objectives of its Founder. Obviously, the Church was well organized. How was it done?

Christ, first of all, spent thirty years preparing His own human nature to undertake the task. Then He took three years and more to develop His own managers, the apostles who were to carry on His mission. Patient and persuasive training it was, as we know from scriptural accounts of His indoctrination sessions. The Sermon on the Mount was repeated in a hundred different ways.

Christ explained to His disciples the job to be done. He prepared them to do it, and then showed them by His own example how it could best be done. By word and work, He preached the spirit of love—a love that reached out for sinners, stood fast before kings, dealt kindly and firmly with the repentant.

But after Christ had inspired them with His own unquenchable spirit, He left His followers at last to their own resources. He remained Himself a constant source of strength and courage, but always in the background. Never did He step forward to take direct command from a faltering follower who had yet to test his own self-responsibility.

Such was the leader Christ proved Himself to be. There is no doubt that He showed in His own life and teachings the responsibility that must accompany all authority. If His followers today are to emulate His work, there is no doubt, either, that they must "go and do likewise."

SISTER M. ROBERTA JONES
A Sister Considers Chastity

¶How explain this concept that to many modern minds seems
wholly negative?

What can chastity mean to the contemporary world, where *Sex and
the Single Girl* is a best-seller and a woman's sexual attractiveness is
used to sell everything from cigarettes to automobiles? What meaning can the lifelong virginity of a religious sister possibly have for
the pop artists in their discothèques? For modern Ephesians, who
consider the legitimate and wholesome exercise of sex passé, who
seek and express the gamut from titillation to ennui in abnormal
and psychotic sexual attitudes and habits? Can Christian virginity
show them the living Christ?

To ask this question is tantamount to asking whether Christ can
still save the world. "I came to save that which was lost," He said.

But will the exposure to the world and its influences that the
renewal in the Church is urging upon modern sisters pose a threat
to their vow of chastity? Will the din of a sex-sodden age over-
power the 2,000-year-old evangelical counsel to forgo marriage and
sexual pleasure for the sake of the kingdom of God? These are
among the questions that vocation counselors are asking themselves.
This is the basic re-evaluation of themselves that American sisters
are making today.

Our Lord's words are universal; in them are the answers to the
problems of every age. He said of celibacy: "Take this in, you
whose hearts are large enough for it" (Matt. 19:12). St. Paul expanded His words into: "A virgin is concerned with the Lord's
claim, intent on holiness, bodily and spiritual" (Rom. 7:34). Both
of these are positive statements; there is nothing negative about
them. In every age the mission of the Christian virgin is to give
witness—to show an unbelieving world that there is a living God
who will share His eternal life with anyone who accepts Him.

Not every modern pagan has rejected Christ. Some have never

met Him, and the only images apparent to them have been weak reprints of an age that has been outgrown. Even the Christian struggling in the world needs reassurance that the battle does have meaning, that the life of grace is real. The virgin's calling is to focus the light of Christianity to a point where every man who has eyes to see can read plainly: "The fight is a good fight; it can be won. There is a higher path, and it carries men to eternal life."

But the vow of chastity doesn't look positive to most people—even to many Christians. When I was in high school, my great aunt, who was a Sister of Saint Agnes in Wisconsin, went to Arkansas for a home visit. She was a salty character in her sixties. On the train, a woman who had been sitting beside her suddenly asked: "What's the matter with you girls? Can't you get a man?" "I could have had a man," my aunt snapped back. "And what's more, I could still have one if I wanted one." I think she was right: the American nuns who could still have a man if they wanted one are countless. But the love of Christ impels them to a higher love, to a more universal love, than they could reach through one man and his children.

Now, if chastity really is so positive a force, then that unselfish love should have more power to sanctify the world than the world has to corrupt their purity. Cardinal Suenens has written in *The Nun in the World*: "Loving Christ does not mean loving an abstraction. It means loving Him who is living within the Church of today." And how are sisters being asked to love Him? They are being asked not just to tolerate lay people, not merely to welcome them, but to seek contacts with them. They are not being pushed directly into the world of the discothèques to give living witness, but they are being implored to make the vow a vital experience in themselves and the Church. Before it can communicate with unbelievers, there must be existential reality in their love for laymen as persons, in their projection into the lives of others.

Many spiritual advisors are urging sisters to attend an occasional CCD meeting. Cardinal Suenens has suggested that they engage in adult education, continue correspondence with former students and patients, and visit homes of students to develop mutual understanding. Michael Novak has urged sisters to attend universities, teach on university campuses, work with Newman Clubs. Many of these things they are already doing. So is there any real problem?

Even at the risk of being compared to Oliver Wendell Holmes' maiden aunt, I think we must admit there is. His grandfather's needless worry that some lovesick youth might follow his daughter home from finishing school was delightfully funny. She remained the "one sad, ungathered rose" on his ancestral tree. Let those laugh who think my question absurd. As one retreat master told me: "Sisters are assuredly not old maids. Their psychology is totally different."

One of our sisters, who returned recently from studies on a university campus, said she had observed what seemed to be an alarmingly repetitious pattern of sisters leaving their community, abandoning their religious vocation. She said she couldn't ignore the evidence that those who left were most noticeably friendly to patients, student nurses and other nonreligious. It would seem that multiple contacts with many people, men and women, can be a source of temptation. If a sister really tries to love people as persons, to listen to them, to sympathize with them, to appreciate their personal uniqueness, her heart can get sidetracked. Isn't that the way most human affection grows into exclusive, possessive, marital love? By frequent contact? By sympathy? By mutual interests and appreciation?

But is this the only danger to her vow of chastity, or even the greatest one? A sister can also dry up in her spotless convent till she has little more meaning than a mummy—to herself and any who see her. The lack of genuine human love and openness in convent life could be driving sincere sisters to leave. There is no husband to bring a sister back to renewing her love when she goes off on womanish tangents: mean, picky frustrations. There are no little faces like her own making demands on her generosity. She has to see the one she loves in ever-changing features. Isn't the danger of desiccation really a greater threat to the fulfillment of her vow to love Christ in every creature than the risk that she might love one or the other too exclusively?

What about the peril to the vocations that never materialize? The girls who are not attracted to Christ because sisters' lives do not show forth a greater love? When chastity degenerates into selfishness, it loses all its radiance. There is no girl who is not drawn by love, and we all know there is no love to compare with Christ's. I believe sisters could bring it into sharper focus and project it for more young women to see.

Are we to believe that safety lies in fleeing the world, in preferring the warning of the *Imitation of Christ*: "Every time I am among men, I return less a man" to Cardinal Suenens' challenge: "The world is my convent"? ("A religious house," the cardinal tells us, "is not a world of its own. It must take its place in the world and do its share of the work to be done, while still not losing sight of its main object.")

Surely the answer to this question lies in the delineation of the Christian vocation in Scripture and in the living tradition of vigorous religious men and women who communicated the faith to pagans on every continent. It is voiced by many today: the Holy Father, the Council Fathers, the great Scripture scholars and theologians who are the glory of our age. The vocation of sisters is in the Church, in Christ—it is organic. They are to go to God in the intimate, personal relationship of the Bride of God, which is the whole Church, and with that Church they are to show forth Christ to a skeptical world.

Recently, one of our sisters had a caller on a Sunday afternoon. Sister had been working hard all week revamping the biology and chemistry labs in our high school, and, extremely tired, she was taking a much needed nap. When she was called, she inquired whether the person asking for her was an adult. I couldn't tell her; I had only relayed the message. I knew only that the caller was adult enough to have driven to the convent, because I had noticed the car from my window. "Tell the guest I'll be down," she said. The visitor happened to be a former student, now married, bringing her first baby and her problems for sister's appraisal. By the time the visit ended, prayer time had arrived, and there was no more nap. To me this was an honest fulfilling of the vow of chastity, rather than a reneging.

The solution, it seems, lies primarily in a sister's motivation and maturity. In a recent issue of the St. Louis *Review*, there was an article telling of the changes the Sisters of Loretto have made in their relations with the laity. "The Sisters visit homes when their presence reflects their apostolate . . . a human-rights meeting, a CFM meeting, [visits to students' homes] to allow the sisters to understand the home environment of the student, but also to enable the parents to know the sisters better." Almost any activity with lay people that brings Christ to them is compatible with the vow of chastity. Celibacy has to take on positive meaning for the

Christian laity before it can make sense to a self-centered world. The layman's spontaneous response to news of a vivacious girl's entrance into the convent must not be: "But she would have made such a good mother." It must be: "Thank God! So many persons will share such a wonderful girl's love."

What Abbot Christopher Butler told the Council Fathers about Scripture studies can equally well be said of the sister's devotion to the needs of others: "Doubtless some will turn liberty into license—but we must risk this for the sake of a greater good." Sisters are not adolescents. The youngest sister in the country has shown enough maturity to follow the call to a life of self-denial as a means toward fulfillment in Christ. That is not the act of an immature person. If a sister uses the apostolate as a way to escape the sacrifices and restrictions that are inseparable from her vocation, she knows she is insincere. If particular contacts with the outside world become a source of persistent disturbance to prayer and community living, they must be set aside by the individual involved. But then she must make new approaches to the same end of bringing Christ to the world.

As Père Congar has said, a convent must be "the Church in miniature." A religious woman cannot simply dispense with the discipline and ceremony of community life. She cannot give way to frantic haste and pressured business. The Gospels do not give this picture of Christ, and He had the whole world to redeem.

The people to whom a sister gives Him know—and those still clamoring or yearning for that service are ready to know—that there are times when she can minister to them and times when she cannot. There is rarely a week when the only time she can possibly give is in the professional role of teacher or nurse, when she simply cannot find time to give a fuller service to persons outside her community. But prayer in common with her colleagues is, for almost every sister, the first service. To nurture a personal relationship, to make a better environment in her home, doesn't a successful wife have to spend time with her husband? And so must the sister with Christ.

Even when she is convinced that she must offer meaningful witness, make her life a real and constant confrontation with the persons inside and outside her convent, there are still problems. What about time? Even though she rearranges her schedule, there will still remain only 24 hours in each day. If her schedule for prayer and community exercises makes personal contacts with lay people virtually impossible, she must present this problem to her superiors for a possible change in schedule.

We need more than nun auditors at the Council; we need articulate sisters in the parishes and dioceses, to make their needs known, to make it possible for them to devote more time to direct apostolic works. Sisters must be relieved of some of the tasks they have done during the formative centuries in the American Church. School clerks or secretaries could be employed to relieve principals of some of their work-load in the parochial schools. Lay readers could help teachers with some of their paper-correcting load. More efficient maintenance programs could be used in our parishes to facilitate the sisters' work.

Every sister is called to spiritual motherhood; this is the real fulfillment of her vow of chastity. It would seem to me that a mother's love makes time for the deepest needs of her children. And if the man of the house wants to do more for the children than merely meet their physical necessities, he must help to make that possible for her.

JOHN LaFARGE

Sister for Lunch

When a young girl announces to her parents that she has decided to enter a religious community, it's just as likely as not to cause a considerable shock, even if the parents are the best and most pious people in the world. What a shock it can be is told by columnist Joe Breig in an issue of *Ave Maria* not long ago, right from his own experience. Well, that's part of the personal sacrifice, and the life of entire religious dedication would lack meaning if it did not occasionally occur.

We can be grateful, however, to Mr. Breig for raising a point about which a little frank talk does not seem—to me, at least—quite out of place. This is the matter of permission to revisit the parental home. Says Mr. Breig: "I would not be at all surprised to live to see this never-go-home rule changed in communities that have it." His own daughter's community, according to his account, permits her to come home once a year, at first for a few days, and then for a week or more as she becomes more of a veteran in religious life. "I know this is good for her," says her father, "good for us, and good for religion."

At the risk of seeming to be a troublemaker, I would like to say that I definitely agree with Mr. Breig. I am not suggesting any homecoming on the part of the canonically cloistered orders, such as the Discalced Carmelites, for instance, or the contemplative Dominicans or Franciscans or Cistercians. With these, the total and lasting separation is an integral part of their vocation itself. The same principle would apply, doubtless, to the various types of semi-cloistered nuns, who combine the strict enclosure with an active life of teaching or service.

I am talking of the great number of noncloistered religious communities engaged in the active life. Such active communities treasure the sacred inner life of their respective houses, and rightfully fear any weakening or dilution of its genuine family spirit by letting down the bars that protect its members from a very inquisitive and secular-minded world outside.

Yet with all these reservations, I cannot escape the belief that in our present world, at least here in the United States, under our modern surroundings, much good could be accomplished if at certain times, under suitable safeguards, a closer contact could be established between the good Christian home and the dedicated member or members who have "taken the veil." I consider this particularly necessary in our modern, highly secularized society.

May I put it this way? I believe it is only by an occasional presence of the order-member right in the home, that the full import of the positive, joyful, constructive elements of the dedicated religious life can be made sufficiently vivid to the modern mind, which is so grievously threatened by spiritual cowardice and fastidious doubt.

This seems to be one of the ideas behind the new "secular institutes": bodies of men or women leading in secular life the full exercise of the religious vows of poverty, chastity and obedience. If they can "take it," who live all the time immersed in the profane world around them, cannot the members of an active religious community gird themselves—by a bit of special training, by a sense of mission, by an awakening of live charity—to exert once in a while, under all the proper conditions and safeguards, a similar apostolic or mission function?

The Little Brothers and Little Sisters of Charles de Foucauld observe the contemplative life immersed not only in secular but often in completely pagan surroundings. They accomplish this, of course, only as the result of long and rigorous preparation. Cannot the members of our active religious communities do their part in preparing themselves for the informal but fruitful contacts of an occasional visit to the home folks? I wonder if we do not underestimate the degree to which such informal contact is desired and welcomed precisely by the younger generation. It is on such occasions, rather than in the more formal and professional contacts, that younger people decide for themselves how far the professed dedication of their religious companion is truly genuine.

Specifically, even if changes cannot be wrought in other respects, I would at least plead for some more considered and uniform policy with regard to the sister's presence at private or family meals. Few items that concern the relation of a religiously dedicated person to the outside world seem to be more surrounded with proscriptions and prohibitions. Many of these may be grounded upon excellent reasons, which I do not question, or at least upon reasons that were fully valid in former times and other circumstances. But in point of fact some of them can lead to situations that create mistrust of, rather than reverence for, the religious life.

When a nun, already a "veteran" of the religious life, and an only child, returns home for her mother's funeral, it is difficult for her secular relatives to understand the regulation that prohibits her taking even a modest lunch with her aged and widowed father, but requires that she and her companion be fed at a separate table in the adjoining room. (Even our present Holy Father changed the custom of the Pope taking his meals alone!)

Such rigid proscriptions undoubtedly had their excellent reasons in other times or countries. Today, however, I think an occasional "nun for lunch" should be a part of the observance of every Christian family. One of the earliest and deepest impressions I myself as a child received of the religious life was the much-anticipated day every August when the Little Sisters of the Poor took lunch with my mother and the rest of us. And we children were most impressed by the fact that the said Little Sisters did not talk "piety" but were full of good humor and fun. When on one memorable occasion some "fake" nuns came to us, my sister detected them by the abnormal solemnity of their conversation.

Mind, this is no jovial plea for secularizing the cloister, for any lessening of the dignity and reserve that belong properly with the religious life, for any "Going My Way" shenanigans—and such are always lurking around the TV corner. Certain lines of demarcation must be kept as intact as the DEW lines in the Arctic. In every culture, however, in every age, standardized methods of sharing food and drink form the acceptable way by which bridges can be crossed. In that type of human contact, lasting, mutual knowledge may take the place of crude suspicion.

I don't think I am quite unreasonable in thinking that an occasional "sister for lunch" may at times, in her own special way, bring to our spiritually starved world a bit of insight into the meaning of that service of the Master to which she has dedicated herself. Our Lady herself was not above attending a wedding breakfast—and talking at it. And at the very least, the puzzlement of so many conflicting regulations should be ended.

STAFFORD POOLE
Tomorrow's Seminaries

¶The history of the Church may depend on the course our seminaries take

In recent years it has been fashionable for Catholic intellectuals to look down on the training of priests with a mixture of tolerance and amused condescension. Seminary training, they point out, has usually been shallow, isolated from reality, and confined to a few medieval and scholastic subjects of little immediate value.

In a recent article on Catholicism, *Life* magazine (Oct. 18, 1963) made the following observations: "Compared to the priests and nuns of the middle ages, the religious of today are, without question, men and women of good quality—clerical scandal, for example, is so rare now as to rate newspaper headlines when it happens. But many Church leaders are frank to admit it is less clear that these servants of God are particularly well equipped by their spiritual education to serve their laymen. Seminary education, which has hardly been changed since the reforms imposed by the Council of Trent in the 16th century, is heavy on discipline and old-fashioned dogmatic theology, but light on psychology and sociology."

This same criticism is voiced, but with far greater vehemence, by Daniel Callahan in his article "The Freedom of Priests" in *Commonweal* (Oct. 18, 1963). Mr. Callahan decries the heavy emphasis on passivity to be found in seminaries, and their erasure of some basically human and potentially valuable characteristics. Worst of all, he says, is the physical and intellectual isolation of seminaries: "It is more than likely that the graduate of a seminary will have only the barest acquaintance with literature, psychology, sociology, economics, history and political science. . . . Under such conditions, many priests undoubtedly find themselves handicapped when faced with well-educated, intellectually sophisticated laymen."

Theoretically, the critics of seminary education should have little to find fault with since the publication of Pope Pius XII's *Menti Nostrae* in 1950. The late Pontiff opened the way for the modernization and adaptation of seminary life, particularly in the following famous paragraph: "Particular attention must be paid to character formation in each young man, by developing in him a sense of responsibility, a capacity to use his judgment concerning men and events, and a spirit of initiative. For this reason, directors of seminaries must use moderation in the employment of coercive means, gradually lightening the system of rigorous control and restrictions as the students grow older, helping them to stand on their own feet and to feel responsibility for their actions. . . . If young men—especially those who have entered the seminary at a tender age—are educated in an environment too isolated from the world, they may, on leaving the seminary, find serious difficulty in their relations either with ordinary people or with the educated laity, and it may happen that they adopt a misguided and false attitude toward the faithful or that they consider their training in an unfavorable light."

But what should have been a Magna Charta for seminaries has had little practical effect—if the criticisms already mentioned are as valid as they appear to be.

The vast majority of students entering seminaries at the present time (here I limit the term "seminary" to the years of college, philosophy and theology) were born in the closing years of World War II or after it. They have never known the United States when it was not engaged in either a cold or a hot war. For the most part, their parents are of the generation that grew up during the Depression and the war years. These parents have determined that their children should not have the problems or disadvantages they themselves were faced with. In many cases, this protection has merely spawned a new set of problems.

The sheltered life of many of today's students presents a remarkable paradox; for it is a mixture of great independence and abject dependence. The young man who enters the seminary today is called on to give up a great deal more than his predecessor of twenty or thirty years ago. In the postwar world, the seminary is not the alternative to the bread line or war service. In following a vocation, a student may be giving up an extremely comfortable life. He may have been free in his movements, free as to social contacts (even as to steady dating), free from burdensome restraints at home and excessive work at school—free in everything except making responsible decisions.

In our times, when such a high value is placed on security, the process of decision making is often left to parents. In the seminary, their place is taken by rules, disciplinarians and spiritual directors. And because the ultimate decision in a vocation belongs to the person called, many are unable to face it. Sometimes the realization of all this overwhelms them within the first few days after entering a seminary. At other times, the act of deciding is deferred, and in extreme cases a student will adopt almost any tactic to force the seminary authorities to make the final decision. Students in theology have been known to defer their acceptance of holy orders until they could have positive urging from their directors—or even their psychiatrists.

This basic indecision, one of the most pressing problems that our seminaries face, often finds expression in an excessive group dependence. Such dependence is neither the result of social consciousness nor a manifestation of genuine charity. It comes rather of a vague desire to be lost in numbers—to be accepted, to follow the group and be saved the inevitable, heartbreaking day when a man stands alone, face to face with the reality of a vocation. Students give each other mutual support. Yet this is not the positive kind of support that aids and helps the work of a priest, but a negative type that offers sympathy for "tension" and "pressures," often imaginary, always exaggerated. In its extreme form, this dependence is found in the student who postpones a decision on vocation in order to find out what his friends are going to do.

One of the chief failures of the present generation is its inability to find a challenge in adversity, large or small, and to find the courage to overcome the various minor contradictions that life in the Church continually offers. Yet that is the very thing the Church expects of her seminarians. Admittedly, it is difficult to find a genuine challenge in the routine activities of seminary life. But this routine has its counterpart in the life of every priest.

There is no lack of idealism in today's aspirants for the priesthood. It seems clear that in our present society the greatest difficulty is not in finding vocations but in keeping them. The incoming seminarian has ideals, often very lofty ones; but for a variety of reasons he lacks the perseverance and ability to reduce them to practice. Thrown into a world that does not correspond to his concept of reality, he strives to revise the reality rather than his concept. The only alternative is flight—the return to a more congenial environment. *Life* magazine, in the article mentioned above, quotes Msgr. Michael J. McLaughlin, of Long Island: "You take a boy who is idealistic, who wants to contribute to others. He can go off to South America as an engineer and work in the jungle. His desire to serve is satisfied outside the priesthood." Not infrequently, young men who drop out of the seminary choose service occupations such as medicine, teaching, or the Peace Corps.

What, then, about the seminary itself? Is it really a "quaint institution," anachronistic in our society? It would seem to be, for it comes to us from a distant age and a vanished culture. Does this mean that the entire seminary system should be abolished? Should there be a return to something like the pre-Tridentine system?

Although such a suggestion has been voiced, it is at the present time neither practical nor desirable. Anyone who has closely studied the history of the Church knows that, whatever their faults, seminaries have served the Church well. At least, the scandals of the 10th and 15th centuries have not been repeated since Trent. But this does not mean that improvements and accommodations are not in order.

The fundamental problem of American seminaries is their number and variety. The seminaries agree, perhaps, in essentials, but there is a fantastic variation in the way in which they train their students. Many are progressive, perhaps even permissive; others have changed little in fifty or more years. Differences in rules, discipline, the teaching of classes, faculty-student relations, the degree of freedom permitted, the admission of outside influences, minimum scholastic requirements—all these vary widely from diocese to diocese.

The disturbing aspect of this situation is that so little is known about it. To my knowledge, no one has ever made a close study of American seminaries comparable to that made of medical schools at the turn of the century. Such a nation-wide assessment should be the first concern of any national association of American bishops. Seminaries should be evaluated and then standardized within reasonable limits, ample room being left for individuality, prudent experimentation and adaptation to local needs.

The discrepancies of seminary standards are most distressing in those areas that concern the acceptance or rejection of students for intellectual or disciplinary reasons. Some seminaries are notably easier than others, and students who fail to make the grade in one seminary are often accepted and eventually ordained in another. There will never be real progress until it is an established rule: 1) that the involuntary drop-out from one seminary cannot enter another, and 2) that voluntary transfers be so closely regulated that change of diocese cannot become a convenient escape mechanism for inferior students. This would be a self-denying ordinance for dioceses pinched by the shortage of vocations; but only when it has become common practice will the heresy of numbers finally give way to a zeal for genuine excellence.

One hindrance to obtaining this excellence is the proliferation of small, poorly equipped seminaries. It would be highly desirable to have more regional seminaries composed of high-quality teaching centers and diocesan houses of study. This would be a partial solution to the chronic problem of inferior and uninterested teachers, small faculties, inadequate libraries and narrow, unrealistic curricula.

All seminaries, without exception, should be accredited by the State and regional accrediting agencies. The principle can be questioned, but in our society this is the practical standard of evaluation for education. Impartial accreditors can turn up more than a few defects in seminary education that the authorities on the spot have missed. In the light of Pius XII's statement: "the literary and scientific education of future priests should be at least not inferior to that of laymen who take similar courses of study" (*Menti Nostrae*, §88), it is at least open to question whether the existence of a non-accredited seminary can be justified at all. In addition, accreditation assuredly helps the large number of students who do not continue on to the priesthood.

Then, too, the six-year system of major and minor seminaries should be abandoned in favor of the separate college of liberal arts and philosophy. The so-called six-six system, which dates back to St. Vincent de Paul's division of the *grand* and *petit séminaire* in the 17th century, has no relevance for our times. The liberal arts must be removed from both the high school and the shadow of the theological curriculum and restored to their proper importance. In this way, too, as he enters and leaves the college division, the seminarian would have two opportunities to make a decision on his vocation.

Once they are accredited, seminaries can offer a recognized A.B. degree, and no student incapable of achieving this degree should be allowed to enter the priesthood. One of the most reprehensible practices of American seminaries is that of permitting students to enter their strictly professional training of theology (the equivalent of graduate work) when they are unable to meet undergraduate standards.

What about the nonaccredited seminaries? Ideally, theirs should be a temporary state, an interim against the happy day when they will achieve some sort of outside recognition. But that day, unfortunately, may be a long way off. Meantime, the fact of nonaccreditation does not absolve those seminaries from the obligation to measure the quality of their education in relation to similar courses of study in outside colleges and universities. This is the minimum required by *Menti Nostrae*. The administration of such seminaries would be obligated to assure itself, by means of standardized tests, by follow-ups on the work of former students, and by any other means available, that their education is at least on a par with what could be had elsewhere.

Normally, the undergraduate concentration in seminaries is scholastic philosophy. Every seminarian should have a thorough grounding in philosophy, both for his future theological studies and for the intrinsic value of that study as an intellectual discipline. But there is no reason why every seminarian must make it his major in his bachelor's program; for not all are endowed for such a program or inclined to it by nature. Seminary curricula should be expanded to include other majors in the liberal arts, and thus give scope for individuality, free choice and the cultivation of needed talents. But whatever the major field, every curriculum should contain basic courses in contemporary philosophy, sociology and social work, anthropology, experimental psychology and the behavioral sciences, counseling techniques, art and music appreciation, and at least one modern foreign language. Some of these courses should be taught by qualified laymen.

The European background of seminaries, which was responsible for the six-six system, has also dictated that they be isolated from the world. This requirement was prompted in part by the European concept of chastity in the adolescent, but all too often it has come to isolate the faculty as well as the students. In our society, however, separation from the community, from the intellectual trends of our times, from a practical knowledge of the world and the people that the future priest must deal with, is little short of criminal. The priest with narrow horizons, incapable of intellectual growth after ordination, convinced that he has all his answers at hand in a series of formulas drawn from standard manuals—this man will be at best a mediocrity, never fulfilling his promise or potentialities.

Every seminary should have a well-planned program, beginning with the first year of college, that brings the student into contact with the needs of our times and the various ways of meeting them. Liturgical renewal, ecumenism, the laity and their place in the Church, civil rights, urban renewal, the conservative movement, automation—nothing is outside the scope of seminary training if it prepares the future priest to meet the problems of his time and society.

The answer to the problems of our time is not necessarily permissiveness. Some have felt that all the restraints of the past must be removed in order to teach responsibility and self-reliance. The flaw in this reasoning is that the seminary's primary duty is to train. This training for the priesthood is specialized and difficult. The difficulties that form an inevitable part of the priestly life must have counterparts in the seminary, lest the newly ordained should encounter some rude shocks.

What the Church wants is a prudent gradualism that, in moderate steps, will emancipate the student from the seminary routine. By the time a man takes up his theological studies, he should be able to govern his life—his rising, retiring, study, spiritual exercises—without the tyranny of bells, reminders or admonitions. If he cannot, there is scant hope that he will ever be able to. The seminary must still judge him, but it should not have to spy on him or compel him.

Basically, the Church in the United States must decide what it wants and expects of the diocesan priest, and then choose the methods and draw up the standards for training such a man. The history of the Catholic Church in the United States may well be determined by what developments take place in our seminaries during the next generation.

JAMES J. KAVANAUGH

The Missing Dimension

¶A product of seminary training points out the one thing overlooked by its critics

When I read the eloquent criticisms of seminary life by the Michael Novaks and Daniel Callahans, I am reminded of the social worker who wandered through the slums. She was horrified at the dirt and garbage, the beds without sheets and the diets without green vegetables. From the pedestal of her bourgeois balance, she condemned the social system that produced this tragedy of life without bathrooms and vitamin C. She saw the poverty, the unemployment, the winos and prostitutes, she saw everything but the parents who loved their children and the kids who loved their neighborhood. And hence she didn't understand the answer of a little boy she spoke to. When she asked: "Whose shack is that?" he looked at her and said: "That's no shack, that's my house."

I am a priest who was raised in the seminary slums portrayed by the modern critics. Michael Novak tells me about the faculties that are "small, ingrown, overworked and not contemporary in their outlook." He tells me about the spiritual formation that is "irrelevant and could not in fact be continued except in the hothouse isolation of the seminary." He reminds me of the books of spirituality I read, in which I was "led away from the experience of God to the observance of discipline." He feels bad because the works of St. John of the Cross and St. Teresa are "not read with near the frequency or attention" they deserve.

And Dan Callahan continues the touching picture of the "garbage along the curb" and the kids batting stones in a vacant lot. We discover that "the majority" of seminarians, during their formative period, are systematically deprived of any "significant contacts with the laity." And the same isolated seminarian is "given a very scant education in those disciplines which loom so large in the modern world." He tells me that my training in spirituality was produced by stressing the "ascetical superiority of the clerical to the lay life." He warns me of the "incipient anticlericalism among the laity," blissfully unaware that his embittered pen may be producing a good bit of anti-laity in the clergy.

Now let me explain. I am glad to exchange Tanquerey for Rahner, Congar and Schillebeeckx. I like to hear the talk about a seminary settling on a university campus. I am glad that our Scripture courses don't have to be an effort to modernize a poorly revised Vulgate. I'm happy that canon law may not make the future priests learn about all the penalties and refinements of excommunications. I'm glad that moral theology will work its way back to the Word of God, and liturgy will take a place of prominence. I approve the efforts that the Paulists, for example, are making to cut down the number of class hours, to give more academic freedom to the gifted student. I think that private meditations and fewer organized religious exercises will be a help to the restless American seminarian with the "puritan blood."

In fact, I think the old seminary men feel much the same way. I believe that their only hesitation is motivated by the same love they showed us throughout our training days. They have lived in the priestly life, most of them admirably, and they know its unique difficulties. They know them better than Michael Novak and Daniel Callahan; they know them better than the newly ordained wonder who mistakes enthusiasm for faith. The one dimension the critics seem to avoid, and to me it is an important one, is the real manly love and absorbing devotion that the seminary professors had for the students. And I think that the lack of this dimension lends a hysteria to their critique that creates distorted judgment. What they say about the seminary profs, the modern generation says about its parents. And yet no one panics about that.

We just accept with gratitude the new enlightenment, sometimes question its validity, and hope that the new forms will produce as much love as the outmoded ways did. Everyone knows that our theology was too defensive, our seminaries a bit too disciplined, our message a little less than kerygmatic. But the men who staffed them were at our disposal as few parents are. They laughed with us, prayed with us, answered our questions with painful research, sacrificed social contacts to belong to us. They calmed our fears, told us of Christ's love, asked us to be gentle, humble and patient, and showed us what Christ looked like in a cassock.

I can remember in my first year of college deciding I wanted to quit. I can remember the priest who listened to me, praised me, made me laugh, told me what it meant to say Mass and forgive a frightened sinner. I remember the priest in philosophy, laboring with the meager textbook that Grenier was, taking a whole class to answer a question I'd asked, after he had spent an evening in research. I can remember the rigidity of Noldin, our moral theology book, but I remember far better the love of the man who walked us through those definitions. I remember him telling us not to deny absolution if there was a glimmer of hope. He asked us to be at our gentle best in confession. He told us of people's fear, of love as the goal of moral theology, of the need to ask advice of doctors and lawyers—and parents.

I recall the nightly talks by the rector, when the splendor of his own priesthood warmed our hearts. I remember his homily on the Pharisees, and the night he told us that "what we give up is peanuts, what we receive is everything." He described the sacrifices of parents, the sacrifice of solitude they make for their children, the sacrifice of interrupted conversations, of their worries, failures and financial concerns. I can remember my confessor never hurrying, always encouraging, always trusting. I remember with a smile the mimeographed notes of *Mystici Corporis*, revised and revised again, with the simple inscription: "Tear up what I gave you yesterday." I can remember our dogma prof struggling with the Trinity after a night of reading and discussion.

Our theology certainly lacked the spark and kerygma of today's. But the men who taught it taught us, and what they were kept leaking through in love. They knew we needed changes, but not even the advanced voices of Europe spoke with conviction. And when they spoke, we had to admit that they spoke from empty churches, social and economic fury, two wars, a divided continent, and a rising mound of murdered Jews.

We were searching for answers amid a generous people, who smiled and tipped their hat to "Father," who built churches and put up schools and raised big families. Ecumenism was great, but many of us (I for one) had lived in Protestant neighborhoods where we weren't allowed across the street, where dogs had more freedom in yards than we did. We had lived in communities where Catholics were condemned from the pulpits, where the presence of an ex-priest in a Protestant church was a stellar event, where our mothers were laughingly called "rabbits" when they hung the week's thirty T-shirts on the line.

When my generation (which is Michael Novak's generation) had survived the era of Catholics versus Protestants and (let's be realistic) Protestants versus Catholics, we entered the phase of Catholics versus the world. We were willing to carry our signs to ban *The Moon Is Blue*. We listened to the dangers of secularism as proposed by our bishops. We nodded our assent, and we stayed away from B-movies, ignored trashy books, attended Holy Hour and said the daily rosary. We were also happy, exuberant, and loved football and hot-dog roasts. We feared Margaret Sanger as destructive of homes, we despised Paul Blanshard and his half-truths, we read *Our Sunday Visitor* and believed in Fatima.

About the time of my ordination in 1954, we began the new phase of Catholics in the world. We'd had a half-dozen years to study *Mediator Dei*, and its message was beginning to filter through our defenses. Scripture studies began to open up when the scholars decided that *Divino Afflante Spiritu* meant what it said. Monsignor Ellis warned us about our inbreeding and our lack of scholars. John Cavanaugh of Notre Dame spoke of ecumenism and Catholic intellectuals. Catechetical studies began to question our teaching methods. We went from unit systems to textbooks, and back to the units. But we were dealing with people and not machines, and it took time. And many of us were happy in the Church.

We discovered in our young priesthood that converts flocked to the faith. We saw grown men, Americans all, weep when they were baptized. We saw searching eyes grow moist in our instruction classes when we told them of the wonders of Christ we had learned in our intellectual ghettos. We found the laity—with whom we had enjoyed no "significant contacts"—keeping us so busy that we hardly had time for prayer. We found that the high school kids loved our classes and told us the secrets of their beginning love. They told us their dreams to have a holy marriage, to keep their bodies pure that love might pass through the crucible. We discovered that public schools invited us to talk about marriage and dating, the meaning of faith and morality in the age of the atom. They didn't seem bored or oppressed, nor did they find us "irrelevant." We would become irrelevant if we stood still.

We found it difficult to talk of indulgences—but who didn't until Rahner came along? We found it hard to discuss the Pope's infallibility, but there wasn't much written on collegiality. We—or at least I—found it difficult to speak on Mary every Tuesday night at novena, but I had not seen her as the image of the Church. Our sermons lacked the power of today's homily, but the parables and the words of Isaiah and Tobias held attention. It took the lessons of wars and atom bombs and the charism of Pope John to spark a renewal. Even Teilhard, with all his vision, knew that the freedom of the spirit would move step by humble step.

I don't regret the first decade or so of my life, when it was Catholics versus Protestants. There were honest reasons for our brawls. We fought them out like men and moved on. I don't regret the priests who led us through that age. I love them and thank them for my vocation, although they honestly believed Vatican I had said it all, and lived that belief with courage.

I don't regret phase number two, when the slogan said: "Catholics versus the world." It taught me courage and the value of the "pearl of great price." I don't regret the seminary days, when the textbooks were so defensive and partitioned, the rules so stiff and demanding, that the men who directed and taught us had to be filled with love. What the textbooks didn't say, these men told us with kindness and patience that readied us for the renewal.

Nor do I regret the present phase, when every book gives a new insight, every journal holds out new dimensions of the faith that Christ has given. The new liturgy thrills the priesthood nourished in the seminary. The new lay involvement justifies the asides of men who looked beyond the textbook when they taught—and they looked with their hearts, because our modern theologians had not put their dreams into words. The courage and humility of Vatican II make me glad to be alive, give me added zest to plunge into a world I more clearly see as Christ's. The catechetical proposals and kerygmatic plans give me no rest if I should grow complacent in the work of Christ. I see more clearly my failures, I sense more realistically my opportunities and responsibilities. I know how hard it will be to be a priest, a layman, a human being, in the world in which I live. And yet I regret it not at all.

I only regret that the critics can't understand the love that lived in the seminary, the friendships that were formed there, the courage and faith and humility that were fostered there. I found myself no stranger to the world, I found myself not isolated from its thought or its hopes. And I will be ever grateful to the men who taught me from an untiring devotion that I have never been able to match. The readiness with which I face renewal is the readiness born of their love. I bucked the novelties, and the new-found freedom, the outspoken witness—until I discovered their value. But it was the loyalty to Christ they inspired that taught us that if we listened to the united Church, we'd make no mistakes.

I guess what I regret most of all is that those "who bore the heat of the day" for me should be stereotyped as some kind of unenlightened Torquemada. When Michael Novak quotes the seminarian who found his professor as "one of the best minds of the 15th century," I just hope that 20th-century thought will produce his kind of love. It's nice to come at this particular eleventh hour: the pay's good, the clothes are not ruffled with sweat, the energies are well rested and dynamic. I just want us latecomers to remember that some great men nursed those vines and bore many a harvest before we got here. And our harvest isn't old enough to test the taste of its wine.

SECTION III

LIFE, SEX AND SANITY

JANE HANOVER ADAMS

Love, O Love, O Careful Love

¶Will tomorrow's mothers look on childbearing as a threat to their
fulfillment?

Our daughter was recently being catechized on the sacraments, in
preparation for confirmation. Having grown accustomed, though
reluctantly, to hearing the "new thinking" on marriage expounded
far and wide, I half expected an analysis of "family planning" in
the text. Hence I was enormously pleased to find a simple and
stately exposition of the family, including such traditional thoughts
as: "Parents must work and sacrifice together to provide for the
spiritual and physical needs of their family," and "If they keep
God's law in their marriage, they can depend upon God to give
them the graces they need to fulfill the purpose of their marriage."
This latter, our daughter was able to tell me, is "to continue the
human race."

I fear that she has encountered such straightforward, uncom-
plicated teaching about her possible future vocation for about the
last time, and that when she takes up the subject again, later, she
will find it cloaked in enough clauses, conditions and concern to
confuse even the subtlest mind.

If she attends one of our Catholic high schools, she will presently
take a course on marriage. For the most part I envy her this opportunity. Though the discussion of canon law, impediments and
divorce may not just fascinate her, there will come some common-
sense talk about dating, to augment the running dialogue at home.
There will be, I know, inspiration and motivation, and, in the
main, a thoroughly Christian perspective on that vocation of love
and generosity and service which is marriage. Whether she plights
her troth to a husband, whether she becomes a consecrated virgin,
or whether she stays single in the world, she needs to have this
outlook, and I am grateful for the help.

But one fine morning there is likely to be an "additive" for which I will not give thanks. She will hear—from a priest, a doctor, a married couple (perhaps from all of these)—that even though children *are* the primary purpose of marriage, there are some important whereases in the contract. A truly prudent married couple, it will be explained, expects to space and limit their offspring judiciously so as not to overproduce. They must do this in a morally permissible way, of course, as God expects them to; and "control" is the password.

She may even be advised to start compiling a record that will enable her to keep an eagle eye on her cycle at all times (though by then a urine or saliva test may make the whole process simpler, if more clinical), and so accomplish prudent reproduction. But whatever the current "how to," it will be presented on the theory that she will eventually practice family limitation if she marries, and that this is the way to keep her safe from the evils of contraception. (Meanwhile, if certain proposals are adopted, the man-to-be in her future may even be getting drilled in conditioning his reproductive reflexes.)

I well know that in a public high school she could encounter a "life adjustment" course instead, and learn about self-expression and feminine fulfillment and the contraceptive way. I know, too, that there is agitation to introduce the subject at the fifth-grade level.

But in either case, and even if the matter were ignored academically as of old, other teachers wait anxiously in the wings. For instance, she can pick up Catholic periodicals around the house, at the doctor's or dentist's office or at church, and find articles, sometimes interspersed with related advertisements, on "responsible parenthood." There will likely be a ban-the-babies piece by a lay or professional person, or by a priest in sociology or demography; or a survey in which married couples reveal bitterness about their fecundity and the Church's intransigence; or the afterthoughts of a middle-ager who perhaps took a fling at large-family life during the heady days of the 1940's and 1950's and is now ready to concede. (Were the neighbors and the in-laws right after all?)

Editors who surely would blanch at the thought of exposing a mentally sick priest to public view will no doubt still be filling their columns with case histories of disturbed mothers (as a warning to the foolhardy) and illustrations worthy of the Neo-Malthusian League. Not to mention an occasional series in the secular press by someone, Catholic or otherwise, who: a) agrees with the birth-control movement in everything but the *means*, and is able to quote one or more responsible theologians to support his position, or b) agrees with the birth-control movement and considers it only a matter of time and patient understanding on both sides until the Church, pushed forward by an aroused laity, catches up with the 20th century.

Another eager teacher may be right in the parish, in the person of the young curate who works with the teen-agers—who is rightly a hero and mentor to them, and who is "nervous about large families."

At this point, it would be unnatural indeed if she didn't begin to wonder about her parents and whether she and her brothers were "the effect of blind passion or the fruit of nature's unknown whim" (as one writer expresses it), or whether, since our family is not a large one, they were the result of prudent planning. She may begin to wonder, also, considering the more densely populated homes of some of her friends, if their parents have the "rabbit-warren morality" referred to by yet another Catholic spokesman, or whether they just hadn't heard that whereas "formerly the problem had to be left to Divine Providence," there was now "a new dimension in Catholic family thinking." (We'll have news for her on these points—one item of which will be that if you're looking for libertines, don't waste your time on the parents of numerous children. Even Margaret Sanger recognized that *one* marital act a year "might be sufficient to keep a woman with one child in her womb and another at her breast during her entire childbearing period.")

Then college, if she goes. We're rather glad that worries about the expense of college didn't interfere with *her* advent into the world. If she wants and can make college and we can't afford an expensive one, there are excellent "streetcar" colleges in our city—scholarships and student-aid plans for the deserving, too. College can somewhat enlarge her knowledge of the new thinking, though the young rebels who used to say (and mean): "No church is going to tell *me* how many children to have," will have turned to other quarrels because it will seem evident that this battle has long since been won.

We hope she will be stimulated to learn about the social teachings of the Church; but we predict she may very well hear all about

Mater et Magistra, for instance, *except* those embarrassing passages on Providence and population. (How else explain the almost simultaneous appearance of an article urging students to take up this encyclical and a hearty endorsement, by the same writer, of Dr. Rock's book?) She may also learn to quote verbatim Pius XII's three well-worn sentences about the hoped-for refinement of the licit method for regulating offspring, and remain ignorant of the literally thousands of eloquent sentences he spoke on the blessing of offspring and the significance to Christianity of the large family.

Perhaps in time this girl of ours will choose marriage. Well, then, a refresher course on "responsible parenthood" may be included in her preparation for the sacrament of matrimony. At her nuptials, incidentally, the Church will pray that she may be "rich in children," but I suppose that's just the vestigial remains of an ancient agrarian society, utterly irrelevant to modern life. Still later, she and her husband can review the whole subject and its "mystique" at a renewal day for young married people. Very possibly a book will be recommended that paints a beautiful picture of married love, only to destroy it by recommending a compensatory sexual practice, which readers of Aldous Huxley will recognize as the exquisitely pleasurable yoga of love practiced by the most enlightened inhabitants of the "Island."

All in all, I wonder if our girl will stand a chance of approaching her vocation in the frame of mind and heart befitting a Christian bride—not so much because of pressures from a hostile and worldly society, but because the very guides she has reason to trust will unwittingly have handicapped her. Throughout this time, of course, we parents will not be sitting idly by. But we wish conditions were not being systematically set up that can only make it more difficult for young Christians to approach the maturity asked of them by the Sermon on the Mount.

The kind of responsibility we should like our daughter to acquire is a loving response to a loving Father who speaks to her through the people and the circumstances of her life, a humble and "resolute willingness to undergo inevitable fatigue and sacrifices in the fulfillment of a mission so noble and often so arduous as is the cooperation with God in the transmission of human life and the education of offspring" (*Mater et Magistra,* §195).

We think she should develop a great respect—awe, really—for the vocation of marriage, be sure it is *her* vocation, and then be ready to give herself to it with courage and good cheer, instead of foolishly standing on her fictitious rights against her own God, fighting the very love that is meant to make her into a fully developed human being.

The kind of prudence we would see grow in her is not the anxiety of the fainthearted, the apprehensive caution of the fearful. In the words of Father Gerald Vann: "One might suppose that our Lord had said He had come not that we might have life but that we might have safety. And therefore prudence has come to mean, quite simply, caution, the caution necessary to avoid all danger and ensure complete safety. To such an extent has the greatest of the cardinal virtues come down in the world."

Prudence about marriage, for her, ought to mean a prudent decision to marry or not to marry, when to marry, whom to marry. If she is unable to exercise prudence on these questions, which will directly affect numerous lives, then a future decision to "plan" will likely not be the sudden blooming of prudence, but caution masquerading as prudence. Let her rather take counsel and be wise in her choice of vocation and preparation for it, and then let her live it with a stout heart.

The kind of control she ought to cultivate is chastity—that of the virgin while she is unmarried, that of the wife if she marries. Such control would rule out her yielding to intemperate desire either through fornication or through contracting marriage too early. (In marriage, it might be added, this would not only rule out adultery, but also the touch of Jansenism which counts it somehow more godly for married people to eschew the marital act, or the touch of hedonism which implies that there really isn't anything much else.)

I cannot understand why anyone would want her to think that control in marriage is a matter of successfully avoiding "too many babies," or that temperance can be acquired by deliberately sowing the seed of life on barren ground. Or that periodic continence is not merely a remedy for medical, social, economic and eugenic ills, but is, in fact, the "prudent" way of married life. Or that, anyhow, given the conditions of modern life, she will inevitably have one or more of the licit reasons for family limitation. Or that babies (after the first four at least) may somehow be an evil to be avoided instead of a gift to be cherished. Or that family limitation does not exact a stiff toll in moral, psychological and spiritual problems. Or that every couple will produce an excessive number of children unless controlled—when in fact sterility, complete or partial, is a major medical problem. Or indeed that any thinking couple must view with alarm the fast multiplying world population and decide whether they have the right to add even one new hungry mouth (in our overfed country).

At an age when her idealism is at a peak, her mind alert, her capacities growing, she will be receptive to the words of life. Should she not hear them, instead of the dismal predictions of those who tremble at the thought of more human life? Will there be someone to call forth a joyful echo in her heart with words like these from Pope Paul: "Efforts to re-establish the equilibrium between growing population and means of livelihood are therefore not to be directed toward violation of the laws of life or interference with the natural flux and flow of the human family. Such an attitude or renouncement of life, indeed, kills the noblest aspirations of the spirit; while a declining birth rate, aimed at by such systems, has always proved sooner or later to be, in the history of the nations, a sign of defeat and of doom."

We want her to see the dignity of Christian marriage, to consider soberly, but not morbidly, the gamut of possibilities implicit in the marriage vows. We want her to have confidence in her innate ability to cope and to hope, to meet difficulties with composure instead of panic.

Nature has equipped her to receive and carry and nourish the gift of new life. Her heart will grow to embrace her spouse and the whole harvest of their love—if she is not conditioned to reject them. The grace of matrimony, perfecting nature's gifts, can fashion her into a wise and inwardly tranquil wife and mother whose best contribution to Church and State is good sons and daughters—their number now hidden in the inscrutable mystery of God's creative love.

If there are those who would assist us as we try to prepare this girl for her life, if they would earn our gratitude, let them try to apprehend the mysterious making of the family as its natural and supernatural destiny unfolds; reverently study the norms implanted in nature by God; resist all temptations to reduce marriage and family to a mechanical formula acceptable to human wisdom.

Granted this approach, we think a certain husband-to-be, if he exists, may one day have cause to be grateful, too.

As for now, we hope she will always remember that the Vicar of Christ who reigned in Rome in the year of her confirmation said: "Don't be afraid of the numbers of your sons and daughters. On the contrary, ask Providence for them so that you can rear and educate them to their benefit and to the glory of your fatherland here on earth, and of that in heaven." And again: "Every night I say the third decade of the rosary for all the babies born in the last 24 hours, because they are the treasure of the future." And, in his last letter to the Roncalli family: "Oh, the children, what a richness the children are, what a blessing!"

FRANCIS CANAVAN

Reflections on the Revolution in Sex

¶Must we still say that premarital sex is immoral? And what of homosexuality?

Sex is here to stay. But the sexual moral standards of Christian civilization may not be. They are being attacked today as seldom before. "For the first time for centuries," said the British magazine *New Society*, in its January 24, 1963 number, "the Judeo-Christian code is under fire, not just from people who wish to break it for their own pleasure's sake, but from people who believe that it is actually wrong."

This revolt against Christianity, which is comparable to the Enlightenment in the 18th century, is the Sexual Revolution of the 20th century. It is taking place in almost every Western nation; in the United States it is already well advanced. But since the advocates of the revolution are somewhat more outspoken in Great Britain than they are here, this article will report on what they are saying in the United Kingdom rather than in the United States. No invidious comparison is intended. The Land of the Free, after all, is also the Home of the Playboy Philosophy. In this respect, Americans have no reason to look down on anyone.

At the root of the sexual revolution is the growing awareness that modern contraceptive technology has radically separated sex from procreation. Reflection on this fact is leading many thoughtful persons to ask why sexual relations must be confined to marriage or even, for that matter, to the normal organs of reproduction. The contemporary preoccupation with meaningful interpersonal relationships has only added force to this questioning.

Prof. G. M. Carstairs, of Edinburgh University, raised the question in trenchant form in his series of Reith Lectures on the British Broadcasting Corporation's Home Service in November, 1962. Young people, he said, are rapidly turning British society "into one in which sexual experience, with precautions against conception, is becoming accepted as a sensible preliminary to marriage."

Among the "indications of precocious sexual behavior in our society," he mentioned "the increasing number of cases of venereal disease in young people and the fact that in 1961 no less than 31 per cent of girls who married in their teens were pregnant at the time of their wedding." The professor was not alarmed, however. "The interesting thing," he remarked, "is that this premarital licence has been found to be quite compatible with stable married life."

"Is chastity the supreme moral virtue?" he asked. "Surely charity, that is, consideration of and concern for others, comes first." Besides, he said, the former theological canons of behavior are seldom taken seriously. "In their place, a new concept is emerging of sexual relations as a source of pleasure, but also as a mutual encountering of personalities, in which each explores the other and at the same time discovers new depths in himself or herself."

The distinguished literary critic, Cyril Connolly, proclaimed: "The Reith Lectures are an achievement of which our culture can be proud." Not everyone in Britain shared his jubilation, of course. Some felt more disturbed than proud. But they had even greater cause for disquiet with the publication, in February, 1963, of a booklet entitled *Towards a Quaker View of Sex*.

The authors were a group of eleven Quakers. They spoke in their own name, not in that of their denomination. Six of them, however, were Elders of the Society of Friends. The group included teachers, psychiatrists, a barrister and a housewife. All were married except one, Dr. Anna Bidder, who was a Cambridge University expert in zoology specializing in the giant squid.

Towards a Quaker View of Sex "rejects almost completely the traditional approach of the organized Christian Church to morality, with its supposition that it knows precisely what is right and what is wrong, that this distinction can be made in terms of an external pattern of behavior, and that the greatest good will come only through universal adherence to that pattern." Its own answers, it says, are "tentative and incomplete." They are certainly different from the accepted Christian norms.

The authors note "an increase in transient premarital sexual intimacies generally." They refuse to frown upon it, however, since "it is fairly common in both young men and women with high standards of general conduct and integrity to have one or two love affairs, involving intercourse, before they find the persons they will ultimately marry."

It is even more common, they say, for those who do marry each other to have intercourse before the ceremony. "This is true, probably, of a majority of young people in all classes of society, including those who often have a deep sense of responsibility."

Even after marriage, the group of Friends observe, "the sexual drive differs in strength and frequency in different individuals, and what is customary and normal in one marriage may not be so in another." In this connection, they mention the so-called "triangular situation." It "is too often thought of as a wholly destructive and irresponsible relationship," they feel. "Not sufficient recognition is given to the fact that a triangular situation can and often does arise in which all three persons behave responsibly, are deeply conscious of the difficulties and equally anxious to avoid injury to the others."

(In the second edition of their booklet, published in January, 1965, the authors reject an interpretation of this passage "in terms of an adulterous relationship being good and beneficial to all three persons concerned." But they still feel that "more often than is recognized, the three people concerned behave responsibly," etc.)

Responsibility is also the keynote of their treatment of homosexuality, which "one should no more deplore than left-handedness." They see "no reason why the physical nature of a sexual act should be the criterion by which the question whether or not it is moral should be decided. An act which (for example) expresses true affection between two individuals and gives pleasure to them

both, does not seem to us to be sinful by reason *alone* of the fact
that it is homosexual. The same criteria seem to us to apply whether
a relationship is heterosexual or homosexual."

"Homosexual affection," they explain, "can be as selfless as
heterosexual affection, and therefore we cannot see that it is in some
way morally worse."

It is not surprising, therefore, that these Quakers feel that Christian sexual morality up to the present has been pretty much a
ghastly mistake. "The fulfillment of our nature as distinctively
human beings," they say, "is through relationships that are *personal*,
through the kind of friendship that is its own justification." These
relations cannot be confined to marriage, even when they are sexual
in nature.

This conviction leads them to criticize the Anglican theologian
Sherwin Bailey. They acknowledge their indebtedness to him in
general, but they state their dissent from one of the conclusions in
his book, *Common Sense About Sexual Ethics*. Their complaint is
this: "He holds that to say 'I love you' means nothing less than this:
'I want you, just as you are, to share the whole of my life, and I ask
you to take me, just as I am, to share the whole of your life.' He
further says that it ought never to be said unless marriage is possible, right, and at the time of speaking intended. That such a statement is unrealistic is at the root of our work. Nothing that has
come to light in the course of our studies has altered the conviction
that came to us when we began to examine the actual experiences of
people—the conviction that love cannot be confined to a pattern."

The authors quote with approval John Macmurray's *Reason and
Emotion*, in which he says: "Our civilization, for all its scientific
and administrative capacity, has remained emotionally vulgar and
primitive, unchaste in the extreme. We do not recognize this, of
course, because it is simply the reflection of our own inner insensibility. That insensibility is the inevitable result of a morality based
upon will and reason, imposing itself upon the emotions and so
destroying their integrity."

But it would be wrong to interpret the authors of *Towards a
Quaker View of Sex* as being anti-moral. They themselves say:
"*There must be a morality of some sort to govern sexual relationships*," and put it in italics for emphasis. They explain the basic
principle of their morality by stating that they "accept the defini-

tion of sin given by an Anglican broadcaster, as covering those actions that involve exploitation of the other person." This, they say, "is a concept of wrongdoing that applies both to homosexual and heterosexual actions and to actions within marriage as well as outside it. It condemns as fundamentally immoral every sexual action that is not, as far as is humanly ascertainable, the result of a mutual decision."

On a later page they add: "Where there is a deliberate intention to avoid responsibility and all possibility of being involved and committed, then evil creeps in and the act becomes mutual exploitation. But where there is genuine tenderness, an openness to responsibility, and the seed of commitment, God is surely not shut out. Can we not say that God can enter any relationship in which there is a measure of selfless love?—and is not every generalization we make qualified by this?"

The next round in Britain's controversy over sexual morality came in July, 1963. Dr. Peter Henderson, the principal medical officer of the Ministry of Education, said at a teachers' meeting: "I do not think that it is wrong if a young man and woman who are in love and who intend to get married but who put off marriage, perhaps for economic reasons, have sexual intercourse before marriage. I do not think they are unchaste or immoral. They may or may not be wise if they do so, but I cannot convince myself that they are immoral."

After *Towards a Quaker View of Sex*, Dr. Henderson's views should have seemed almost conventional. But because of his position, his words were nationally reported and stirred up considerable protest. Sir Edward Boyle, the Minister of Education, refused to repudiate Dr. Henderson. "It is not part of my function to prescribe what moral teaching could take place in the schools," he said. "The voice of conscience, not society, should guide people in their views."

A view more radical than Dr. Henderson's was expressed by Dr. Alex Comfort in his book *Sex in Society*. According to a review in the London *Daily Telegraph:* "He starts from the premise that no form of sexual behavior is sinful unless it has demonstrably bad effects, and going on from there examines such vital questions as teen-age morality, extramarital relations, and the law and deviation."

Another review, in the *Sunday Times*, quotes Dr. Comfort as saying: "It is highly probable that adultery today maintains far more marriages than it destroys."

Advanced views turned up even in the Established Church of England. Canon D. A. Rhymes of Southwark Cathedral gave a sermon in March, 1963, in which he announced: "We need to replace the traditional morality based upon a code with a morality which is related to the person and the needs of the person." He also said: "Much of the prejudice against homosexuality is on the ground that it is unnatural. But unnatural to whom? Certainly not for the homosexual himself."

In September of the same year, Canon T. R. Milford published a pamphlet, *Talking of Sex*. In it he questioned the idea that marriage is essentially indissoluble and that divorce is always and in every circumstance a sin. On concubinage or triangular relationships, he quoted a group of professional people who had come to this conclusion: "We should not condemn as simply immoral those who in good faith have chosen this way. But they cannot expect approval of conduct which, taken as an example by others, would be disastrous."

Theory was reduced to practice in the fall of 1963, when the Marie Stopes Memorial Foundation started consultative sessions for young unmarried people in its Tottenham Court Road clinic in London and offered birth control appliances to some of them. The foundation was affiliated to, but not a part of, the London Federation of the Family Planning Association, whose own clinics at that time were forbidden to advise single people, even those about to marry.

In June, 1964, however, the Family Planning Association decided to encourage the setting up of youth advisory centers, at which unmarried people could get medical advice on sex problems, including advice on birth control. The decision was taken after two hours of debate. Mrs. Leah Manning expressed the majority point of view, saying: "We have to face facts; we have to realize that the practice of premarital sexual intercourse has begun to establish itself." Lady Limerick objected on the ground that the Family Planning Association would have to change its name, because it would be dishonest if the motion passed. In certain cases, she said, it would "merely be giving advice to people to help them avoid marriage."

Finally, in December, 1964, despite opposition from its Catholic members, the London County Council approved plans to assist organizations providing contraceptive advice to young unmarried persons. The *Observer* praised the move because "we must guard against the crime of producing children without parents." To clinch the argument, it added: "It is certainly easier to teach contraception than chastity."

International opinion made its impact felt in Britain with the conference of the International Planned Parenthood Federation in London in June, 1964. The *Sunday Times* reported: "There was general acceptance, among most of the representatives of 46 countries attending, of premarital intercourse (even among boys and girls in their early teens)." But attitudes still varied in different countries, they admitted. A 14-year-old girl in Stockholm did not much mind being seen abstracting a contraceptive from a slot machine. But Italy, "still under the dominating influence of the Roman Catholic Church, would appear to be one of the few European countries where a bride is still expected to be a virgin."

American attitudes were revealed by Dr. Alan F. Guttmacher, president of the Planned Parenthood Federation of America. "Parents themselves are becoming more sophisticated," he was reported as saying. "They know, for example, that their son or daughter must go to college equipped with contraceptives." But, he felt, "so long as they are taught responsibility to each other, I think some better humans may come out of this 'new morality.'"

J. Kruithof, professor of moral philosophy at the University of Brussels and Ghent, offered a philosophic analysis of the whole situation. According to the London *Times*, the Belgian professor told delegates to the conference that he believed the traditional system of morality was on the way to complete breakdown.

Traditionally, he said, sex, love, marriage and children were considered to belong together. Today, childless couples were no longer looked down on. Extramarital and premarital relationships were quite common. It was even possible that sex without love—a kind of prostitution for enjoyment rather than financial gain—might be the new pattern emerging among young people.

"We need a new code of morality," Professor Kruithof said. "This new system is in the process of formation. We are going toward a revaluation of the sex act."

The British Council of Churches had already reacted to this kind of challenge to Christian morality. At its half-yearly meeting, in April, 1964, it decided to set up a working party charged with producing a statement of the Christian position on sexual morals in a persuasive, modern style. This was to include the Christian case for abstinence from sexual intercourse before marriage and faithfulness within marriage.

The Rev. Kenneth Greet, chairman of the Council's advisory group on sex, morality and the family, was reported by the London *Times* as saying at the meeting that if the churches were to engage effectively in defense of Christian standards, they must listen seriously to what the most responsible of their critics were saying. Further, the positive things Christians had to say needed to be said more effectively and with a greater sense of urgency. "We must say very much more than we have said in the past about the Christian understanding of sex," he declared, "not merely in terms of procreation but in terms of rich and diversified human relationship."

The churches that form the British Council of Churches have already accepted contraception as a Christian practice. Indeed, it was the Anglican Communion that gave the lead in that direction at its Lambeth Conferences of 1930 and 1958. It would seem difficult, therefore, for the Council to defend traditional Christian standards of sexual morality in terms of the procreative purpose of sex. Whether a successful defense can be mounted "in terms of rich and diversified human relationship" alone remains to be seen. So far as this writer knows, the working party has not yet made its report.

Catholics, for their part, should not dismiss the attack on Christian sexual morality as the mouthings of a few extremists. The sexual revolution is a reality that will grow and spread as time goes by. Its advocates will become more numerous and more bold. They must be taken seriously. They are a direct threat to the morals of every young Catholic. To ignore them, and thus to leave our young people unprepared to meet their disciples, would be folly.

One final reflection on the revolution in sex comes to mind. There are Catholics today who urge Rome to go to Lambeth and accept contraception as a means of solving problems in family life. Nothing that has been reported in this article *proves* that these Catholics are wrong. But the arguments of the sexual revolutionists against Christian morality suggest a thought. It is this: the road to Lambeth may not end there.

FRANK M. WESSLING
Is It Immature Loving?

¶The "problem" may not be birth control but rather a static notion of love

Years of struggling to understand women have convinced me that, though boys may become silly when they discover sex, women, when they make the great discovery, can get downright ludicrous.

The *Saturday Evening Post*, not long ago, contained a piece in its "Speaking Out" department titled "A Catholic Mother Tells 'Why I Believe in Birth Control.'" The writer, Mrs. Rosemary Ruether, is a humanities teacher at Scripps College in California, mother of three children, and wildly frustrated because she can't understand why the Church places love before sex in marriage.

Mrs. Ruether has her Catholic doctrines upside down. She speaks of "a doctrine of birth control that seems to injure marriage." Since the Church does not have "a doctrine of birth control," but rather a doctrine of marriage, and Mrs. Ruether must certainly have heard of it, I can be forgiven for thinking that some women make their own marital problems. It is so easy to lash out at the Church.

True, for various reasons, some rooted in Western history and some in the Jansenist plague, Catholic doctrine on marriage has suffered bad explanation and preaching. Despite all pious disclaimers, it is obvious that very often the way marriage has been preached in the Church has tended to underscore its biological function at the expense of its total human reality.

But Mrs. Ruether has doubtless noticed some of the recent material on marriage and sex in Catholic publications and has fallen for the rather restricted view of sexuality displayed there. It is a view (the newly awakened adolescent's view) hypnotized by the act of sexual intercourse. Too many preachers and teachers in the Church suffer under the same hypnotic spell; so it should be no surprise that married people who agonize publicly over their problems should turn in a rage of frustration against the official doctrine of the Church.

When Catholics are preparing for marriage, they are told that the purpose of marriage is the procreation and education of children. That statement of purpose, as far as it goes, is true. It is a true statement of the purpose of marriage as a human institution. Some kind of stable union between man and woman is needed to raise human creatures rather than half-tamed savages, and that union is marriage. The Church, of course, should have no monopoly on stating the purpose of marriage. But it is good that she continues to state it, since nearly every other spokesman for humanity seems to ignore that purpose.

Unfortunately, the Church also seems to have a near monopoly on treating marriage with a one-sided stress on purpose that makes for easier misunderstanding than understanding of marriage itself.

Despite the penitential breast-beating of St. Augustine, total personal union, including sexual union, is the heart of marriage. And this being the heart, it is this that is at the center of the sacrament —the Christ-finding aspect—of marriage.

Marriage is a promise to make two into one. Two people as different as they can be—man and woman—promise to make an attempt to immerse their separate prior selves into a new self, a synthesis forged in the time-fires of struggle, joy, conflict, pain, ecstasy, fear —all the jolting glory of human life well lived. Two people afraid of life can marry, of course, and have much less of life than this in their love; but then they should not afflict others with their complaints that the half-life isn't satisfactory.

I think birth control is not the real problem of affluent people who complain about it. I think their real problem is a static notion of love.

When people have access to the wealth of erotic literature available to Americans, and are as self-conscious about sex as we are, they manage to convince themselves that the intellectual experience of sex is a liberating experience, making it unnecessary to take all the steps along the path of intimacy in marital love. In reality, Henry Miller and his imitators have inhibited a great many people who ought to know better. *No one* can give lessons on the proper unfolding of the sexual experience in married love. A man effectively cheats his wife and a wife cheats her husband if they do not explore the mystery of each other from the beginning with the guileless honesty of innocent children. They are going to have a lifetime of living together; so they had better decide early to take pleasure in all the possible ways of loving each other, at all the possible times—with a touch, a look, a word, as well as with an embrace.

If a husband and wife have not learned in a few years how to give themselves to each other totally in the intimacy of an understood look, then they had better get busy learning how to love each other. They are simply lousy lovers. And I don't care if they hustle off to bed every night of the week for the so-called marital embrace. If that is the only love-making they do, they are at best only half alive.

The business of learning to love a husband or wife takes some time and discipline. I am not learning to love women in general; I'm learning to love the unique woman who is my wife, and so I have to discipline myself to the need of intimacy with her. It takes time and energy, and there are frustrations; but for one who keeps plodding on, the benefits are decidedly worthwhile.

Mrs. Ruether complains that discipline in married love "is a matter of destroying some positive good in the marital relationship." She is quite wrong. I did not want my wife to be little more than a baby machine, and she did not want to be a baby machine; so we were forced to do what someone should have advised us to do freely. We found that our intimacy, our moments of self-giving, need not be confined to the bedroom, and that there was much to be learned about loving each other if we were forced not to take the easy way—for intercourse is the easy way. True, it is the seal on married life, but it should not be necessary to be constantly sealing the same empty envelope. My wife and I think there is joy in filling the envelope with all the small, daily love-making we can. The seal then takes on fresh meaning each time we impress it upon our lives.

All of us, married or not, will save our lives by learning to love as fully as possible. If I am ever going to learn to love, I shall have to learn it in my marriage by loving my wife first of all. In that love I have got to see and appreciate variety and degrees, so that when I turn outward to the world and other persons, I am able to love the variety and the degrees of goodness I see there.

We aren't angels; it takes time to appreciate the sacrifices, the discipline, that will force us to be as human as possible, to give ourselves in love as fully as possible. A Christian claims by virtue of his name that he is prepared to accept, even without completely understanding, the discipline of loving totally as Christ did. He accepts because he believes that Christ was given to us as the Way to human fulfillment.

We have to love; everyone knows that. But it is so difficult to admit that love really demands a sacrifice of self for the "other." If a man and woman aren't forced by some external pressure in the beginning to sacrifice themselves in marriage, they will more than likely not do an adequate job of sacrifice, of loving, on their own. They will equivocate, they will argue, they will complain that such sacrifice destroys their integrity as individuals. I would agree that it must destroy the *old* individual, but only to create a new integrity in the marriage trinity: I—You—Love. Marriage is a promise to work out a new integrity, more meaningful, more complete, and infinitely more life-giving, more fecund, than the old.

What the Church says about birth control is hard for most people to accept. It is even harder to accept than necessary, because it is seldom expressed within a context that gives it anything more than a simply biological meaning. It need not be so, however.

The immediate cause of children is total sexual giving, a man and a woman's total surrender to each other. The Church says, as a witness to the marriage promise of a man and woman—which is a promise of a man to give his manness, his sexuality, to the woman and of the woman to give her womanness to the man—that the married couple have no right to renege, or to attach later conditions, on the promise of *total* self-giving. Contraceptive birth control is, purely and simply, the giving of self *with reservation*.

I can imagine a kind of marriage promise in which the contraceptive life might be acceptable: a man and woman would not give themselves to each other without reservation in the marriage contract. They would enter a frankly conditional union. People do, in fact, enter this type of union and call it marriage. They are not, however, entering the marriage that we know of as the constant stable unit of Western society and the sacrament of Christian life. And they are not entering a life in which a total commitment of love will take solid root and grow, unless despite the "conditions" the husband and wife learn the full meaning of love.

It would do no good even if the Church could say that birth control is acceptable. The problem posing as birth control is really a problem of immature loving.

What the Church can do to make Mrs. Ruether and a host of other people a bit less frustrated is to take most priests out of the business of marriage counseling. Too many who think they have a right to counsel married people simply have no appreciation of married life. When people come to them with problems, they try to give advice and help, of course; but I'm afraid that too often they succeed only in deepening the problem.

I must agree completely with Mrs. Ruether when she expresses exasperation over priests who tell people that "the only difficulty in the use of rhythm is self-control." Such a statement makes it perfectly clear how little the person who made it appreciates the marital relationship.

The rhythm-determining *process* is a galling irritant to any husband and wife who respect the dignity of their relationship and who live with a true vision of what their relationship should be. It reminds me somewhat of the current civil rights bill, a piece of legislation that ought not to be necessary but nevertheless is, because certain extrinsic disorders prevent us from living freely and completely according to our vision of what human dignity demands. The civil rights bill can thus be accepted, even passionately supported, when it is seen in the proper light. Any necessary discipline imposed on marital love needs to be seen in the proper light also.

I have real hope that the Church will shed a great deal of that light on marriage in the future. Bishops like Cardinal Suenens and theologians like Father Bernard Häring are forerunners of the churchmen who will confront the Rosemary Ruethers of the future.

They will not tell her that "the only difficulty in the use of rhythm is self-control." They will ask her what goes into the total rhythm of her life. They will want to know if she is only playing a one-note tune in her marital love or if she is making an attempt to play a symphony of intimacy. They will not immediately consign her to hell if she is stumbling over rugged problems. But they will try to help her see that she doesn't yet know as much as she thinks she knows about love and about growth in marital intimacy.

SECTION IV

THE LIGHTER SIDE

JAMES POWELL

Closed and/or Open

¶Repartee has always been my forte, but occasionally I meet difficult people

Back in the good old days, when I was a much simpler person than
I am today, I picked up a better-than-middling reputation for fer-
reting out non-Catholics (as we used to call them) at parties and
setting them straight on where they had gone wrong theologically.
Their reaction came in two sizes, depending on how long the party
had been under way. If it was early enough in the evening, more
often than not they would content themselves with shaking me violently by the lapels of my little sailor suit or, throbbing at the tem-
ples with apoplexy, try to shout the smile off my face. But as the
evening lengthened and my smile became more and more insuffer-
able, reaction No. 2 would set in and somebody would take a poke
at me. (I have always felt that the one truth I came to learn from
these encounters—"Protestants never lead with their right"—should
find a place somewhere in our catechisms. I leave it to whoever
decides on such things to frame the question for which it would be
the answer.)

But if I was outwardly calm as I smoothed my lapels or brushed
off the seat of my pants and moved on, smiling, to the next non-
Catholic, on the inside I was teeming with perplexities and hurt
feelings. "Leaping lizards," I would brood with an inward shake of
my head, "all I said was they were wrong. Everybody can't be
right." And sometimes I would add, pensively: "Gee, but it's hard
to be chums with non-Catholics."

All that, as I said, was back in my simpler days. Eventually I
stopped being invited to parties. And with so much time on my
hands, I set about improving myself. I contemplated; I pondered;
I thought. As you can well imagine if your experience has paral-
leled my own, I soon had my share of those anxieties and insecuri-
ties that are the heart and soul of modern man. Yet if I see more

deeply now, it is less clearly—through a mist born of the meeting of my hot Augustinian blood and my cool Thomistic mind. You will say that I have acquired wisdom or something, and you are probably right.

Perhaps it was no more than coincidence, but just about the time I was wondering whether I had the right to keep all this wisdom hidden under a basket, the Ecumenical Council opened. Then and there I decided, as perhaps you did, that at historic moments like this the Church needs all the brainpower she can muster. So I resolved to get back into the swim again, and to this end I added a press to my little sailor suit and stood around with a kind of casual conspicuousness until people started inviting me to parties again. But it was the new me, the wise me, the me who only argues with Catholics.

Not so long ago, at one of these parties, I approached two Catholics of my acquaintance. "Hi there," I said, adding triumphantly: "It sure looks like the liberals have got those darned conservatives on the run at the Council." The fat one winced, and his thin companion glanced nervously left and right for an avenue of escape. "Hi there," I repeated, adding triumphantly: "It sure looks like the liberals have got those darned conservatives on the run at the Council."

The fat one stared at the other side of the room for a moment and then said quietly: "You know, I'm not sure I'm happy with the terms 'liberal' and 'conservative' that the secular press has tacked onto the Fathers of the Council. Oh, I'll grant you it's all very quaint, all very Wild West—good guys with white hats and bad guys with black hats. But let's ask ourselves if we really want to apply it to a spiritual community such as the Church." He paused for a moment so we could all ask ourselves. "No. No, I don't think we do," he continued. "At best it's divisive. At worst it gets us involved in the meanings of words and all kinds of things out beyond our depth."

"Personally," said the thin one, "I've always considered the liberal the only true conservative."

"Somewhat along the same lines," said the fat one, "I've always considered the conservative the only true liberal. Now, looked at from this point of view, as expressed by my friend here and myself, the Fathers of the Council can be thought of as liberal *and* conservative. But," he added, tapping me on the chest, "but I'm afraid our distinction is just a bit too subtle for—no offense meant —the run of the mill, the Joe Catholics of this world, the little old mother superior in Dubuque, so to speak. For them—and confess now, for you—pushed far enough, 'liberal' and 'conservative' boil down to 'right' and 'wrong' or 'wrong' and 'right'." "Ah," I said. He began to chuckle. "Without knowing it," he said, "you've been saying that some of the Council Fathers are wrong." The thin one joined him in a delighted chuckle. "Ah," I said.

"Your preoccupation with right and wrong is all very amusing, all very naïve," smiled the fat one. Then he added soberly: "All very Manichean." "Manichean?" I asked. "That, of course, is a heresy," he said with a little smile. "Well," I said, backing off rapidly, "it's not as if I was saying anybody was immoral or things like that." "You'd be on firmer theological ground if you were," he said. "After all, the bishops are human beings just as my friend here and myself are human beings. They are sinners just like my friend and I are. Call them that and they'll thank you for it. But 'wrong' is something else again. That's pretty strong talk."

"If you must have labels for the Council Fathers—and I suppose you must," said the thin one, kicking me when I was down, "how about shepherds and fishermen? Archbishop Felici speaks of shepherds and fishermen. You've got those who want to protect the sheep from the wolves, and you've got the ones who want to fill up the nets with fish."

"How about traditionalists and innovators?" asked the fat one. "Those who see the big job as keeping the deposit of faith intact and those who want to spread the teachings of Christ through the world."

"Now, Father Küng speaks of bishops with 'open door' mentalities and those with 'closed door' mentalities," said the thin one. "Even Father Küng doesn't speak of right or wrong."

"Even Father Küng?" I asked, suddenly feeling the whole weight of the world on my shoulders alone.

"There you are," said the fat one. "The Church moves forward by a kind of dialectic: existence and essence, form and matter, nature and grace."

"Yin and Yang?" I asked, with a trace of sarcasm.

"Look," said the fat one, giving me the fisheye, "it's like the

main arch of a Gothic cathedral." "That's right," said the thin
one. "Jean Guitton calls it like the main arch of a Gothic cathedral."
"You've got these two columns," said the fat one, "and they rise
up parallel but like they were opposed to each other. Then, at the
top, lo and behold, suddenly they come together forming an arch
under which the faithful—that's us—worship in security and tranquillity for centuries." I followed the gesture of his hands to the
ceiling. "How about we get a bit of air?" I suggested, indicating
the terrace.

"Let me have a go at him, this time," said the thin one to his fat
friend. "Are you ready?" he asked, looking at me. I nodded. "Now
a sower goes out to sow . . . ," he began. "Stop," I said. "I know
this one. Some of the seed falls on . . ." "That's not it at all," he
said impatiently. "What I'm talking about is an image that François
Mauriac, the Frenchman, uses to describe traditionalists and innovators in the Church. Just listen and don't be so contrary. A sower
goes out to sow seeds." He picked up a bowl of peanuts from a
near-by table and made the motion of scooping up a handful. "First
he must hold the seed in his fist. Then—" and he opened his fist in
a broad, sowing motion—"he must open it to scatter the seed. Now,
the fist closed around the seed stands for those who want to guard
the deposit of faith. The open hand, for those who want to spread
the teachings of Christ. But you can't get along unless you've got
both."

"And this isn't to imply, by any means," added the fat one, "that
the closefisted ones don't want to spread the teachings of Christ or,
conversely, that the openhanded ones don't want to guard the deposit of faith. In fact, almost the opposite may be said to be true.
Let's not forget they're all in this thing together. It's just a question
of temperament. And isn't that what makes horse racing?"

"Hold your horses," I said. "You need the closed fist and the open
hand, all right. But not both at the same time. There's a time when
the hand has to be open and a time when it has to be closed. The
big question is, what time is it now?"

"But that's the whole point in a nutshell," said the thin one. "You
have to do both at the same time." "You mean your fist closed and
open at the same time?" I asked, looking him straight in the eye.
He nodded, though not too enthusiastically. "I know it sounds
strange," he said, "but it's a mystery." I kept looking him straight

in the eye. "There's kind of this ineffable moment when the hand is opened and closed," he said, licking his lips. I kept looking him straight in the eye. "Ineffable, you know what I mean?" he asked rather weakly. I took the bowl of peanuts from him. "Now keep your eye peeled," I ordered, scooping up a handful of peanuts. "Fist closed." Then I scattered them across the carpet in a sowing motion. "Fist open." The thin one blinked. I began walking up and down, scattering peanuts left and right. "Fist closed. Fist open." He ran along beside me on his knees, watching my hand. After I had made six or seven turns, he was looking pretty crestfallen. "I thought I saw it there just for an instant," he said dejectedly.

"Of course, this whole thing proves almost absolutely nothing," said the fat one, who had been watching us with undisguised contempt. "After all, Mauriac is a Frenchman and your French farmer may sow seeds like that—in fact, nothing a French farmer did would surprise me. But your scriptural sower and your no-nonsense American farmer sow the way the good Lord intended—with the fist closed at all times," and he closed his hand into a loose fist, "and just this little hole for the seeds to get out almost by accident. Otherwise you end up with seeds scattered all over hell's half-acre."

I scooped up the last handful of peanuts. "Like this?" I asked making my fist like his and swinging it in front of me. Nothing came out. I tried again. "It's the salt," he insisted. "Peanuts are no good. The salt clogs up the hole. Now, if we had some of those little cheese things . . . ," he said, looking around the room.

The thin one was still on his knees watching my hand for the ineffable moment. "Fist closed," I said. "Fist open." And I scattered the last handful of peanuts across the carpet. At this point I was seized by the scruff of my neck and the seat of my pants, and my host propelled me toward the door. As I went, I kept my dignity by shouting: "There's a time for the fist to be closed and a time for the fist to be open. Somebody's right and somebody's wrong!"

Alone out in the hall I said to myself: "Well, somebody is." And I fought back a tear, because I was certain in my heart of hearts that another bowl of peanuts, or even those little cheese things, and I would have convinced them.

KATHARINE BYRNE
School Is Where You Learn Stuff

¶A four-year-old with a brief case has his first brush with formal education

This is a story that I have never been able to edge into the competitive field of dinner-party conversation. Since I am what is known in the trade as a late-in-life mother, I have had few opportunities for success in the cutthroat realms of parental small talk. My friends' children, you see, have always been years in advance of my own.

I began to suspect the social implications of my position long ago, when a first-born's first tooth looked like headline material to me, but someone else's little girl had just been named valedictorian for her kindergarten graduation. Then came the realization that you can't brag about your pediatrician's fees to persons who are already supporting the orthodontists. This was followed by the knowledge that there is no point in working up a story about what happened when you took the Cub Scouts touring the pretzel factory if the woman across the table has just survived the chaperone's job at the eighth-grade class picnic. When my life-goal was "Everybody Dry by a Year From Next Christmas," the rest of the world seemed already to be dug in for the Battle of the Car Keys.

Then, quite suddenly, or so it seemed to me, the first of my friends' daughters brought home *her* baby. Then I knew that conversationally all was lost and forever. If I were ever going to get in a few words about *my* little boy, it would have to be in print. No one was going to *listen* to anything I might have to say about him.

John is the last and the loneliest of this line-late-started. At his age all the others had at least one other person left at home to fight with. So we decided to fill that void, supply that need, and send him to a nursery school. Nothing fancy, you understand. No station wagon with "Kiddie Kollege" or "Park-a-Tot Prep" or

"Mommy's Idle Hour" inscribed across the doors. No kiln-fired ceramics or even a resident psychologist. Just a two-hour-a-day session offered without charge by the new community center a few blocks from home.

This brief encounter with basic education, we thought, could give John something to do besides waiting all day for bigger kids to come home. Importantly, too, it might help to straighten out his size trouble. So often he would observe bitterly: "Everybody in the whole world is bigger 'n me." You could point out passing infants in arms or in buggies, tiny children playing in the park, or those newspaper pictures of the First Baby Born in the New Year. But since no one under the age of six or seven ever came to our door, for all practical purposes (and he had no purposes which were not practical), everyone in the world was bigger than John.

He already knew what a person going to school or business should wear. Long accustomed to getting up early, competing with six others for the use of one-and-a-half bathrooms, he would often appear for breakfast wearing a white shirt, cuff links, old school tie (his brother's) and a tweed jacket (size 10) deeply cuffed. To any protest that a garment was years too large for him, John would insist that all it needed was a "good cuffle." Thus arrayed, however, he was likely to sit around all morning like a retired executive who had never cultivated a hobby, or follow his mother with a string of complaints about life and a brainwashing repetition of: "Now is it time to go to the corner and wait for the kids?"

The Nursery School might give some point to John's day. He thought so, too, and entered seriously into the work of getting ready for the great day coming. He set out to acquire as many as possible of the adjuncts to learning. Passionately devoted to the right way of doing things, he began to accumulate the things he would need in order to enter the world of educated people. I say "educated," because in the beginning John seemed to think that everyone else at this place would already know how to read, how to write, and "how to arithmetic." This in spite of his sister Peggy's patient insistence that "a school is where you learn stuff."

Still, she did teach him how to count to eleven, how to print a "J," and how to read TEL AVIV on the bakery where they go to buy Long Johns or jelly-filled sugar-crusted bismarcks.

Since he watches five other persons leave the house daily, each with some kind of carrying case for text books, library books, work books, note books, pens, pencils, sandwiches, apples and thermos jars, he knew that an appropriate receptacle is basic to the whole idea of education. For himself he fancied a certain Top Grain Cowhide Attaché Case he had seen in a Christmas gift catalogue. Dean Rusk might have carried it with distinction. But then, there has never been anything humble about John's aspirations. Before he was three he wanted a power lawn mower so that he could "get out and make some money." Settling, with very poor grace, for a discarded zippered bag of his father's, John began to pack, so that he would be ready for the day when his school opened. During this period he kept the things he thought he needed in an old Navy footlocker, far from his family's interested gaze. Only his sister Jody, a conspiratorial type, full of educational folk lore, acted as consultant.

On the day appointed, we set out for the halls of learning, the community building now known to all of us only as "John's School." For several weeks, whenever the car passed that impressive monument to the high tax rate, he would say: "There goes my school!" As we stood in the beautiful tile and terrazzo corridor with perhaps twenty other sets of mothers and children, waiting for the teacher to appear, I noticed that John was the only four-year-old carrying a brief case. There was no other gray-haired parent in view, either.

After a few moments of nervous foot-shuffling and nose-wiping on the part of those assembled, the teacher, wearing gray sweatshirt, black pants and a gym whistle rounded a corner at a medium trot. I recognized her uneasily as the same young woman who is in charge of tap dancing, ladies' weight redistribution and tumbling.

Approaching the group, she let us know in a voice which would inspire respect in an opposing soccer team that we would "dispense with formalities," as she just wanted to "give the kids a little workout" on the first day. The mothers, she suggested, could come back in an hour. With this she opened the doors to one of the largest and best equipped gymnasiums in the Middle West, a place big enough to house a college basketball game and several thousand spectators. As she herded in the children, the more reluctant and the less, she plucked John's school-going materials from his grasp.

"You won't be needing that, Bud," she boomed as she tossed the brief case in my direction.

The huge doors swung shut. Most of the mothers went off to home or market, but I told myself I had nothing else to do, and sat on the stairs at the end of the hall, propped bolt upright against the newel post.

From inside the gym came muffled noises. A phonograph of very low fidelity ground out "The Stars and Stripes Forever," accompanied by some uneven footwork, perhaps a primitive form of marching. Then there was something which sounded like bodies piling up against a wall, followed by several sharp blasts on a gym whistle. A few minutes later the doors opened wide enough to admit a janitress carrying a pail and a mop.

Time passed slowly. I decided to look inside John's carrying-case to see how he had planned to fortify himself for his first day of school. He had packed the bag with the precision of a parachute rigger. There was a foil-wrapped peanut-butter-and-jelly sandwich which must have been made very early in this project; a long, thin pad of paper (each sheet inscribed with a long, thin, wobbly "J"); one-half of a slide rule; Jimmy's report card; a beat-up copy of *Madeline;* six well-sharpened pencils; another book, gray with the dust of the topmost bookshelf: *British Poets of the Nineteenth Century, Wordsworth to Landor.*

At last the great doors swung open again, and the children came reeling out into the hall. John was wearing a look like thunder. His ears were red, too; always a bad sign. He picked up his brief case and demanded: "Why are you all the time telling me this place is a school?"

This why-are-you-all-the-time clause is a favorite debating device of his, a kind of offensive defense, as in "why-are-you-all-the-time giving me a bath?" or "why-are-you-all-the-time out looking for me?" Or the melancholy and unanswerable "why-are-you-all-the-time making stuff to eat that I don't like?"

"This place," with a wave of his arm which disposed of the entire $1.5-million worth of public property, "is not any school. A school is where you learn stuff. This place is nothing but a gym-a-sium." Looking like an editor of *National Review* who had just stumbled into a den of progressivism, he walked out of the building, his passport to learning under his arm, and he never went back.

Shortly afterward, his sister Kathy instituted the To Go Club, an organization whose one clear purpose was to-go-to-the-drugstoreto-buy-a-gumball. Involved with meetings, bylaws and secret hand-clasps, our boy seemed to have lost interest, as well as faith, in formal education.

But even now, when table talk moves around to whose head was smashed against the schoolyard fence and how the blood spattered, or who became ill—and where—John, like the fond alumnus for whom any academic unpleasantness is now lost in a nostalgic haze, will dig up his invariable reminiscence: a brief, dramatic bit about a certain girl in *his* school, with a strong sup-porting role for the lady with the mop.

STANLEY VISHNEWSKI

Spare Us, O Lord!

¶It takes a pretty spry person to keep up with the pace of liturgical changes

Don't get me wrong—I have nothing against the recent changes in the liturgy. To be truthful, I'm all for them. In fact, I believe our liturgists are going too slow. It would make me happy to see the restoration of the Kiss of Peace and an offertory procession where fruits and vegetables are brought up to the altar. I'm also strongly in favor of married deacons. I am the type that wants to rush in and take a more active part in the liturgical functions of the Church. I have been a cross-bearer, an acolyte, a taker-up of collections and a distributor of envelopes. I have always wanted to participate more fully in the divine worship—and there, per-haps, lies the source of my woes.

For many years, many more than I care to remember, I con-sidered myself a faithful subterranean worshiper in the Church. I recall the dimly lighted churches where I ruined my eyes trying to decipher the small print of my missal. I felt that I was in the catacombs. And in my youthful zeal I would from time to time whisper an *Et cum spiritu tuo* to the priest's invitation of *Dominus vobiscum.*

Oh, yes! Is there a lay apostle alive today who doesn't remember the time when it took a great deal of moral courage for a lay person to carry a missal to Mass? Is there a lay apostle alive today who doesn't recall the raised eyebrows and puzzled looks of his fellow parishioners? I used to sneak into the back pew and pray that if anyone saw me engrossed in my missal he would assume that I was a seminarian.

Today, when it is the custom for lay persons to say the divine office in private and recite compline together at their meetings, it is difficult for me to recall that period (before Catholic Action) when our pathetic attempts to recite compline were frowned upon as a dangerous innovation and a complaint was made to the chancery office about our "theatrical prayers."

I remember how anxious I was in those "dark days" (before this glorious renaissance of active lay participation) to take my rightful place in the divine worship. It was not right, I thought, for the clergy to do everything and limit my activity to placing small coins in the collection box. I wanted to be a co-participant with them. I remember how eager I was to recite the Divine Office —the books in those days were all in Latin. My zeal must have outrun my discretion, because I really believed that the Collect was the time set aside for taking up the Sunday collection.

But—alas for my pretensions and my desires—I had no ear for music and no talent for the study of Latin. For many years, I was forced to stand or kneel in the pews as a silent adorer of the Mystery taking place.

I was determined, however, to participate. I would learn to sing the Gregorian Mass. It took me 20 years (and this is no mere boast) to get to the point where I could with confidence sing an entire Gregorian Mass. One of the reasons for my difficulty was the fact that my mentors were a group of zealous apostolic women who delighted in coming up with little known Masses and motets from obscure provinces and centuries. I spent a year learning to sing the Hymn of the Flagellants, but I am not in favor of restoring this quaint custom.

But then came the glorious day when I knew I had it. I was able to sing the Mass of the Angels in its entirety, from Introit to the closing procession, with a few extra hymns to boot. O happy day! I rose early in the morning and carefully ran through the notes that my voice was to transmute into glorious melody. And, lugging my *Liber Usualis*, I manfully strode to church.

But then what happened? A new melody, beautiful in its simplicity, swelled up from the massed throats of the choir. I listened in silence, my mouth formed in a cavernous O—until a nudge from a fellow chorister brought me back to reality. "Gelineau Psalms," he whispered. "The latest rage in Church music."

Back to my music lessons I went, forgetting about Gregorian chant, now immersed in the study of Gelineau. It took me a year to get to the point where I could stand up and sing the new melody with any confidence.

It was a lovely June day when I hurried to church to participate in the singing. The church was crowded; those present seemed to be a much younger group than usual. Proudly I took my place in front, ready to give my voice in worship. Then! Yes, you are right —it was the gaily rhythmic tunes of the *Missa Americana*, the American Mass composed by Fr. Rivers.

It took me two months to learn the folk melodies of the American Mass, and when I rushed to church to sing, I discovered to my consternation that my pastor had decided to have a series of dialogue Masses. Not one to be an obstructionist, I went back to school and studied the correct Latin pronunciations.

Next time, I was determined to be ready. I took my *Liber Usualis*, my copy of the Gelineau Psalms, my notes for the American Mass and my Latin missal. I was sorely tempted to take my record of the *Missa Luba*. I even took a candle—just in case there was a procession. I was determined to participate.

The Mass was in English!

P.S. I have found a small chapel in a run-down section of the city. Its worshipers are all elderly men and women. The interior of the chapel is dark, and the only light visible is from the flickering candles on the altar and the vigil lamp. It is impossible to use a missal or a psalm book, and one can meditate beautifully to the comfortable clicking of rosaries.

SECTION V

LONG, LONG THOUGHTS

ERNAN McMULLIN

The Symbol-Makers

Man is above all a curious animal. Uncomfortably situated somewhere between the two great realms of matter and spirit, he has
enough matter to tie him down and enough spirit to make him unhappy about it. And he is curious in another sense, too—curious to
know, to *understand* the situation in which he finds himself. It is
this inexhaustible gift of wonder that has given rise to all the greatest
achievements of the human mind: theology, philosophy, science—
all different ways of understanding the things that are.

But understanding is a laborious business. It is not just that it is
hard work in which the freshness of that wonder with which the
child looks out at his unpredictable world tends somehow to get
lost. Nor is it just that understanding is so easily hindered by
prejudice and swayed by passion.

No, understanding is laborious above all because we must ourselves forge the instruments of our search. Our principal instruments of inquiry, words, seem to come to us ready-made. Yet, like
many other ready-made things, they do not fit very well, and this
is where the trouble begins.

Words and their meanings have been shaped and buffeted by
the accidents of human history; there is no such thing as a perfect
language, one whose distinctions perfectly mirror the reality of
which I wish to speak. I have to use vague words, words with a
sort of fuzziness about them, words with many different meanings.
I have to use words in new senses or even coin entirely new ones,
when I don't find anything appropriate at hand. Since the very
evidence from which my quest begins must be stated in language,
my very *starting* point may be difficult to articulate and, therefore,
to understand.

But if we want to push beyond our starting point—and this we
must do if we are to understand anything more than a very small
corner of space and time—we need symbols that are far more
complicated than words are. They may be made up of words, like

the poem that helps me understand a little more of man's loneliness or his exaltation. Or they might be made up of abstruse algebraic signs that help a physicist gain a single complex insight into a molecule or a telephone circuit. Symbols such as these stretch out to all corners of the universe and pull in its inmost strands for my wondering inspection. But constructing them is hard work, the work of generations, an unending work. What does it require? Well, patience, of course, and genius at times; help, maybe, when the matter gets too difficult.

We know more today than our forefathers did about the striking differences between the different families of symbols. We are no better than they at *creating* new symbols—not as good, perhaps —but we are much more self-conscious than they about the ways in which such symbols are made, the controls one must use, and so on. For a moment, then, we can allow our minds to go back in time, three or four thousand years, to let us see the symbol-maker of that day at his work. He had little to draw on, no instruments to extend his reach in space, no written records to give him a foothold in time past—only a deep and sure knowledge of what was in man, his greatness and his littleness, his virtues and his vices.

So it was of man the poet sang; it was in the likeness of man that the worshiper made his gods; it was with manlike spirits that the inquirer peopled his heavens and his earth. These were the symbols he could understand and manipulate. They gave him the great epics of Odysseus and Ossian; they filled his folklore with powerful, mythlike accounts of God's dealings with man, and of men with one another.

They gave little insight, however, into nature, where the seasonal regularities seemed to have an eternity far removed from any human caprice. And so a different sort of symbol-making began, very slowly; one that required patient observation of the regular courses of star and season and the creation of new symbols to count and chart them. This was the beginning of what we have come to call "natural science," but three thousand years would pass before it developed beyond purely descriptive symbols to the powerful explanatory "theories" of Newton and Boyle.

In the meantime, however, two other very important developments were taking place. In the bright sunlight of Greece, men were for the first time beginning to put ambitious questions like: What is the best form of government? How can truth be eternal, since all things seem to pass away? Where can a compelling basis be found for codes of human conduct?

You will notice that these questions have much in common. They are *reflective*, that is, they ask us to reflect upon our immediate experience and analyze it carefully; and they are *critical*, that is, they force us to evaluate assumptions we have been hitherto making about what is so or what is best. Questions like these we call "philosophical." They are difficult to answer because of the complexity of the symbols they involve. The philosopher has no special sources of evidence open to him; he takes the loose-knit terms of our everyday usage, terms like "perceive" and "substance" and "change," and tries to unite them in a coherent and tightly organized structure in order to make our experience as a whole more intelligible to us. The quest of Socrates and Plato and Aristotle can be seen on the one hand as a quest for the symbolic forms, the definitions, the rules of logical inference they needed and, on the other, as the patient and penetrating analysis of what we know and how we know in terms of these forms.

On the other side of the Mediterranean something very different was happening during these centuries. There was a small obscure people there, a desert people who knew little of science or of philosophy, yet who claimed a special knowledge of the most important subject of all, God. This knowledge, they said, God had given directly to them through the mouths of their prophets. He let them know about Himself, about His creation of all that is, about the origins of the human race, about the rules by which He wished human conduct to be governed, about the very special destiny He had assigned to them as a people.

This message was conveyed to them in the simple unsophisticated symbols of their everyday usage, the only language in which the prophets themselves could think or be understood. Sometimes they used more elaborate symbols: metaphors, parables and the like, which abounded in the folk literature of that day as a means of teaching where simple words failed. But God had no special language whereby He could communicate to men, and so His message was hard to penetrate sometimes, not only because God is so far beyond our understanding, but also because the human symbols in which He had to speak were so inadequate for what He had to say.

Then in the fullness of time, Christ, the Son of God, came

among men and, for a few short years, spoke to them of the things of God. He was the Word of God, the perfect symbol of the Father. Whoever knew Him, knew the Father too. He came to bring not only knowledge but also redemption. His life and death were meant to save and not just to instruct. He left behind Him a new knowledge of the mysteries of God, a new message of hope to the simple and the sinful and the suffering, and a small handful of dedicated men were to carry that message into all the world. Such was the power of the gospel story that the Word of God struck a chord in every heart that opened itself to His love.

As the years went by, people talked over that familiar story from all angles. They asked what Christ had meant when He said that the Father and He were one, or when He said over the bread at the Last Supper: "This is my Body." Man cannot help asking questions like these; he wants to *understand* to the best of his powers. In trying to answer such questions, terms like "person" and "nature" and "substance" had to be introduced and defined. And so the philosopher's help had to be enlisted, since, as we have seen, he is the professional when it comes to the analysis and criticism of complicated common symbols.

This collaboration between theologian and philosopher is seen in the works of great thinkers like St. Augustine, in whom Plato speaks to the problems of Christianity, and St. Thomas Aquinas, who brought the wealth of Aristotle's philosophical insights to the formation of a Christian world view. St. Thomas' *Summa Theologica* is like a single vast symbol in which all he knew of God and man is organized in a powerful unity. He knew, none better, that the methods followed by the theologian and the philosopher, the sorts of evidence they relied upon, were quite different from one another. But he saw that there could, and should, be some communication of terminology and insights, some utilization by the theologian of the wisdom concerning God and human nature that the philosopher had been able to glean unaided.

The domains of God and man were explored, in so far as the imperfection of human symbols and the weakness of the symbol-maker permitted. But how about the third great domain, that of nature? There, little was known and that little was filled out by symbols drawn from the Bible or from the philosophers of Greece. The images of Dante's great medieval panorama, *The Divine Com-*

edy, come about equally from the two. Looking back on it, it is easy to see why this should have been so. The Bible speaks little of nature; its aim is not, as the theologians knew perfectly well, to give us a science of nature. Yet some of the authority it enjoyed in the things of God inevitably rubbed off on its passing references to the motion of the sun or the waters above the heavens, simply because there was no physical science there to act as a corrective in these matters.

Now, let us take a leap forward in time and ask about the situation in this regard today. Three centuries of careful observation and endless theorizing have given us an insight into nature that our forefathers could scarcely have dreamed of. We have found the secret of constructing ever more complex scientific symbols, symbols that give not only understanding but great power as well. Power commands attention, and the attention of mankind, alternately anxious and triumphant, is today fixed on the works of science. So great is the magic of the scientific symbol that by comparison older symbols tend to look pale and drab.

It is this, far more than any actual conflict, that has led so many to describe the relationship between science and religion as one of tension. It is true that scientists and theologians have come in sharp conflict in a few (actually in surprisingly few) instances. But these were due to the inevitable clash between a new mode of understanding and an old, and they are, for the most part, resolved today. It is clear to us now that the ways of describing natural events used by the biblical writers were simply those familiar to the people of their time, and no further significance than this is to be attached to them. This still leaves one domain of possible dispute, man himself, his nature and origin, toward the understanding of which theology, philosophy and science must work together in an easily upset harmony. Such collaboration demands mutual respect and understanding, a feeling for the special character of the other's procedures and types of evidence.

Before the advent of modern science, theologians were faced with a serious problem. There seemed to be some reason to suppose that the earth's history had been very short, a matter of some thousands of years. If this were so, then each of the diverse natural kinds of animal, vegetable and mineral, of nebula, star and planet, would have needed a separate act of creation on God's part, a whole series of "interventions," as it were, and creation itself would have lacked any complete inner causal plan. This was hard to reconcile with the Christian notion of God as an all-wise Creator, and of creation itself as a single timeless act, in which all that nature needed was given it. St. Augustine, for one, went to great pains to try to effect this reconciliation with his theory of the "seeds" that contained within themselves the potentialities of the future.

Today science has resolved this problem by showing beyond doubt the immense age of the universe, and suggesting ways in which the different natural kinds may have evolved from the original desolation. This has proved a great, though sometimes unrecognized, contribution to Christian theology: God does not have to keep filling gaps in the scale of being. We know Him not so much through special interventions of this sort as through His total support of all that is. We reach Him by meditating on the fact *that* the universe is when it might not have been, rather than on particular aspects of *what* it is. As science continues to explain formerly unexplained features of the universe, nature itself comes to take on more and more the unity and intelligibility that we would expect in the work of an all-wise God.

We have come a long way from the symbols of Homer and the early Hebrews. It would be a tragedy if the power and beauty of our new-found scientific symbols should blind us to the truth that the Word of God came once for all on earth to bring us a truth that saves, but one that demands a faith rooted in integrity and humility.

NEIL HURLEY

The TV Commercial: Window on Mass Culture

¶Advertising practice in the TV world mirrors our modern system of values and corporate image

Mass consumer advertising makes up a very large part of the psychic air we Americans breathe. Unfortunately, we find it difficult to evaluate its effects. That, perhaps, is why a visitor to our shores can help us to assess more accurately a phenomenon which we take so much for granted. Bernard Hollowood, the editor of *Punch*, recently commented on the appalling intrusion of privacy which advertising has wrought in America. Focusing his criticism on television commercials, Mr. Hollowood felt that the inordinate influence exercised by this species of advertising on the mores and purchasing habits of the British man in the street was bland compared with the situation here. In fact, his only word for the constant interference with what limited pleasures one derives from watching TV in the U.S. was "brainwashing."

Of the 1,600 advertising impressions to which each American is estimated to be exposed daily, the most annoying are undoubtedly the TV commercials. When one recalls that the ordinary U.S. family watches television on the average of five and a half hours daily (six hours in the winter months of January and February), then it is easy to see why businessmen view this medium as a sales weapon without peer.

Considering, moreover, that both the hours of prime time in the evening and the number of channels are limited, one can readily appreciate why manufacturers in any competitive industry must challenge their rivals' efforts to capture TV's mass markets.

In no other country is the TV commercial so significant as it is in the U.S. This is true for a number of reasons.

Our country is saturated with TV sets and accounts for 77 per cent of the world's TV advertising expenditures.

No other nation has a television broadcasting system financed so heavily by commercial advertising.

Unlike Canada, Australia and Great Britain, we do not have the "magazine concept" of TV advertising. This means that sponsors do not buy indiscriminate time. They buy a particular show.

Thus the system of TV advertising now in effect means that all television fare shown in the home represents an indivisible unity consisting of three parts show and one part commercial. In America, therefore, the TV commercial is virtually the Siamese twin of all programing.

Curiously enough, even the commercial portion of this package deal has been transformed into a "show within a show." In publicizing their products, why do companies support entertaining, rather than informational, commercials? The reason is simple. In an affluent society, where people are not so price-conscious and where products are more similar than dissimilar, the brand name and corporate image have become more important than differences in product or price. The adman tells a psychological story, hoping to change the consumer's way of reacting to a specific product.

Hence, with the aid of the behavioral sciences, the TV commercial has acquired a psycho-economic character. It tries to create and deliver an escalating standard of living on the basis, not of use-value, but of psychological value. The symbols and subjective feelings employed have little, if any, connection with objective selling points inherent in the product.

In keeping with such an approach, Harry Wayne McMahon, author of *The Television Commercial: How to Create and Produce Effective TV Advertising*, gives advice on how to use the imagination to suggest something without actually saying it. A TV commercial, as a "show within a show," stirs a picture in the mind's eye. If this technique can be harnessed properly, it can be used to stimulate one of the four basic buying urges which lie beneath the threshold of consciousness: self-preservation, ambition, love and economy.

The noted motivational researcher, Dr. Ernest Dichter, would paraphrase this fourfold classification, more alliteratively, as sustenance, status, sex and security. In either case, the underlying philosophy is a mixture of materialism and hedonism. Harry Wayne McMahon maintains: "Yes, the viewer is basically selfish. That's advertising primer." Dr. Dichter's own analysis is that "it is almost an essential characteristic of American culture that the average individual wants an exaggerated amount of fun, entertainment and escapism. Yet, at the same time, he has not freed himself from the guilt feelings which he has every time he enjoys himself."

In the postwar era, advertising has grown into such an instrument of social control (by conditioning people to new purchasing habits) that it provides the social scientist with a window from which to view the value system of contemporary America. Because advertising, if it is to be successful, cannot conflict with the nation's value system, the TV commercial cannot help but furnish the trained sociological eye with a tool for examining our most cherished goals.

We must remember, however, that the TV commercial, as all mass consumer advertising, does more than mirror the country's values; it also molds them. The commercial is both an agent of change and an index of national values. If, then, we drop the commonplace perspective we ordinarily have with regard to TV commercials and adopt a more analytical stance, we shall have an admirable schoolmaster to instruct us on the patterns of mass culture which have grown up in our midst.

A great deal of the spot advertising that goes on outside of prime time is of the hard-sell variety: jingles, catchy slogans and pseudoscientific demonstrations. Such advertising does not interest us here as much as the unconscious buying urges exploited by the heavy TV advertising spenders. Because a company must let each of its many products create its own image and attract its own audience, the number of leading TV sponsors is relatively low.

In one year recently, for example, 45 companies paid out $480 million—almost one third of the total $1.3 billion spent in the nation on all spot and network advertising. As a result, viewers were most exposed to commercials featuring autos, cigarettes, cigars, soap, cosmetics, toiletries, beer, chewing gum, soft drinks, oil and tires. (Fortunately, TV liquor ads have been banned till now.)

What do we note about these commercials? Price is rarely mentioned, and product claims are not heavily stressed. Rather the sales appeal is carefully designed to evoke emotional resonance in the viewer, not intellectual assent. The next time you sit before your TV set, look for the subtle subconscious—even irrational—appeals to pleasure (cigarettes, cigars, beer, chewing gum, soft drinks); status (automobiles); super-hygienic attractiveness (soap, cosmetics, toiletries); security (oil and tires). You may notice, too, that some beer and cigarette commercials are focusing on the teenage market by means of allusions to athletic prowess, popularity, "datability" and sexual allure.

It is no secret that certain manufacturers are intent on cementing a mass consumer franchise with the youth in the audience, since it is estimated that in 1970 some 40 per cent of the national population will consist of those who are 20 years or under. With less discrimination than their elders, with discretionary income to spend and with a vast potential as tomorrow's affluent citizens, youth represents an enticing market for TV advertisers.

The only way to measure the impact of TV commercials on impressionable children is to recall that from 3:30 in the afternoon until 9:30 at night the TV sponsor can count on the attention of millions of children, many of preschool age. That appeals to the imagination, rather than to the mind, should fill the commercial slot is not surprising. This effort to reach children explains why the TV commercial has evolved into a "show within a show."

If a mass-advertising culture is growing up in America, then, it is because it is profitable to invest millions in a brand name or a company image, and then associate this name or image with some psychic satisfaction which assures the potential buyer that he or she is lovable, kissable, respectable, honorable, clean, odor-free, immune to insecurity and, in general, not missing any pleasure which others may be enjoying. In other words, economic considerations have enlisted the behavioral sciences in order to modify the psychic states of TV audiences. Brand names and corporate images are made memorable so that a mass market is presold before buyers are confronted with myriad products at the point of purchase.

Take Bristol-Myers as a dramatic example. This company makes such products as Ipana, Vitalis, Mum and Bufferin. In a recent year the company spent $40 million to nurture a sales volume of less than $150 million. The TV budget of this company alone ($10.7 million) was substantially greater than that of such giants as National Dairy Products, Du Pont and General Electric, with sales volumes ten, fifteen and even thirty times as great.

Through repetitive advertising and by means of appeals to hygiene, personal attractiveness and comfort, the products of Bristol-Myers were successfully presented to mass TV audiences. That people are buying an image and not a utility is evident from the fact that Bristol-Myers' Mum sells as much as fourteen per cent higher than a comparable jar of Colgate's Veto. Moreover, a bottle of Bufferin tablets sells for $1.23, while Bayer aspirin costs 73 cents and unbranded aspirin just 49 cents.

In the psycho-economic age in which we live, the competition among manufacturers of products that are only marginally different is taking place in the imagination of the American people, young and old alike. A random, but broad, sampling of television commercials gives boundless evidence of that fact.

The Hollywood ectoplasm compounded of romance, happiness, physical attraction, comfort and wealth is now rolling into the the living rooms of America—thicker than it ever was in the old movie palaces. The kinetic image which Thomas Edison projected

in his New Jersey studio in the last decade of the 19th century
has now invaded the parlor, with color and sound added. The
psychic impact is incalculable, since the motion picture is more
effective than the still in the transmission of values and implicit
attitudes. With a few socio-psychological clues it is possible to
identify these values and attitudes. This is the reason why the
sum total of commercial skits, lasting from one to three minutes,
provides an admirable barometer of the cutural temper of our
times.

The most successful advertising campaigns are those that overwhelm the senses. The sultry woman's voice; the society setting;
the rich, rough scion with the tattooed, hairy hands; the attitude
of complacency and apparent lack of anxiety—isn't this the typical
TV approach for much cigarette advertising? It is basically a
narcotic dream with an inexcusable dosage of dishonesty.

Can TV commercials, as the editor of *Punch* maintained, rightfully be termed "brainwashing"? They certainly represent a coun-
terpsychological force against which the adult viewer is beginning
to develop a sense of need for self-protection. What else would
cause such concern except a type of Pavlovian technique which,
for insistence and boldness, is almost as repulsive as any "recondi-
tioning" process the Communists have devised?

Just recently, an engineering firm conducted a scientifically controlled experiment on three TV stations in Boston. On 65 per cent
of the programs monitored, the commercials were louder than the
accompanying programs. On 20 per cent of the shows the commercials were on the same sound level, and on 15 per cent they
were softer. In extreme instances, the commercials were 78 per
cent louder than the main portions of the program, while in
other cases the figure ran, on balance, to 59 per cent. Despite
regulatory prohibitions on sound levels, all sorts of sonic mayhem
can be perpetrated within the authorized levels. Consequently, this
prime nuisance of our mass culture is not likely to disappear in
the near future.

Since the public is offended by so colossal an affront to its
judgment, the only real defenders of the TV commercial are those
who make their living by it. Relying on TV to capture lucrative
national markets and to counteract competitors' appeals, sponsors
will continue to invest large sums in commercial television. The
agencies reaping the sacred 15 per cent commission on gross billings

are likewise loath to see the TV commercial decline. Needless to say, the broadcasting networks will not bite the only hand that feeds them.

What about the owners of the TV sets? What of the public to whom the air waves belong? Despite the fact that they finance the original investment in the receiving sets and pay the price of advertising through customer patronage, they are powerless to alter the unilateral contract which so-called free advertising implies: either leave the program or take it *with* the commercial—sound volume, frequency of interruption and shallowness of content notwithstanding. In other words, if the owner of the TV set does not wish to boycott the networks completely, then he is constrained to accept the package deal. This means that in the midst of TV's present potpourri of blatant and tasteless sales messages the viewer is asked to pay a surcharge in terms of psychic costs. If the surcharge includes only exasperation and jangled nerves, it is cheap compared with the possibility of credence which impressionable minds may give to a hedonistic and epicurean system of values. That is why television cannot be called "free" in any significant sense. It would be hard to conceive of a higher consumer tax than the one which has been actually levied on the emotions and imagination of our people.

There is, alas, no easy way of correcting the asymmetry of power which has caused this pitiful situation. One dreams longingly of a solution suggested by a recent research project. In an ingeniously devised experiment, a TV set was so rigged that the tube would stay lit only if the viewer pressed a button near his hand. The question: Would the viewers keep the tube lit during commercials as well as during the programs? The answer was a resounding No. The moment commercials appeared, the tube went off. If all TV sets in this country were similarly constructed, all the false ballyhoo about free TV would disappear overnight.

In the absence of such rigged sets, I am afraid that the mass annihilation of privacy will continue. It is not a consoling thought to look at one commercial after another and say: "That's us!"

And the TV commercial is a success. No matter how gaudy or trivial or treacly it may seem, it gathers the necessary votes at the cash register. No sensible, sensitive person wants to identify with mass man or mass culture. That is why countless Americans deem the majority of TV commercials reprehensible. Nevertheless, these commercials mirror our culture, whether we like it or not. Mass man is always the other person, but the other person turns out, upon closer inspection, to be oneself.

ROBERT J. ROTH
The Importance of Matter

¶An assessment of Pierre Teilhard de Chardin's appeal for the American mind

Recently the *Saturday Evening Post* published an article on Pierre Teilhard de Chardin entitled: "The Priest Who Haunts the World." It gave dramatic recognition to the French Jesuit's influence in the United States—though for a half dozen years Americans have become increasingly aware of him through wide sales of English translations of his books *The Phenomenon of Man* and *The Divine Milieu*. Symptomatic of this trend was the lead Fordham University took among American colleges and universities in sponsoring a series of six lectures on Père Teilhard by a Belgian Jesuit, Fr. Maurits Huybens, S.J., European editor of *International Philosophical Quarterly*. Originally scheduled for a limited audience in a small seminar room, the sessions had to be moved to a large lecture hall jammed with some 500 students and professors from Fordham and neighboring colleges.

What is it in the thought of Père Teilhard that is catching the imagination of Americans? Undoubtedly each one, from his own reading, will answer this question from a slightly different point of view. But perhaps what most of all has called forth a response in the hearts of the people of America and of the world is his confidence in the value of man's involvement with matter. His position is that of an evolutionist who accepts the origin and development of living things from elemental matter.

Now that evolution has reached its culmination in man, he holds, future progress will be made principally in the direction of man's growth as a person. Such growth, though moving along moral and religious lines, will depend on man's continued interaction with the world, which includes inorganic matter, social institutions, cultural development and—very importantly in our age—science. It is by active engagement in all these that man will be able to achieve his fulfillment on the natural and supernatural levels.

This message has given hope and encouragement to all who had begun to feel overwhelmed by the imperious demands that worldly concerns make upon their time and energies. Men have suddenly become aware that interest in this world can have meaning for their enrichment as humans. Matter, then, becomes important—one might even say, sacred. "By virtue of the Creation and, still more, of the Incarnation, *nothing* here below *is profane* for those who know how to see."

This growing enthusiasm for Père Teilhard, with his stress on the importance of matter, will not be surprising to those who have accepted without question the "old tag of American materialism," as Jacques Maritain called it in his *Reflections on America*. Even we Americans become embarrassed and apologetic when it is mentioned. Prof. Maritain, however, who knows us well from having lived among us as teacher and friend for many years, has called this label a "curtain of silly gossip and slander."

Respect for matter, not as sense gratification but as a means of human growth on its highest levels, has been basic to the American experience. The conviction has deepened that the world of matter, of people, of events, of cultural and scientific progress, is important and that, indeed, human growth depends very much on active involvement in all these things. Hence, in spite of the novel form in which Père Teilhard's message is expressed, combining as it does a basic scientific theory of evolution with philosophical and theological vision, this message should not be entirely new to those who know our history.

Critics of American materialism, of course, would see the development of American experience as a movement from a deeply religious to a thoroughgoing naturalistic spirit. And yet, is the latter primarily a negation of religion? Is it not rather an affirmation of matter—along with a conviction that, in affirming it, one cannot at the same time say yes to religion? Attention to certain aspects of our history may serve to suggest an answer to these questions.

The origins of America had strong roots in theology, though it

was Protestant rather than Catholic theology that was most influential. It is easy to exaggerate, but one must admit that there were
strong religious convictions animating the first Pilgrims who came
to America. They were imbued with a biblical sense of the sacred-
ness of history and with a belief in divine intervention in human
events. Yet, though the City of God was their absorbing interest,
they could not long ignore the City of Man. They had to commit
themselves wholeheartedly to the world of matter as they struggled
to build homes and provide for the necessities of life.

As America grew, there grew also a tension between man's
orientation to God and his commitment to the world. New England
Transcendentalism prior to the Civil War had been characterized
as a reaction against a rising naturalistic outlook, and especially
against what was felt by many to be a growing absorption in
material concerns—a by-product of the industrial and economic
growth of the early 19th century. Witness the flight from the world
of a Henry Thoreau at Walden Pond and of the small Utopian
bands at Brook Farm and Fruitlands. These aspects of Transcendentalism would seem to characterize it as the alienation of man from
the world.

But the movement cannot be understood unless it is also seen
as a reaction against Calvinist-influenced theologies, with their
separations between God, nature and man, and as an affirmation
that man's contact with God and nature formed a single experience.
Dominant in this movement is the figure of Emerson, who, in
opposition to a crass materialistic view of the universe, voiced the
conviction that religious, ethical and esthetic experience could be
found only by healing the breach between the human spirit and
nature.

Within this movement, too, one finds a dissatisfaction with existing (i.e., Unitarian) theological formulations, a shedding of theological categories, an individualistic tendency to stand off and
criticize religious rite and doctrine, and an attempt to explain divine
revelation in natural terms. This tendency is found, in one degree
or other, in the leading figures of Transcendentalism, such as
Emerson, Thoreau and Theodore Parker. Perhaps here, more than
anywhere else, is focused the rising tension between theology and
matter.

The next development in this country's thinking was American idealism, our leading philosophic movement in the latter part of the 19th century. It was a movement criticized in its own day for trying to make philosophy a substitute for theology. If we grant that this is what it actually did, idealism can be seen as a transitional stage between Transcendentalism and the pragmatic and naturalistic philosophies before which it was to give way. And yet it is more than transitional, for in its respect for matter it is continuous with what preceded and followed it. Idealists like Josiah Royce saw man's task as an active engagement in the world, and human knowledge as the means of civilizing the earth for the betterment of mankind.

It is especially in pragmatism, America's first "indigenous" philosophy, and in naturalism, sometimes incorrectly called its logical outcome, that we witness the decline of the traditional religious sense and the thoroughgoing acceptance of matter. The men engaged in these movements resolved the tension between religion and the world of matter by gradually eliminating religion, since in their view it no longer made the world intelligible. On the other hand, it is now clear that American philosophic thought in this period was primarily a conscious expression of what the American spirit had always exemplified, namely, a conviction that matter is essential for human self-development.

Pragmatists and naturalists have nurtured what John Dewey called a "respect for matter" because they were sure that it was only by dealing with matter that man could release his potential, fulfill his drive for achievement, and further the progress of humanity on its highest level. From this point of view, nothing that man encounters in his environment is unimportant for human growth. Matter and energy, social, political and economic institutions, science and technology—all must engage man's attention and interest so as to help him achieve his maximum development. To the pragmatist and naturalist, flight from active engagement in the world is a betrayal of one's fundamental responsibility.

In the light of all this, it is not surprising that so many have received Père Teilhard with enthusiasm. His appeal, especially to Catholics, consists in the feeling that he has gone a long way toward providing answers in terms of their own religious experience. There are strong signs of his becoming a prophet in America; and this is a great gain, for we have much to learn from him.

It is a pity, however, that we have not listened to our own American prophets. The importance of matter has already been called to our attention many times. It has been stressed by speakers of varied religious backgrounds and, more lately, by those with no religious affiliations at all. What they have proclaimed, basically, has been man's need for involvement in matter if he is to reach a fulfillment that is truly human and ennobling. They have called for a reassessment of the possibilities of matter, for a reaffirmation of the world as sacred and as demanding our respect because it holds the key to the development of man's highest ideals.

We Americans may and should regret that in our more recent history our prophets have tried to exclude God from their vision of human fulfillment (though these men, in turn, would indict theism for failing to make the world meaningful). But we need not be ashamed of such prophets. Materialists they have been, indeed, but their materialism has been one that has seen matter as a means of human enrichment. True, we have had our share of crass materialism, too, but more often than not this has been due to our material advantages. One is justified in asking whether other peoples, of other cultural backgrounds, would have had the spiritual resources to resist the degrading effects of an "affluent society," any better than we have.

From one point of view, the thought of a man like Père Teilhard is more congenial to the American temperament than to that of any other people. We do not need to have the importance of matter proved to us. This orientation has been native to us from our beginnings. On the other hand, there are certain elements of Père Teilhard's thought that will evoke strong reservations on the part of Americans.

One such element is his position that evolution has a direction—a position he admits is undemonstrable by science, even though his standpoint is that of a scientist. G. Gaylord Simpson, in an otherwise sympathetic critique, has called attention to the inconsistency of this position, and it is bound to receive further criticism. Another such element is what Julian Huxley called his "gallant attempt to reconcile the supernatural elements in Christianity with the facts and implications of evolution." Mr. Huxley indicates that this is unacceptable to many scientists, though he acknowledges the "positive value of his naturalistic general approach."

Moreover, the world of matter that the American faces includes not merely science, but science as it is applied to a highly industrialized and technological society. There are those who are appalled by the overwhelming possibilities of human depersonalization implicit in such a society, and their wish would be to prevent or at least limit the growth of technology. For America, this is an impossible solution; our society is destined to become even more technological. A future respect for matter must face explicitly, and in detail, the many problems for human fulfillment presented by such a society.

There is also the fact that we live in a democracy—though one would be hard put to it to state clearly what the specific nature of that democracy is. In this context, human development will follow lines quite different from those of a highly individualistic or an authoritarian society. There is need in America of a carefully delineated theory of the individual, the community and their mutual interaction, and need of an application of this theory to a democratic way of life.

One could go on to indicate similar problems that arise in other areas, such as social order, economics, and education. But enough has been mentioned to indicate the extent of the difficulty.

Hence some interesting questions remain. Has Père Teilhard raised a problem and suggested an answer precisely in *our* terms? Is it possible literally to transplant a set of ideas from a foreign soil so that they may grow and flourish as truly our own? This latter question deserves serious consideration and should not be too hurriedly discarded. On the other hand, to shirk responsibility by letting others do our thinking for us may be too easy a solution. If that be so, we must then ask whether America has sufficiently shed its intellectual "colonialism" to work out once more an "indigenous" philosophy, and a theology too, which, though stimulated and enriched by the thought of peoples of other times and places, will meet the problems that are somehow uniquely ours.

Whatever the answer, the future thought of America must move in terms of greater, not less, respect for matter—with corrections dictated by man's need for God and religion. I am convinced that we Americans can make this synthesis in a way that will be meaningful to us, and when we do, we may well have a prophecy of our own to proclaim openly to the world.

THURSTON N. DAVIS
The Loneliness of Man

A young Viennese artist, Erich Sokol, published a dozen pen sketches of "American Natives" in an issue of *Harper's* a few years ago. Sokol's "gag," as he calls it, is "to show that normal people, in their normal environment, engaged in the normal routine of their everyday lives, involuntarily are tragically ludicrous and ludicrously tragic." A skinny girl typist, a beer-drinking TV addict watching the late show, a commuter, a teen-ager with a crew cut, an oldster solemnly poised over a barbecue grill in his back yard—to these and other subjects Sokol applies the acid in his pen, dissolving them all into a meaningless mixture of boredom and depressing triviality.

A decade ago these drawings might have turned up in one of our smaller, off-beat magazines. Today we find them on slick paper in *Harper's*. What does this portend? Has our national mood concerning man and his nature and destiny shifted from optimism to pessimism? Have the beatniks given us a new tragic consciousness? Or have we simply "caught up" with the jargon and dogmatisms of European existentialism?

If this sort of self-denigration continues, it might be explained simply as a fad or a temporary posture without real meaning. On the other hand, it might be very significant; for we are coming to realize that there are serious questions to ask and answer about the way of life of contemporary man. This new conviction is leading to new attitudes and concerns. For some time now social philosophers and sociologists have had all of us children of a technological age under their scholarly eyes. So, too, of course, have the poets, novelists and playwrights. Today in the United States there is a large and growing literature on the subject of baffled, confused and lonely modern man—a creature described as alienated, estranged, lacking a sense of direction or even a tag of self-identity. Metaphysicians probe him to discover and discuss what they describe as his anguish, inquietude, anxiety and desperation. Artists try to capture his image in metal, in stone or on canvas. Recently in New York there was an exhibition of "New Images of Man" at the Museum of Modern Art. An unusually perceptive article discussing the sculpture and painting to be found there appeared not long ago (11/21/59, p. 232) in this Review. Its author, Norris Clarke, declared:

"Almost every artist lays him [modern man] bare in his own arresting way, as a creature of taut, often agonizing tension, confused as to who and what he is, painfully lonely and isolated from his brothers, the depersonalized victim of his own triumphant technology or of dark primitive forces unleashed from his own subhuman depths."

MAN SEEN AS A CLOWN

The late Georges Rouault, a French painter whose oils helped set the pattern for much of modern art's preoccupation with the pathetic quality of our contemporary human situation, used frequently to portray man daubed with the thick paint of a clown. Eleven years ago, Martin D'Arcy, discussing "the prevalent image of the clown," noted how far we had already come in modern art from the old Greco-Roman ideal of the human form. Fr. D'Arcy found instead "a pitiable resemblance to that of a man crucified but without grace. The would-be hero (the image of God) is covered with grease paint and exhibiting himself before a faceless audience in a play without meaning, without even the wisdom of the child, and certainly without its innocence" ("The Clown and the Philosopher," *The Month* [London], January, 1949).

As we read these lines years later we think of *J.B.*, the current play by Archibald MacLeish. Here, in the setting of a little traveling circus, and to the accompaniment of commentary by two popcorn salesmen playing the parts of God and Satan, a successful and happy suburbanite—some sort of modern Job—is made to confront, through a series of cataclysmic personal tragedies, the empty face of a meaningless universe. J.B. is neither clothed nor painted as a clown, but the circus tent stretches over his head and he plays out, minus the buffoonery, and clear up to the play's makeshift and inadequate conclusion, the grotesque role of a clown threading his way through a clown's standard pattern of irrational frustrations.

J.B., as Professor MacLeish portrays him, is a symbol of alienated and tortured modern man, abandoned without grace in a world in which, by hypothesis, God is dead, and where man faces and must answer the dilemmas of life with the sole resources of human love and an atavistic yen for survival. Such is the "philosophy" behind the play, a philosophy totally unacceptable to a Christian.

Belief in Jesus Christ and His redemptive life and death makes *J.B.* a frightful caricature of man's true state and destiny. The fact remains, however, that a growing number of our contemporaries have come so to assess our human situation. Moreover, gigantic forces in the modern world—forces and influences external to man himself, his nature and his destiny—do seem to be pressing him into a strange new strait jacket of frustrations, out of which, without all the divine help that faith, hope and charity afford, there is no escape. These forces oppress us all, believer and unbeliever alike.

ISOLATION AND BEWILDERMENT

Let us acquaint ourselves briefly with one recent analysis of the causes that underlie this mammoth contemporary problem. The October, 1959 issue of the *Review of Politics* (Notre Dame, Ind.) featured a provocative article by Glenn Tinder, professor at the University of Massachusetts. Entitled "Human Estrangement and the Failure of Political Imagination," it is a searching critique of our currently crude and unperceptive public thinking about man, his wants and his socio-economic and political ends. The essay deserves to be studied closely for this, its central thesis, which does not directly concern us here. I cite Professor Tinder, however, in order to focus on one section of his article, where he asserts and plausibly demonstrates that today "almost every basic relationship into which a human being might enter has been dangerously attenuated."

The author of the above-mentioned study makes five points: 1) Man today, in large part, is alienated from Nature; this results from enforced urbanization and its consequence, protracted indoor habits of life. 2) Man no longer has roots in a particular region or place. 3) Man in our age has no secure hold on his possessions. 4) Uprooted in time, sundered from past and future, modern man leads a life which, to himself at least, is historically meaningless. 5) Relations today between persons are either nullified or unsettled; if maintained at all, they are apt to be precarious and anomalous achievements.

I trust that this barren listing of arguments fully developed in the article will not serve only to obscure Professor Tinder's point. His conclusion is that today man is rootless and homeless and deprived of a sense of identity and community—and this to a degree that would have been unthinkable in simpler ages and within less kaleidoscopic cultural frameworks.

Now if Professor Tinder's analysis is correct, it should to some degree at least correspond with our experience. Many will agree that it does. From books and plays, from conversations heard on college campuses, often from what is to be seen in the faces we encounter on the streets of our cities, something important can be deduced, namely, that today's world is being increasingly populated by inexpressibly lonely and confused people, persons who have not only lost touch with a community (of understanding, interests, shared values) in which they might hope to find meaning and fulfillment, but whose very search for such a universe has become impossible and ridiculous—because, for themselves, that universe has apparently ceased to exist.

We would expect to have met such persons (the word "persons" is used with some irony, for they bear more resemblance, even in their own estimation, to *things*) in the incredible atmosphere of one of the big concentration camps of World War II. For those who can bear the experience, they are there to be met in a new book by Primo Levi, *If This is a Man* (Orion), which is as shattering a report as Michel del Castillo's *Child of Our Time* (Knopf). Both tell the monstrous story of the complete depersonalization of man in the barbarous conditions of life in a concentration camp. For the most part, Americans have been spared any but a vicarious experience of such a world. To taste its bitterness, however, even in a book, is to learn in how "broken" and irrational a world some even of our younger contemporaries have had to drag out their lives, and what it means, at this lowest point on the scale of human existence, to sustain total and enforced alienation and estrangement.

ESTRANGEMENT ON THE CAMPUS

Curiously, an almost identically sad cry reaches us on occasion from a totally different quarter. It does not come, as the other does, from a dreary bunk in a hut near a gas chamber. It comes from our campuses, and is just as genuinely the voice of men who speak for still other men baffled by their own estrangement from a community of values.

Five years ago, in an address honoring the second centennial of Columbia University in New York City, J. Robert Oppenheimer, the physicist, thus described the interior struggle of a modern scientist: "This is a world in which each of us, knowing his limitations, knowing the evils of superficiality and the terrors of fatigue, will have to cling to what is close to him, to what he knows, to what he can do, to his friends and his tradition and his love, lest he be dissolved in a universal confusion and know nothing and love nothing."

More restrained, but none the less a cry of the heart, are these words, written to honor the same university on the same occasion. Prof. Mark Van Doren stated: "Knowledge is difficult for men to possess if it means knowledge of the truth." And again: "It is enough to know that Pilate's question, 'What is truth?' will always be impossible to answer to the satisfaction of every man. When this is known, then knowledge exists in the most humane of all its forms —the recognition that any man may be right. . . ."

To the man and woman of faith, however, the universe in its essential lines is no such jumble of unassorted jigsaw pieces. For such persons there is possible, and therefore attainable, an ordering of knowledge within a house of truth. What, then, they may demand, have these quotations, books, plays, and reflections on painting and sculpture to do with us? The beginnings of an answer is to insist that all this does indeed concern us. The clown is more of a blood brother than we imagine. As has been suggested above, a thousand intricate influences in contemporary life have conspired to produce him, even in the mind and imagination of those whose inner citadel of faith apparently stands firm against so many mammoth irrationalisms. For the impact and resonance of these forces also touch those whose interior life of sanctifying grace thrives somehow even in an atmosphere made heavy by the death of so many ancient sanctities.

Consider one limited area, so much discussed at the moment, in which we feel the impact of such pressures—the TV medium. Testifying in December before the Federal Communications Commission in Washington, William F. Lynch, author of *The Image Industries*, said the mass media were engulfing us in "oceans of fantasy and dreams and distortions." The evil lies not only in the fact that we are constantly projecting, for home and foreign consumption, he said, a "basically mediocre image of ourselves," but also that we are unwittingly fostering "a national imagination and culture that is not worth living for." Fr. Lynch would undoubtedly agree that in dozens of other fields as well similar corrosive and unsettling forces, more subtly at times, but always with immense pervasive power, are currently undermining—in the minds of all who are exposed to them—the meaningful structure of life itself.

Thus, there is a valid sense in which we are all in this contemporary trouble together: *all* men are troubled because of the encircling spirit of insecurity that is abroad. When the boat of our society is tossed, all its passengers are afflicted. Where so many are religiously starved, even those who habitually eat of the Bread of Life have a keener edge to their hunger. In a world where all are stunned by the immensity of the problems and dilemmas of peace and war; where all, even those who hold fast to old certitudes, must locate themselves and find their way in a milieu in which, for so many questing persons, both faith and reason have "lost face," a touch of this universal confusion rubs off on everyone.

Several reactions are possible with respect to the situation sketched here. One is to reject the whole business as unreal and irrelevant. Another is to concede the reality of the problem and its relevance, but then to plot a strategy of psychological and spiritual withdrawal into some kind of "value ghetto" where one might presumably be immune from contamination. The first "solution" is, of course, no solution at all. The second, save in a limited and sharply defined sense, is unrealistic and impossible for anyone but a hermit, and not too practical even for him. A third and more fruitful approach is that of the Christian who tries to understand what is happening to himself, his family and the world around him, and who, armed with such understanding and with whatever genuine competence he can muster, resolves to work wisely and patiently with existing institutions, and together with other persons of good will, in a common effort to check the decay of our society and to shore up its values. In this enterprise the stakes are perhaps higher than most of us yet realize.

SECTION VI

WHO IS MY BROTHER?

WILLIAM GREMLEY
Negroes in Your Parish

Negro family movement from crowded central areas of cities to outlying sections and, increasingly in the decade ahead, into suburban areas, poses a severe challenge to America in the field of race relations. While this challenge can be defined at several levels, the response to it of religion and religious institutions is, and will continue to be, of vital importance. This is particularly true for the Catholic parish.

Historically, the Church in America has been a central city Church, but its new suburban growth has been the pride of virtually every diocese. From the Catholic point of view, therefore, consideration of the Negro population movement into outlying or suburban communities cannot be undertaken without examination of its effects on the Catholic parish.

On occasions, competent observers have made sound suggestions to strengthen this relationship. For example, at a recent annual meeting of the National Conference of Catholic Men, in Pittsburgh, Fr. Robert Howes, city planner and urban-renewal expert, emphasized the importance of appointing diocesan community-relations officers who would express diocesan and parish concern and involvement in the fields of urban renewal and intergroup relations.

That suggestion and others are worthy of serious attention, but there may be other factors in the situation that are interwoven with the role of diocese, pastor and laity. One important point we consider is the attitude taken by a pastor or the laity toward actual or potential racial change in a parish neighborhood.

New Negro home-owners in a middle-class community are seldom Catholic. The national percentage of Negro Catholics ranks well below the percentage for the total population, and this is often reflected when a neighborhood changes racial make-up. If the neighborhood is significantly Catholic—and many Northern urban and suburban areas are—this change may be disturbing to both parishioners and pastor.

Many outlying parishes are relatively young, and the pastor may be the same priest who was originally assigned there some twenty or twenty-five years ago. He may justifiably feel that the parish is to a large extent a result of his leadership, and he may thus have a pardonable pride in its growth. Since, in city after city, Negro population movement is usually accompanied by panic and flight on the part of white residents, the pastor is often in the unhappy position of seeing some of his leading parishioners moving elsewhere.

The pastor's view of these developments is a matter of crucial importance. If his approach is one of fear that his life's work is in jeopardy, that he may soon see a time when he cannot meet mortgage payments or maintenance bills from parish funds, that his school population will decline, with the place of departing white children taken by only a few Negro children, it is understandable that he should be apprehensive about the future.

If, on the other hand, he does not so limit his concern but sees the whole development as a basic challenge to his function as a Catholic priest, he will promote conversion activities as an ongoing and important part of parish programing for the community. He will react to race-relations problems in the light of Catholic principles and teaching on the subject.

The approach the pastor takes will greatly influence parishioners and actual or potential lay leaders. What he says or does, in sermons, private conversations and parish affairs of any kind, can give a tone or direction for the laity. If he emphasizes the financial aspect to the exclusion of intergroup spiritual values, the laity will exclude those spiritual values—except the more liberated and unprejudiced, who will disagree with him. However, if he vigorously stresses Catholic truth regarding the equality of all men, he will have another kind of influence, although he may find himself criticized by the more backward members of his parish. In any case, when a racially changing neighborhood situation finally confronts him, a pastor must make a personal choice that will be vitally important to his parish's future.

The role of the laity is equally critical. It is they who are besieged by unscrupulous real-estate agents pressuring them to sell their homes. It is they who also have a legitimate self-interest in their homes, their associations, their children's future, the neighborhood in which they have chosen to live. It is they who must meet the challenge, if they so see it, of a new Negro neighbor. They face it with whatever fears, anxieties, hopes or good will their individual make-up has instilled in them. Fundamentally, it is they who carry the image of the Catholic Church and its teachings to their non-Catholic friends and neighbors.

With reference to this problem, much has been written about the responsibility of the Catholic parish to welcome new neighbors, involve people in church activities, etc. A point possibly overlooked is that the responsibility of the laity cannot be divorced from the responsibility of the pastor or, even, of the diocese.

If there is apathy, fear or hostility on the part of pastor or laity to the racially changing neighborhood for the reasons cited, or if the diocese is reserved and distant concerning a Catholic Interracial Council and similar group efforts to meet this challenge, Catholic lay activities in the field of race relations are likely to be weak and futile. If, however, the pastor applies Catholic principles of racial justice to the situation, if the diocese encourages and supports a Catholic Interracial Council and community-relations activities in the various parishes, lay action can be strong and meaningful and contribute much toward neighborhood stabilization when racial change occurs.

These remarks lead to the central point, which is: How can a parish, its laity and clergy in cooperation, adequately apply Catholic principles of human dignity to racial neighborhood changes? With the assumption that sound motivation to meet this goal is either present in the parish or can be developed, the following suggestions are offered:

The pastor should be willing to permit, and should even encourage, community groups to use parish facilities for meetings when they wish to discuss a racially changing situation. However, he, or an assistant, should attend all such meetings and make clear that the facilities of a Catholic church cannot be used for expressions of bigotry, racial hatred or plans to keep Negroes out of a community. When such expressions or dealings take place in a church building, they become blasphemous, and any pastor would have a basic obligation to take firm action.

The pastor should willingly donate his time and talents to such organizational pursuits without attempting to dominate the situation as a personality. To stay aloof from lay discussions or meetings when they involve a moral principle affecting the basic rights of man is, in effect, to diminish the pastor's spiritual responsibility.

Usually, such organizing attempts are encouraged and aided by an agency outside the parish boundaries, e.g., a municipal inter-group-relations office, a Catholic Interracial Council or a local Urban League. When this friendly outside help is offered, the pastor should willingly co-operate with the agencies and welcome their representatives as persons who can give good advice and help rather than hinder.

In most large cities, the pastor can make use of excellent inter-group educational resources in the parish school, such as classroom materials, audio-visual aids, group-dynamic techniques and other intergroup media available to any school, private or public, from the agencies cited above as well as numerous others.

The pastor should take special care that new Negro pupils are welcomed and made to feel secure. Of course, the responsibility of teaching sisters in this respect is obvious. They should make extra efforts to see that Negro children join whatever school groups exist and not assume they will join of their own accord. Sensitivity in this respect involves awareness that the Negro child usually comes from a segregated background and may come to his new school fearful and suspicious of his new white schoolmates. Sensitivity can also be exercised in urging Negro parents to join and take active part in the PTA.

The pastor who is aware of intergroup relations and their impact on his parish will seek to develop leadership in this respect among his laity. Apart from sermons devoted to the subject and whatever activities he encourages in church organizations, he could seek, through private conversation with parishioners, to determine who have the right attitudes and personalities for leadership. He will also inspire and stimulate his curates to play a similar role.

Like the pastor, the lay leader who is sensitive to the problem can seek help from local intergroup agencies. In many places under-going these population movements, agencies have used the approach of stimulating area and block organization. It must be open to, and based on, a concern for all residents. If it is not of that nature, if its leaders persist in advocating anti-Negro concepts, no intergroup agency, private or public, is likely to give any effective co-operation at all to the organization.

The intergroup-relations resources that are available to schools can be used by community groups to combat the fears and distortions of truth that arise when Negroes move into a white-occupied neighborhood. Most agencies can furnish speakers who are qualified to discuss and answer questions on this and other phases of the problem. In addition, an agency can often refer to proper authorities, such as a real-estate licensing board, complaints of harassment of white owners by real-estate agents. One happy note about this type of assistance is that it is usually without charge except for travel expenses, if they are necessary.

The lay leader, in co-operation with his pastor, should seek to involve as many of the new Negro residents as possible in church organizations—Knights of Columbus Council, Holy Name Society, women's Sodality, Altar and Rosary Society, Council of Catholic Men, CYO group or other structure designed for genuine Catholic fellowship. For the new Negro Catholic resident to make his presence known at the church only through Mass and the sacraments, because he knows he is not welcome in the various church groups, is a denial of Catholic lay action as we understand it. The Catholic lay leader and neighbor who takes a lead in this respect can make a valuable contribution by implementing Catholic principles of interracial justice. Usually he will also discover that there is real leadership among the new Negro residents.

The position of the concerned lay leader is admittedly difficult where the pastor is reluctant to take action. He can, more or less, work around the edges of the problem, but without pastoral help he is handicapped. In such situations the intergroup agencies mentioned can be helpful and effective. Through their aid, the pastor may increase his understanding and knowledge of the total problem. Failing that, there is the possibility of obtaining diocesan concern and interest in the situation.

The sociology of Negro population movements is such that at times the trained observer with a grasp of facts can predict months or years in advance when there may be a specific movement into a certain area. Residents of many communities take comfort in the fact that distance or time separate the problems from their doorstep, but it is certain that the present decade will see extensive Negro and, possibly, other minority groups moving into communities which at this time think they are "safe." The informed pastor and lay leader will seek competent advice to help them analyze the problem should it occur in their community. They will be more fortunate if they can lay the groundwork to prepare for it in advance. If they have sufficient knowledge of the fears, myths and distortions that victimize many white people regarding Negro population movement, they will act with prudence and courage to reduce them or eliminate them.

These suggestions are adaptable to almost any kind of community made up largely of home-owners. They are offered as guides or stimulants, whether the problem is at hand or distant. A strong case could be advanced that the sensitive pastor and lay leader should do all or some of these things anyhow, whether the problem is there or not—or even if it will never occur. The world we live in and the importance of intergroup problems to us nationally and internationally impose a responsibility on people, not only as Catholics or members of any other denomination but as citizens, that they mature and develop as fully as possible in this area.

In addition, it is both a parental and a school responsibility to insure that our young people be well informed and without prejudice in their approaches to, and relationships with, people of different races and religions. It is they in the years to come who will inherit these problems, or what remains of them, and it is only common sense to prepare them now as fully as possible.

A final consideration involves co-operation with other community institutions, both secular and religious. The Catholic Church is not alone, of course, in the teaching of basic human dignity as God-given; it is a teaching which other denominations, Christian and non-Christian, can share equally. If the teaching itself, derived from our Judeo-Christian heritage, can be shared, then co-operative efforts to put these teachings into effect can be shared. Previous insularity or aloofness by any religious institution should not hamper such efforts.

The percentage of Negro Catholics, being what it is, suggests that conversion efforts are a must for parish self-preservation and maintenance. This is not to say that conversion motivation is, or should be, anything other than what it has been throughout the history of the Church. The techniques of conversion activities are in the domain of the pastor and will succeed or fail depending on his ability and persuasiveness. But this much can be said: if he remains apart from the entire problem, if he views the presence of new Negro neighbors in his parish with reluctant resignation and a heavy heart because so many of his older parishioners have "For Sale" signs in their front yards, his conversion efforts, if any, will have a very scant chance of success.

The Negro of the 1960's is in many respects a new Negro. He is testing many things in his society besides lunch counters. He is testing all institutions to see if they are ready and competent to meet the challenge of his presence and his integration into the body of his society. In many communities he is testing the Catholic Church.

DENNIS CLARK
City Catholics and Segregation

¶Some reflections on the persistent problem of desegregation in the North

If America has the greatest cities in the world, it also has the greatest ghettos. South Africa has the only population pattern of racial separation approaching ours in size. In some countries Muslims, Jews, Hindus or Christians are segregated, but not on the irrelevant basis of race. We are the outstanding Western nation that makes a man's skin an indignity. Neither South Africa nor the other countries that permit segregation are heirs to the democratic claims and ideals that are the bedrock of history and civil life in the United States. This is the reason our ghettos are the most extraordinary. They are an utter contradiction of all that our nation stands for. Our twisted tradition of racial separation is like a scar that marked the American giant in youth and that grows more and more fearful-looking as he develops.

Catholics in the United States in the 1960's are now inheritors of the massive segregation problem in a way that challenges their religious and cultural system as it has not been challenged on this continent since the spread of the Spanish empire. For Catholics in the United States the racial problem is no longer something far removed in the South where the faithful are usually only sparsely settled. Nor are Negroes any longer solely the concern of missionary orders or specialists in the apostolate to colored people. Negroes are now present in huge numbers in the areas of heaviest Catholic population in the Northeast, Great Lakes and West Coast regions. In the areas where Catholics are best organized and most active, Negroes are locked into the same central city districts that were the social battlegrounds for generations of Catholic immigrants. There is hardly a chancery office in any of the nation's fifteen largest cities that is not surrounded by tens or hundreds of thousands of non-whites.

Negroes are massed in the major cities because there has been a historic transposition of the American segregation problem since World War II. From a Southern, rural issue it has been transformed into a nation-wide, urban issue. Segregation is no longer a stagnant legal and regional phenomenon. It is a dynamic, sophisticated 20th-century system, as devious and deceptive as the city labyrinths in which it is practiced. It is based upon housing restrictions that effectively partition whole areas of the cities into uneasy racial compounds. This is the basis of our streamlined segregation.

How will Catholics react to their full-scale encounter with the race dragon of American social life? The Catholic Church served as one of the most effective forces in Latin American life for countering racism throughout the long history of the nations of Hispanic culture. Can the youthful but energetic Catholics of the United States unravel the racial enigma that has bedeviled this country from its very beginnings?

An examination of the assets and liabilities of U. S. Catholics with respect to race relations may at least give us an understanding of what factors will be involved in this epic encounter in the years ahead. Although ready predictions of the course of Catholic history in this respect may not be forthcoming, at least we shall have some inkling of the terms in which the challenge will present itself.

On the positive side there are several features that must be classified as helpful influences in any campaign to bring about Northern desegregation.

CLEAR DOCTRINE

The emphatic clarity of Catholic teaching leaves no question about the antithesis between ideas of racial restriction and the ideals of Christian liberty growing out of the Catholic concepts of divine order, human unity and social justice. Not only is the teaching about race comprehensive and uncomprising, but it has been force-fully enunciated by Popes, bishops and teachers like Maritain, Con-gar and Sturzo in our time. The 1958 statement of the American Bishops on "Discrimination and the Christian Conscience" is an acute and specific illustration of the guidance to be found in this deeply instructive fund of doctrine.

PAST PERFORMANCE

During the 1940's the Catholic Church built up an excellent image in the eyes of many Negroes. Catholic schools in St. Louis, Washington, D.C. and elsewhere were desegregated before the 1954 Supreme Court decision. Catholic mission and hospital work in the South, as well as the lives of such remarkable people as Father John LaFarge, S.J., and Msgr. John A. Ryan, spoke eloquently of the Catholic concern for interracial justice. The consecration of Negro bishops and the sympathy of Catholic social-action leaders, like Chicago's Bishop Bernard Sheil, with civil-rights causes placed the Church in the forefront of the movement for interracial progress.

COMMON SOCIAL PROBLEMS

In the past, Catholics and Negroes shared a broad working-class affiliation. The problems of job opportunity, unionization, working conditions and the social difficulties of working-class status cut across racial lines and were common to both Negroes and the off-spring of Catholic immigrants. This is still true to a large extent today, as Gerhard Lenski points out in his study of religious groups in Detroit in *The Religious Factor*. This community of interest led Catholic and Negro leaders to speak in similar terms when express-ing the desires of their constituents for advancement and complete acceptance in American life.

LIMITED NUMBERS OF NEGRO CATHOLICS

The proportion of Catholics who are Negro in the major cities rarely exceeds eight per cent. The isolation of Negroes in the South from widespread Catholic influence and the Baptist and Methodist traditions among Negroes themselves partially explain this. Social problems impeding conversions have resulted in relatively small numbers of Negro Catholics in the big dioceses. This has meant that in schools, parishes and institutions, Negro Catholics could be represented without constituting a threat to the nervous racial psychology of the whites. The fear of inundation could often be suspended. Catholics could integrate their facilities in many areas without having to fear total racial turnover—the racial avalanche.

A LIVELY APOSTOLATE

In recent years, Catholic activity on behalf of interracial justice has been particularly lively. Beginning in the 1930's, a succession of notable leaders engaged themselves in full-time commitment to race-relations work. This led up to the establishment in 1934 of the Catholic Interracial Council of New York, with George K. Hunton as executive director. (Mr. Hunton became director emeritus on February 11, 1962.) A galaxy of distinguished women, such as the late Mother M. Katharine Drexel, foundress of the Sisters of the Blessed Sacrament for Indians and Negroes, and her sister, Mrs. Louise Morrell, made interracial justice a daily part of their works. Others were: the late Mother Grace Dammann, R.S.C.J.; Dorothy Day of the *Catholic Worker;* Baroness Catherine de Hueck Doherty, foundress of Friendship House; Mrs. Anna McGarry of Philadelphia; Mrs. Roger L. Putnam of Springfield, Mass.; Dr. Lydwine van Kersbergen of the Grail Movement. (It is interesting to note the prominence of women in this apostolate.)

Today, Catholic Interracial Councils in over three dozen cities carry on programs aimed at combating race prejudice and furthering equal opportunity for minority groups. Since 1958, the National Catholic Conference for Interracial Justice has operated a vigorous program aimed at the same goals on the national level. The campaign for interracial understanding is attracting more and more young Catholics every day.

These factors provide the Church with some of the conditions for success, if wise use is made of them in the crusades and controversies that will focus on civil rights during the coming decade. But, there are other considerations that are not so encouraging.

CIVIC INERTIA

In many communities Catholics are absentees from the organizations and efforts involving civic affairs. In other places Catholics are "represented" on boards and committees but are seldom broadly

involved in community activities or civil-rights matters. Whether
this is due to a failure of Catholic education with respect to the
responsibilities of citizenship or to an American Catholic hangover
from the days when Catholics were not welcome in civic circles,
the condition does exist. Perhaps there is, too, a certain inbred conservatism among Catholics that leads them to be skeptical about
joining groups in the general community. Whatever the cause, this
retardation of civic participation must be overcome if Catholics are
to work constructively on racial problems.

SCARCITY OF NEGRO CATHOLIC LEADERS

It is quite true that there have been men of excellent qualities in
the Negro communities of our cities who are Catholics, and many
of these have worked hard on civil-rights issues. But the economic
difficulties of Negro families have kept many potential leaders
from going on to Catholic colleges and universities where they
could join heartily in the apostolic ranks of an educated laity. We
have not used to its fullest potential the Catholic Negro membership
that the Church has. The top echelons of Negro city leadership
still include heavy complements of Protestant clergymen. We
should hasten to make available more well-trained Negro Catholic
laymen who will carry a larger share of the work of ushering the
American Negro into the democratic mainstream. Too often Catholic organizations reflect only scantily the Negro membership of
our Church.

THE DIEHARDS

There are some strongly Catholic neighborhoods where Negroes
are considered utterly foreign outlanders, unwanted and unwel-
come, no matter what their personal credentials may be. Ironically,
some of these diehard neighborhoods are foreign language communities occupied by ethnic groups that have had turbulent histories themselves. This, of course, is one reason why they often react
negatively to racial change. In these areas, the Church is part of the
traditional way of life. It is a fixture, the center of social life, accepted like the air the people breathe or the names they were born
with. In such areas there is a complex job of intergroup education
to be performed. These communities are often sitting right next to

the expanding Negro ghettos. They have frequently had a rough-and-tumble past with juvenile gangs and have shown strong resistance toward intruders, white or Negro. The Church in these neighborhoods must find a way of neutralizing hostility and bringing about peaceful circumstances for racial change.

THE GOOD GENERALIZATIONS

Although the Church has the tremendous advantage of hard and clear lines of doctrine, this advantage too frequently is squandered when teaching is puffed up into vague generalizations. We need much more specific teaching on matters of race relations. Kindly slogans and airy platitudes simply will not do. If they help to set a benevolent climate, they are self-defeating later, when the well-motivated person seeks guidance about some concrete ways in which he can apply his Christian principles to current situations. More study and preparation on the part of Catholic teachers and leaders in this respect is badly needed.

The 1960's will be a decade of stepped-up social pressures for American Catholics. The race problem will demand especially strong commitment. In the vast metropolitan centers Catholics will have to play an enlarged role in reorganizing urban civic life to include as full partners the heretofore excluded minorities. In Catholic education we face a grave problem of serving those portions of the Negro population in the depressed central areas of our cities. The social-service and school demands that this task alone will place upon us will be formidable. If our institutions are placed at a disadvantage economically by Federal aid to public education, not only will the Catholic schools suffer but innocent Negro families will suffer, and our ability to adjust our cities to racial change will be that much more diminished.

Finally, in a time of increasing interest in religious unity, it becomes daily more absurd for men to be denied the fullness of Christian fellowship and Catholic unity, not because of doctrinal differences but because of the scandal of harsh racial attitudes.

It should be our prayer and urgent motive to prepare our Catholic citizens for the challenges of race relations in coming years. Our spirit is not that of laggards, for St. Paul tells us that we are sent upon this earth as to a race. Let us run well in our race to outstrip racism.

EDITORIAL

Abraham Lincoln: Unfinished Business

Ten years ago Carl Sandburg prefixed this inspired first paragraph to a little essay called *A Lincoln Preface:* "In the time of the April lilacs in the year 1865, a man in the city of Washington, D.C., trusted a guard to watch a door, and the guard was careless, left the door, and the man was shot, lingered a night, passed away, was laid in a box, and carried north and west a thousand miles; bells sobbed; cities wore crepe; people stood with hats off as the railroad burial car came past at midnight, dawn or noon."

The man was Abraham Lincoln. The time, a few scant days after Robert E. Lee's surrender at Appomattox Court House had ended our Civil War. Now, a full century later, and with a vivid interior sense of what it means for a country to be suddenly bereft of its President by assassination, we recall, on his 155th birthday, the memory and the imperious message of our 16th President.

When death strikes, we leave our desks clogged with unanswered letters, our appointment pads studded with dates we shall never keep—our business in general unfinished. So, as it is inevitably for all, it was for Abraham Lincoln. His work was not done when he died. Now, almost a hundred years later, we the executors are still engaged in winding up his affairs.

The work of Lincoln will finally be done only when the American Negro is at last fully freed from the bondage of slavery. Emancipation was formally decreed on January 1, 1863, and three million slaves were given a new life by the adoption, December 18, 1865, of the Thirteenth Amendment. A century has rolled by since then, but we are not yet through with the long process of translating these high principles into palpable elements of genuine equality and opportunity for the nearly 20 million American Negroes of the 1960's.

We are moving slowly onward with this task, but we have a long road in front of us and not much time in which to complete the journey.

Before we crown Lincoln's work with final achievement, there are hard decisions to be made by government officials, home owners, employers, school officials, labor unionists, members of fraternal organizations—in a word, by all of us, North and South. We have got to "cut Negroes in" on the normal benefits of a white-dominated society. We must create decency and respect for Negroes in a hundred thousand suburbs across the country. Negroes must get better pay, find more doors open to opportunity, be given jobs with wider responsibility and a more meaningful challenge to their talents.

In order to help our Negro brothers pull themselves up out of the subnormal status to which they have been condemned by the segregation the rest of us devised, we now have to *exaggerate* efforts at intensive remedial education, job-training and the building of confidence and morale. And let no one think that this can be done without heroic effort on the part of Negroes and an almost complete about-face in the attitudes of most of their white fellow citizens.

Talk is cheap. But actually getting this job done reasonably soon is going to be immensely expensive in time, money, energy, imagination and purposeful hard work. We say "reasonably *soon*" because, while a project of this kind cannot be accomplished overnight, we have wasted so much precious time already that comfortable old slogans of a discredited "gradualism" have no more meaning. The work must be done now.

In the concrete, we have to destroy at once all the ridiculous roadblocks that hinder Negro citizens from registering and from voting. Moreover, we must provide better schools, more schools and a more intensified school program for Negro children, along with vastly improved opportunities for adult education among older Negroes. There must be freer and easier roads of access between Negroes and whites all across the spectrum of business and social life. Then, along with schools and socializing, there must be those indispensable jobs and the cultural and economic opportunities that go with jobs. If these objectives are secured, then out of such a brightening civic, social, economic and educational climate will come the morale and confidence the Negro rarely if ever had a chance to cultivate in his ghetto.

Such, then, in briefest review, is the backlog of Lincoln's unfinished business. It is the business of everybody in modern America. For decades we neglected to concern ourselves about it. Then, in the last year or two, if we hadn't understood its urgency before, we suddenly had our eyes opened. We heard the words and grasped the meaning of "We Shall Overcome." TV sets filled our living rooms with the undaunted faces of Negroes quietly protesting along the tawdry Main Streets of fifty American cities. On August 25, 1963, we watched with fascinated insight as those who had marched on Washington swayed to the unforgettable singing of Mahalia Jackson and fell silent before the sacred eloquence of Martin Luther King. At last we saw what had to be done.

That day, from the high seat in his Memorial, Abraham Lincoln seemed to be looking down over the 200,000 faces that massed before him. In fact, it was not difficult to imagine him, in that historic hour—and again during the 1965 March on Montgomery—looking out over the whole land, weighing each one of us, telling us that the time had come for us to complete the unfinished work of 1865.

G. ROBERT BLAKEY
Discrimination, Unions and Title VII

¶An attempt to assure minorities the vitally important right to join a union

On July 3, President Johnson signed the most comprehensive civil rights legislation enacted in the 20th century. The signing ceremony was held in the East Room of the White House and seen by a nation-wide audience. Signing the bill, the President called on all Americans to join in an "effort to bring justice and hope to all our people—and peace to our land."

A product of a bipartisan coalition of Republicans and Northern Democrats, and of some of the most intensive lobbying the Capitol has seen in recent years, the new act deals with, among other things, discrimination in public accommodations, voting, Federally assisted programs, and, most importantly (in Title VII), employment and union membership.

On August 4, labor gave its official reaction to the newly enacted statute. Meeting in Chicago, the 29-member executive council of the AFL-CIO, not unexpectedly, pledged labor's full support to the new act. At the Chicago meeting, the council adopted a multi-point program designed to assist in implementing it by instituting an educational program among union members, starting community committees to work for desegregation of various facilities, bargaining for fair employment clauses in contracts, seeking to make sure that unorganized employers comply with the act, lobbying in Congress for adequate enforcement appropriations, and observing the operation of the act so that developing inadequacies may be brought to Congress' attention. A civil rights conference for national, State and local leaders has also been scheduled for September.

The significance of Title VII to the Negro and other minority groups in our society—and of labor's support of its antidiscrimination policy—can hardly be overestimated. Anyone possessed of even a superficial understanding of our modern industrial life long ago realized the need of collective bargaining. For America's minority groups, however, today's problem is not the right to form a union, but the right to join a union without discrimination.

Union membership has in many areas of our industrial life become a prerequisite to employment and thus to a measure of economic freedom. A distinction, of course, must be drawn between the craft union and the industrial union. Generally, the industrial union exercises little control over employment. Not so the craft union. Despite the prohibitions of the Taft-Hartley Act, many craft unions operate under a virtually closed shop. Such shops are found most frequently, and have their most significant impact, in the building and construction trades. In these and similar areas, job control is, more often than not, a matter of union policy.

Even when not an economic necessity, union membership remains a valuable asset. Only through it can the worker achieve a voice in determining the policies to be promoted and adopted in his industry—policies that deeply affect his everyday life. And only through the union can the worker effectively prosecute his individual grievances against the company. To be sure, the nonmember may have access to the union grievance procedure, but it will ultimately be a union man who will speak for him. Exclusion from the union actually amounts to a sort of industrial disfranchisement. It has more meaningful implications to the individual than a denial of the right to vote or equal educational or housing opportunities.

Politics still has only an indirect impact on the average citizen's life, and without a degree of economic freedom, education breeds only frustration and open occupancy is meaningless.

Few unions, of course, want to restrict membership. They both want and need members. Most unions, such as the Steelworkers, not only freely admit members without discrimination, but actually state in their constitution that all workers, regardless of race, color, creed or national origin, are eligible for membership. Indeed, the constitution of the AFL-CIO contains such a provision. The fact remains, however, that some unions follow discriminatory policies. Traditionally, most of the Railway Brotherhoods have explicitly resticted membership to "white males" or members of the "Caucasian race." Only last July the Brotherhood of Locomotive Firemen and Enginemen belatedly removed the "white only" clause in their constitution. Officially, discrimination in trade unions is, in the words of George Meany, president of the AFL-CIO, "a bootleg product, sneaked in by the back door and nowhere condoned." And yet it exists. In many cases it is impossible to become a member of a union unless you are a relative of a member or belong to the same racial or ethnic group as the present members. Locals in the building trades often consist entirely of Italian-Americans. The lily-white admission practices of Local 28 of the Sheet Metal Workers in New York, recently the subject of an anti-discrimination order by the State Human Rights Commission, are an example in another trade.

A further example is Local No. 2 of the Plumbers (embarrassingly enough, Meany's home local) in New York City. According to report, the hiring of three Puerto Ricans and one Negro was enough to bring on a walkout by 35 plumbers on the Terminal Market project in the Bronx. Local No. 2 officials explained the dispute in terms that emphasized the non-union status of the men. One of the plumbers on the job was more blunt: "Animals don't mix; why should people have to?" Another observed: "God created me white. Is it any fault of mine they're created another color?" The walkout was not settled until Mayor Robert Wagner, Secretary of Labor Willard Wirtz and Meany himself intervened. Ironically, it was then settled only when the men failed the union's qualifying test, which apparently was fairly administered according to spokesmen for the NAACP, who observed the test.

The sometimes subtle discriminatory practices found in the

North are often more objectionable than the overt discrimination of the South. Under a fraternal system of voting, for example, when an applicant receives two or more "blackballs," his petition is rejected. Such a system eliminates the necessity of giving reasons for the exclusion; the applicant is simply told he is not wanted. The apprentice program in some unions, too, may serve as a vehicle of discrimination; it is often impossible for certain groups to attain the required degree of "proficiency" to be admitted to journeymanship. Companies and unions sometimes work together. Isaac Borges, age 43, father of three children and a plumber for 23 years in New York and in Puerto Rico, and one of the individuals involved in the Local No. 2 dispute, tells a familiar tale: "When I went to the union to apply for membership, they said: 'Well, first you have to go and get a job in a union shop and then come back.' So I went to a union shop and I was told: 'First you have to be a member of the union, so get your membership.' So—what can you do?"

Late in the 19th century it became settled that no one had a legally enforceable right to belong to a union. The power to exclude, even arbitrarily, was felt to be inherent in the nature of the union as a "voluntary" association. (True, at that time unions were no more than "voluntary" associations.) Much has taken place since then. In 1900, less than a million of our 29 million gainfully employed persons were unionized. By 1950, there were 15 million workers in unions, and practically every large manufacturing industry was either completely or almost completely organized. Today, approximately 17 million men and women are members of our various labor organizations. Union assets, minimal until about 1942, today conservatively exceed in value $1.5 billion.

The attitude of the law toward the early labor movement was one of reluctant acceptance, if not active animosity. The use of the labor injunction was widespread. That was the era of the *Debs* case, where Federal troops ended a railroad strike, and the *Danbury Hatters* case, where a hostile Supreme Court, in obvious contradiction of legislative intent, applied the Sherman Act to a labor union. Now much of this has changed. The union's position in society is maintained not only by its internal strength and a relatively favorable public opinion, but by positive Federal and State legislation, which provides affirmative legal protection for organizational activity and collective bargaining and frees it from antitrust prosecution. As the legally protected, exclusive bargaining agent of employees in an industrial area, the union weighs, determines and implements policies that vitally affect the everyday lives of all those whom it represents. The union in a very real sense has become the employees' industrial government.

Realizing the inadequacies of the traditional approach, a number of States have passed statutes making it illegal for a union to discriminate on the basis of race, color, religious creed or national origin. Twenty-five States presently have some sort of fair-practices legislation. A few courts also have adopted a more realistic view. The California Supreme Court is one example. In 1958, in *Thorman v. the International Alliance of Theatrical Stage Employees*, it directed the admission of an arbitrarily excluded applicant. But these statutes or cases have efficacy only on a Statewide basis, and they are most often found in the industrial North, where the problem of racial and other discrimination is present but does not loom large. Indeed, roughly 60 per cent of American Negroes live in States with no antidiscrimination legislation, and these are precisely those who need it most. (It must be added, of course, that the Negroes in the largely unorganized South suffer as much from the unorganized but bigoted employer as from the racist union.)

The effect of the existing general pattern of discrimination of both union and employer, however, is clear. Many assume that the non-white has made gains in recent years. The converse is true. The medium family income for the non-white over the past decade has slipped from 57 per cent to 53 per cent of the White. Herbert Hill, labor secretary of the NAACP, estimates that only one-half of one per cent of all the skilled mechanics among plumbers, electricians and operating engineers are Negroes, and according to Department of Labor statistics, the unemployment rate among non-whites is over twice as high as among whites.

The history of the passage of the civil rights bill, particularly Title VII, by Congress is remarkable. Many felt that Title VII would never survive the Senate filibuster. Had Senator Russell of Georgia, the leader of the Southern forces, sought to bargain, it might have died, and the bill might well have been otherwise weakened. Yet Russell remained adamant, perhaps hoping for a white backlash (whipped up by Gov. George Wallace's primary campaigning) strong enough to defeat the motion for cloture. When the vote came, it was too late; compromise was out of the question. Despite the vote of Arizona's Barry Goldwater, and his opinion that

Title VII was unconstitutional, on June 17, the 81st day of debate and the 57th of the filibuster, the Senate by a vote of 76 to 18 passed the bill, Title VII included. The mood of the Senate was aptly described by Senator Dirksen's reference to the saying of Victor Hugo: "Stronger than all the armies is an idea whose time has come."

The final version of Title VII remains largely the F.E.P.C. bill, H.R. 405, which the House Education and Labor Committee, with the backing of leaders like Meany, had reported on July 22, 1963, and which Rep. Emanuel Celler's House Judiciary Committee had bodily incorporated into H.R. 7152, the House bill. The chief difference is that enforcement is placed in the Federal courts rather than an administrative agency.

The measure has been subjected to severe and often misleading criticisms. Sen. Joseph Clark of Pennsylvania has aptly termed them "fantastic." Critics, including such people as Governor Wallace, who has already announced he will have no part of enforcing it (other Southern leaders, such as Senator Russell himself, urged compliance rather than lawlessness) have said it would abolish union seniority and set up racial "quotas" to achieve some sort of racial "balance."

Title VII, in fact, outlaws just such a policy. Policies like "preferential hiring" advocated by Negro spokesmen like Dr. James M. Nabrit, president of Howard University, and James Farmer, national director of CORE (also criticized by men like Roy Wilkins of the NAACP) stand clearly condemned. Under the provisions of Title VII, discrimination by unions affecting commerce *for or against* anyone on the grounds of race, religion, sex or national origin is explicitly made illegal. (Here it should be parenthetically emphasized that Title VII will also have a significant impact on the largely unorganized white-collar worker; it applies equally to unions and employers.) Title VII is designed to encourage judging on the basis of ability. Professionally developed ability tests, administered in good faith, for example, are explicitly approved. Title VII does not set up any system of reverse discrimination.

Like the bill itself, Title VII, however, is not a panacea; the millennium will not arrive now that it has been passed. The enactment of Title VII cannot with a stroke of the pen end discrimination in our industrial life. One commission in Washington, as the

New York *Times* noted editorially, cannot effectively check the admission practices of every local union or employer. The greatest effect of the statute, in all probability, will derive from its mere passage.

Unquestionably, the great majority of union leaders will obey the law. The adoption of the Chicago program may be taken as evidence of their attitude. Unfortunately, however, the declaration leaves a far more significant question unanswered: What will be the feeling of the rank and file? For it will be their feeling that will be decisive. That there is anti-Negro sentiment among even the most enlightened unions is not to be doubted. David McDonald, president of the Steelworkers, for example, is reported to have told the President at a White House dinner of widespread anti-Negro sentiment in his union and, what is more, of a private poll indicating that Senator Goldwater leads the President in popularity in the union. The problem facing union leaders everywhere, on the race question, is not unlike that facing America's religious leaders. There is a real gap between professed principle and actual practice. Here creative leadership is surely called for.

While not the final answer—that lies in men's hearts—Title VII nevertheless makes an honest attempt to strike at the vicious circle of poverty and ignorance, which is the crux of discrimination. People cannot be expected to become educated unless they have an opportunity to use their education, and the poor today without education will surely be poor tomorrow. Given effective and sensible administration—and most importantly, reasonable acceptance by the rank and file—Title VII will go about as far as law can go in helping us to realize in our industrial life the ideals of our democratic society. We can only hope, therefore, that union people everywhere will—along with Rep. Charles Longstreet Weltner, the courageous Congressman from Georgia who changed his vote on final passage in the House—"accept the verdict of the nation."

SECTION VII

POPE JOHN'S LEGACY

JOHN COURTNEY MURRAY
Things Old and New in "Pacem in Terris"

¶Initial reflections on certain key accents in Pope John's latest encyclical to serve as guidelines for a fuller understanding of its
meaning

An adequate interpretation of the encyclical *Pacem in Terris* must
wait on lengthy study, because the reach of the Pope's words, in its
breadth and depth, is greatly extensive. What follows are some comments on certain salient points of the encyclical, on the quality of
the Pope's thought and its major accents.

It is obvious, in the first instance, that the Pope here offers a
shining example of everything that he means by his own word,
aggiornamento. He situates himself squarely in the year in which
he writes—1963. There is not the slightest note of nostalgia, nor
of lament over the past course of history or over the current situation that history has evoked here on earth. The Pope confronts all
the facts of political, social, economic and cultural change that have
been the product of the modern era. Generously and ungrudgingly,
he accepts those elements of historical progress which can be
recognized as such by the application of traditional principles as
norms of discernment.

The Pope then proceeds to speak to the postmodern age, to a
new era of history that has not yet found its name but that is
clearly with us. His acute sense of the basic need of the new age
is evident in the word that is so often repeated in the encyclical
and that sets its basic theme. I mean the word "order." This does
seem to be the contemporary issue. The process of ordering and
organizing the world is at the moment going forward. The issue is
not whether we shall have order in the world; the contemporary
condition of chaos has become intolerable on a world-wide scale,
and the insistent demand of the peoples of the world is for order.
The question is, then, on what principles is the world going to be
ordered.

The basic principle of the Roman Pontiff is as old as Plato, for whom society was "man writ large." The "man" whom the Pope puts at the basis and center of a human world order is not the abstract human nature which is presented in certain older textbooks on ethics. His "man" is the man of today, that is to say, the human person upon whose structured nature history too has left its mark. This strongly personalist accent of the Pope should quiet the fears and win the sympathies of those to whom the phrase "natural law" is uncongenial.

In dealing with the problem of political order, Pope John XXIII represents a development of the tradition. He leaves behind the predominantly ethical concept of the society-state which was characteristic of Leo XIII. He adopts the more juridical conception of the state that was characteristic of Pius XII, and he carries this conception to new lengths. For instance, he clearly accepts the distinction that seems to be missing from Leo XIII, namely, the distinction between society and the state. His general conception of the political ideal is fundamentally that of St. Thomas, "the free man under a limited government." The Pope states, with a new firmness of accent, the three principles that constitute this ideal. The first is that society must afford men "the sphere of freedom." The second is the ancient principle of constitutionalism: that the state has its foundations in constitutional law, whereby the powers of government are limited. Even the modern conception of the written constitution is endorsed by the Pope, for the first time (if I am not mistaken) in the history of papal utterances. The third principle is that of popular participation in the public administration. Though this principle is deeply rooted in the liberal and Christian political tradition of the West, the strong emphasis given it in this encyclical again represents a welcome newness.

One can hear in the Pope's words a contemporaneous echo of John of Salisbury and his broad definition of the function of the Prince, which is "to fight for justice and for the freedom of the people." Only here it is not the question of a Prince, but of the whole order of constitutional and statutory law of public administration. The first function of the state and of all its officers is to guarantee the juridical order, that is to say, the whole order of human rights and duties whose roots are in the human person as situated in the contemporary world.

One of the most striking aspects of the encyclical is the generosity, the breadth and the contemporaneity of the Pope's statement with regard to the rights and duties of the human person. An outstanding instance of his full acceptance of modern progress is his affirmation of the place of woman in society as conceived in the world of today. Even more important is his strong insistence on racial equality.

In the past, papal pronouncements on political and social order have always been suspended, as it were, from three great words—*truth, justice* and *charity*. These three great words are repeated in this encyclical, and the demands of each are carefully particularized. But a fourth word is added, with an insistence that is new at the same time that it is traditional. I mean the word *freedom*.

Freedom is a basic principle of political order; it is also *the* political method. The whole burden of the encyclical is that the order for which the postmodern world is looking cannot be an order that is imposed by force, or sustained by coercion, or based on fear—which is the most coercive force that can be brought to bear on man.

By sharply accenting this theme, the Pope clearly takes sides against movements on the march today that would organize the world and create an order in it on the basis of force and not on the basis of the principle, which we are proud to call American as well as Christian, that the ordering forces in the world must be the forces of "freedom under law." These forces of freedom and for freedom emerge from the depths of the human person, which in the end is *the* creative force in human affairs.

The summation of the Pope's thought is in the sentence which asserts that all order, if it is to be qualified as reasonable and human, must be "founded on truth, built according to justice, vivified and integrated by charity, and put into practice in freedom." Elsewhere the Pope makes clear that freedom is *the* method for the "realization" of order in human affairs as well as a goal of the order itself.

In another respect the Pope manifests his clear intention to be guided by the traditional axiom by which Leo XIII was likewise guided, "*vetera novis augere*," the principle that the Catholic tradition is a growing tradition, a tradition of progress, which requires that the "old things" be constantly affirmed at the same time they are completed and complemented in organic fashion by "new things."

I refer here to the distinction that the Pope draws between "historical movements that have economic, social, cultural or political ends" and the "false philosophical teachings regarding the nature, origin and destiny of the universe and of man" which originally animated these movements. The basis of the distinction is the fact that "those movements, insofar as they conform to the dictates of right reason and are interpreters of the lawful aspirations of the human person, contain elements that are positive and deserving of approval." It is therefore possible to divorce these movements, in all that is of practical merit in them, from the erroneous doctrines with which they were historically allied.

I am not sure just what "historical movement" the Pope chiefly had in mind. I suspect that it was Continental socialism, whose primitive inspiration was largely atheist. Perhaps the Pope's distinction has some relevance to the whole Marxist movement, but here its application would have carefully to be made. In any case, I should think that the distinction may be given full application in regard of the 18th- and 19th-century movements toward political freedom. So applied, the distinction dissolves the whole problematic of Leo XIII, whose great conflict was with Continental, sectarian Liberalism. In his time, he was not able to draw a distinction between the animating principle of this movement, which was that of the "outlaw conscience" that recognized no authority higher than itself and no law that was not of its own making, and the free political institutions of which this movement was the protagonist.

At his distance from the 19th-century state of the question, which is now outworn, Pope John XXIII is able boldly to make this important distinction. The significance of its making will, I think, be felt particularly in regard of an urgent problem that continues to face us, namely, the problem of an organic development of traditional principles touching the relations of Church and State in such wise that we may come into possession of what we still lack —a complete and unitary Catholic doctrine capable of prudent application in the political and religious conditions of our own time. A further welcome contribution to this end is the Pope's unprecedentedly broad affirmation of the "right to worship God publicly and privately" as a "right conscience" dictates.

I should say a word about the Pope's thought with regard to the constitution of a world community. He is clearly in the tradition of Pius XII, whose insistence on the need for a juridical organization of the international community is well known. John XXIII seems to develop the thought of Pius XII by his call for "a public authority, having world-wide power and endowed with the proper means for the efficacious pursuit of its objective, which is the universal common good in concrete form." This authority must, he adds, "be set up by common accord and not imposed by force." Again the principle of freedom, as a principle and as a method, is affirmed.

The Pope proposes this goal in the spirit of "confident hope" that is the dominant spirit of the whole encyclical. But it will not be clear to many, including myself, how this hope is concretely to be realized, given the fact that no moral or political consensus presently exists within the total international community that would furnish the basis for the existence of such a public authority and for the effective exercise of its powers. It is clear that the Pope is intimately aware that our postmodern era is characterized by what he calls a "pronounced dynamism" toward change of all kinds. It is also clear that he has most correctly indicated the right direction of change toward the remedy of a "structural defect" in the international community. For the rest, it is clear that he puts his hope in the efforts of those, who are still "not many" but whose numbers must grow, who are "scientifically competent, technically capable and skilled in the practice of their professions," and who will be able therefore to "create a synthesis between scientific, technical and professional elements on the one hand and spiritual values on the other."

His hope, therefore, is not utopian idealism. It is possible of realization. It seems to be sustained, in the last analysis, by the confidence that breathes through the whole encyclical—a confidence in the power of the human person, in association, to "insure that world events follow a reasonable and human course." It is therefore a hope that no reasonable man can fail to share, no matter what the difficulties in the way may be.

The encyclical will be perhaps most closely scrutinized for the guidance that it may give to Christians and to men of good will in regard of all that we mean by the Cold War. There will be those who will think, as I do, that we have been given only limited guidance. The Pope did not choose to deal with an aspect of the matter that has been carefully covered by his predecessors, notably Pius

XI. I mean the profundity of the current crisis of history out of whose depths the Cold War itself has arisen.

The Pope has indeed made it entirely clear that the future must not be permitted to belong to the conception of political and social order that is inherent in the Communist revolution. He declares himself openly against "political regimes which do not guarantee for individual citizens a sufficient sphere of freedom within which their souls are allowed to breathe humanly." The encyclical shows no disposition to come to terms, in some manner of false peace, with the doctrinal content of the world revolution, especially its conception of Promethean man as the creator of himself and the rightful single ruler of the world. There is no encouragement in the encyclical for those among us who take a shallow or mistaken view of the depths of evil that are inherent in Communist ideology. On the other hand, there may be some warrant for the thought that the spirit of confident hope which the Pontiff courageously embraces fails to take realistic account of the fundamental schism in the world today.

On this difficult subject, about which there will be much argument, I have only one suggestion to offer as a help toward an understanding of the encyclical. I think the Pope deeply understands the disastrous extent to which men today are gripped by the myth of history which the Marxists have so diligently inculcated. In many ways, a deterministic view of history has gained much ground among us. In this view, man has lost command of his own destiny on this earth; his destiny is determined by the events of history, and he is himself powerless to control these events. The conclusion is that history today is surely and certainly carrying man toward catastrophe with an inevitability against which man is helpless.

I think that the Pope wishes to take a strong stand against this myth of history as the master of man. I think this intention stands behind his confident assertion that "the fundamental principle on which our present peace depends must be replaced by another." Today the principle of such peace as we enjoy is simply naked fear. No one will deny that this principle must be replaced by another. The difficulty arises when the Pope goes on to say that we not only must, but also can, move forward to a new and more solid basis of peace. We must not, he seems to be saying, feel ourselves to be trapped in history, unable to change its course, unable to control world events, unable to avoid the disaster that waits for us if the world continues on its present course. At least in this respect, the Pope will command the agreement of all men of good will who believe that there are energies in the free human spirit whereby man may fulfill his destiny on earth, which is to be, not God, but the image of God. All men who believe in God are agreed that He is the Master of history. Man, therefore, manifests himself as the image of God chiefly by his intelligent, confident efforts to master the course of historical events and direct it toward the common good of the peoples of earth.

MOST REV. G. EMMETT CARTER
Conciliar Rome

To choose among the almost infinite variety of impressions that remain after the experience of the Council is a confusing task. So much has been said about the external events, the politics, the human strengths and weaknesses, that I would prefer to limit this brief article to an attempt to search the profound Christian dynamics, to seek the spirit of the Council, under the shifting sands of daily events.

To come directly to the point, it is my conviction that what we are witnessing is a crisis in the age-old struggle of the Christian to decide whence comes his power. This has always been the agony of the Church, and we are arriving at a consciousness of our dilemma in a spectacular way.

The appearance of Jesus, Son of God and son of Mary, did not represent a simple evolution of man's ability to achieve and a quantitative development of his power source. It was a revolution, a deviation, a whole new set of dynamics.

Jesus paid fully for His novelty. "Is not this the carpenter's son? And they despised Him." When His new spiritual force began to cut across the political-economic-military forces, as sooner or later it had to, He paid the final price.

His early followers fared little better. They received the contempt of the Romans for their lack of an administrative and political

complex, the raillery of the Greeks for their hopelessly unsophisticated philosophical system. "To the Jews a stumbling block; to
the Gentiles, foolishness." Paul's only attempt at philosophizing
finds him caught in a wave of Areopagite laughter as he tries to
regain the high ground of supernatural thought power and—rather
lamely on this occasion, in my opinion—to leap the gap from their
gods, whom they did not take seriously in any case, to the risen
Christ, who was everything to him. Was this why in the future
he would preach "only Jesus and Him crucified"? Had Paul understood forever the source of his power?

But the Church moved on and soon found that supernatural
power was not her only stock in trade. Men came to love or
fear the Church, and powerful monarchs—at some times in well-
meant gestures, at other times as a calculated scheme—made her
rich and powerful. Charlemagne created the Papal States; bishops
became princes and warriors as well as pastors; Church and State
became practically indistinguishable, while Emperors called Councils and Popes deposed Emperors.

Nor could anyone accuse us any longer of failing in complicated
philosophical systems. The great and legitimate need of the early
Councils to probe and define theological truths, the splendid syn-
theses of Augustine and Aquinas, in which faith sought intelligence, raised the Christian Church to the pinnacle of thought and
human penetration of the divine mysteries. But neither Augustine
nor Aquinas ever lost sight of the original power, of the source
of such soaring; and when the former cried out: "O ancient Beauty,
ever old and ever new, too late have I known you, too late have
I loved you," he was referring, not to his philosophical processes
and his subtle distinctions, but to the source of all his wisdom.
And when Thomas Aquinas, toward the end of his life, groaned in
a mixture of ecstasy and despair: "All I have written is a straw,"
he was not being ungrateful for the power of his mind, but was
recognizing that it was but a very humble handmaiden of the
Spirit of Jesus, which led him to the mysteries of the faith.

With the confusion of Christendom in the terrible divisions of
the 16th century, and for a long time after, the need to bring the
power of intellect to the defense of that faith became an all-
engrossing task. Sterile criticism of where this has led us is of
no avail, but neither is there any advantage in dodging the truth.
It is a fact that theology, because it was so philosophy-oriented,

so dependent on reasoning—not to say rationalism—brought it to pass that we failed to stress adequately the true sources of our Christian power. Almost all priests today can recall that their seminary theology was a process of analyzing concepts and arriving at a syllogistic conclusion. Once reached, this conclusion was then put in juxtaposition to a text of Scripture to prove that the reasoning was right. No wonder Péguy spoke of the need of *ressourcement*.

It is naïve and unrealistic to suppose that this emphasis on social power and mind power was at its greatest when Pope John called his Council and that, in a sort of collective voyage to Damascus, the great majority of the bishops suddenly in 1962 saw the light and heard the voice. Through the subtle influence of the Spirit, this Council was being prepared in the minds of men for a long time.

World events and providential defeats were teaching the Church once more its true nature and its true power. A hundred years ago, the Catholic world mourned the loss of the Papal States to Garibaldi. The memory of that event hardly distresses us today. On the contrary, we are convinced that it was the beginning of the modern emancipation of the Church from the shackles of intervention by, and even identification with, the state. The Church of the poor was beginning to leave the power of this world to the princes of this world and return to the poor.

On the side of thought power, a quiet revolution had been taking place since the turn of the century. In catechetics and kerygmatic theology, the best minds of the Church were returning to the simplicity of the Christian message, and the scriptural-liturgical emphasis that was to dominate the Council was already supreme in many of the Catholic communities, particularly of Central Europe.

It was against this background of preparation that we assembled in 1962, although few adverted to it at the time. But it soon became apparent that the dominant thought in the minds of most of the bishops was to renew the Church in terms of a complete return to a Christlike simplicity and an acknowledgement of our supernatural and spiritual power, to the exclusion of all other forms of power.

Instead of the "triumphalism" of yesterday, the idea of the person came to dominate, and God's plan to save man through man's own personal co-operation and involvement, rather than through

the political pressures of a hothouse, closed society or juridical penalties and carefully encouraged fear.

Let us illustrate this movement, however briefly and inadequately,
in its two phases.

First, the temporal power. Pope John and Pope Paul must both
have cringed during the coronation ceremony they were subjected
to after their election. When the tiara was placed on Pope Paul's
head, he was told, in a ceremony reminiscent of the most trium-
phalistic era of the Renaissance Popes: "Receive this tiara adorned
with three crowns and know that you are the father of Princes and
of Kings." Pope Paul's reaction against this pomp was vigorous. The
ostrich plumes in papal processions suddenly disappeared (may
they never reappear!) and the Pontiff promised to reduce the pomp
of the papal court so that, without loss of dignity or reverence, it
may be truly ecclesial in character. But most indicative of all is what
the Holy Father did at the ceremony in which he concelebrated
with the Oriental bishops during the Council's third session.

This has been much analyzed and, in my opinion, falsely or
inadequately reported by most. The gesture had supreme significance. Whatever the origin of the tiara, one thing is certain: it is
a crown, or a series of them, and it has come to signify a certain
worldly and temporal dominion. The Pope removed it from his
head and placed it—not just anywhere, but on the altar. At that
moment, without speaking, he seemed to cry aloud to the world
that he renounced any power but that of his Lord. The altar has
always symbolized Christ—that Christ who, the Alpha and the
Omega, is the source of all power, temporal and spiritual. To his
Master, the Pope remitted his crown, to stand before the world
with the miter of a bishop—of the Bishop of Rome, successor of its
first Bishop and claiming no other jurisdiction, no other power than
that given by Christ to Peter.

As to the Council Fathers' view of the Church's mind power,
it is expressed in the documents that have been promulgated as the
fruit of the Council. If we were able to do this Council over again,
some of us would like to believe that there might be only one
schema, with a number of *adnexa*, or appendixes, or developmental
decrees. This central schema would be the magnificent text of the
Decree on the Church. In it no one is condemned, no heresies are
exploded, no threats are uttered. It is a powerful document, but its
power resides in its Christlike simplicity and in its substituting of

personal considerations of peace and love and co-operation for abstruse philosophy or sterile claims to superiority.

The power in it is the power of personal involvement. It presents
the mystery of the Church in terms of those persons who are
called to share in it. The central figure is, obviously, Christ. But
with Him and in Him are the people of God in all their totality:
the Blessed Virgin, the Pope, the bishops, the priests, the religious,
the laity, all men of good will, each contributing in love to the
fullness of the mystery of Christ.

To illustrate the Christ-centered mode of our participation in the
mystery of salvation, we have the Council's great constitutions and
decrees. What they express in regard to the Church's answer to the
question put to her Founder: "What do you say of yourself?"
is carried out logically in the Decree on Ecumenism, where, once
more, we go to our brothers not as their judges or their accusers
but as persons to persons, as lovers of the truth to our fellows who
also love the truth.

In a similar vein, that which was the first fruit of the Council
in terms of time becomes our lasting and active treasure in terms
of fulfillment and result. I refer to the Constitution on the Liturgy.
The family of God so accurately described, so warmly presented in
the Constitution on the Church, the people of God so eager for
unity and love as presented in the Decree on Ecumenism, come
together in a life of prayer with Christ, who is the power of the
Father and in whose name we can "do all things."

I have been asked what I think the Council means. That is what
I have tried to express. It is much more. But in a way it can be
summed up by this paraphrase: "Whereas I was rich—in worldly
power and sophisticated philosophy—I became poor. Whereas I was
poor—because I had momentarily lost sight of the true source of
all power—I became rich in the supernatural mystery and strength
of the faith."

JOHN COGLEY
Five "Poems on Postcards," about the Council

VIEWS OF THE COUNCIL

As Seen by the Progressives

The opportunity is heaven-sent
More or less to undo Trent
And march with equanimity
Toward Vatican Council Number Three

As Seen by the Conservatives

The Church must move—but not too fast
Its future flows from its placid past
Festina lente, that Catholic boast,
Measures the movements of the Holy Ghost

As Seen by the Middle-of-the-Roaders

The Council would be quite a mess
If we weren't here to check excess
With conservative caution and progressive fuss
It really all depends on us

DISCOVERY

There are Jesuit progressives
To tend the Open Door
And Jesuit conservatives
And moderates by the score
There are Jesuits liturgical
As any O.S.B.
And Jesuits inclined toward
Private piety
There are Jesuits so venturesome
They can't go fast enough
And others who are finding
Aggiornamento tough
There are dialoguing Jesuits
And those who have their doubts
There are Jesuits for the ins
And Jesuits for the outs
There are Jesuits as pacifist
As any British bish
And some who diet strictly
On the military dish
Of welfare plans and such
Some Jesuits are leery
While others of the brethren
Are clearly New Frontiery
And on literary matters
The plural patterns hold
The Jesuit *qua* reader
Fits no common mold

There are Jesuits left and Jesuits right
A *pro* and a *con* for most any fight
So wherever you stand, you stand not alone:
Every little movement has a Jebbie of its own.

ON THE VIA DELLA CONCILIAZIONE

If a certain reporter has it right
There is a Discalced Carmelite
Who has the only straight info
On just which bishops voted no

Secundum a certain C.S.C.
Or maybe it was a Marist
The author of a certain book
Has been unduly harassed

And if one can trust a French curé
The Curia has had its day
At the *troisième* session *les pères* will take up
What must be done to force a shakeup

Cardinal A had a row with Cardinal B
(Something to do with celibacy)
And an Augustinian has the dope
On what the Dutch archbishop told the Pope

For what the Pope said in reply
You'll have to see Monsignor Y,
A Very Reverend who knows his stuff
And frequently talks quite enough . . .

And so it goes along the street
Whenever tipsters chance to meet
But rumors aren't worth a dime
Until they're authorized by *Time*

LITERARY INTELLIGENCE

That George Eliot was a girl, I know
And Evelyn Waugh is a boy
And Pamela Johnson is Lady Snow
And Bloy doesn't rhyme with cloy

Brendan Behan likes his sauce
Newman wrote of Gain and Loss
Joseph Conrad was a Pole
Francis Thompson lived on dole
O. Henry spent some time in jail
And *Moby Dick* concerns a whale
Hans Küng is only thirty-five
Upton Sinclair is quite alive
On Fridays Mrs. Kerr eats fish
Mrs. Rinehart wrote of *Tish*
Sartor Resartus refers to a tailor
And *Esquire* features Norman Mailer
Jimmy Baldwin lives in Paris
Where you can buy the Loves of Harris
Moravia comes from storied Rome
And Papa once called Oak Park home

I know their habits, their next of kin
But who the hell is Xavier Rynne?

FOR MORE VERNACULAR

From Staten Island
To far-off Thailand
The faithful don't *compris:*
Hic, haec, hoc is foreign talk
From see to shining see

Let the Gospel be sung
In the English tongue
On the French wave long may it ride
Lest its impact should vanish
Speak it clearly in Spanish
For the Thais make it fit to be Thai'd

Mass communication
For every last nation!
Let the Word
Be heard!

FERNANDO M. CASTIELLA
Non-Catholics in Spain

¶What rights can religious minorities in that country claim before
the law?

In 1953, on the occasion of the Fifth Convention of Italian
Catholic Jurists, His Holiness Pope Pius XII delivered his famous
discourse on religious tolerance. This precedent and that of the
equally important encyclical *Divino Afflante Spiritu* (1943) on
scriptural studies have been essential steps toward that better understanding among Christians which Pope John XXIII so clear-
sightedly carried forward, by creating the Secretariat for Promoting
Christian Unity, by convening the Council and by issuing his
encyclical *Pacem in Terris*.

In 1953, too, I had the honor of negotiating and signing the concordat that Pope Pius XII concluded with Spain. Since that time I
have firmly believed that an adjustment of the legal status of non-
Catholics in our country is a necessary corollary of the concordat.
It is necessary if the religious peace we Spaniards have enjoyed for
centuries is to be kept intact. It is necessary, too, if we are to pre-
serve, with proper regard for the faith and conscience of dissenters,
that very special blessing of Spain's history which is its "Catholic
unity."

Those familiar with that papal discourse of 1953 will remember
that it asks the Catholic statesman to study the facts of the situation
in which he is involved, so as to determine whether, in concrete
instances, tolerance can be "justified in the interests of a higher
and more general good." In that, however, "which concerns religion
and morality, he will seek also the judgment of the Church. On
such vital questions touching international life, only he to whom
Christ has entrusted the guidance of His entire Church—that is,
the Roman Pontiff—is competent to speak."

This is the road taken by the Spanish State. Hence it is appropriate to ask, as regards the "facts," whether there really is a

denominational problem in Spain. In other words: what is the total number of Protestants (they are the ones mainly involved); what is their significance in the nation's life; and to what extent may they be said to be persecuted or to encounter difficulty in the free profession and practice of their faith?

It should be noted that neither the Jews nor the Muslims—the only non-Christian religious bodies among us of any size—complain of the treatment accorded them today in Spain. There is no need to recall here the official protection that both groups have enjoyed in our peninsular and African territories, nor the manner in which our diplomatic and consular missions have courageously defended and effectively aided the Sephardic Jews in every European country where they suffered racial persecution.

Limiting the discussion to Protestants, let us point out that, according to the most reliable statistics, this Christian minority in Spain comprises, in round numbers, about fifteen thousand Spaniards and an equal number of foreign residents. In addition, there are several thousand members of the American armed forces at bases used jointly by Spain and the United States, who for the most part are not affected by the religious problem. Also to be taken into account is the Protestant fraction of the nine million European and American tourists who yearly visit the Iberian peninsula. The total number of these Protestant tourists ranges from the tens to the hundreds of thousands and is on the increase.

If these figures are compared to our total population of 31 million, the insignificance of the Protestants' role in Spanish life becomes evident.

The Reformation never gained a foothold on Spanish soil. In the first place, the Catholic monarchs Ferdinand and Isabella of Spain appointed new prelates—more particularly Cardinal Cisneros, Primate of Spain—who initiated on our soil the Catholic Reformation, which was to culminate in the Council of Trent. The reforming work of Cisneros anticipated the Lutheran protest in every respect. In fact, it can be said that the renewed scriptural interest that so happily characterizes modern times had its origin in Catholic Spain. Moreover, the first university to unite the spirit of humanism and the spirit of the Catholic Reformation was that founded by Cisneros at Alcalá and enjoined by him to teach theology without being bound by any school, "along the three paths" of Thomism, Scotism and Nominalism.

It must also be remembered that the driving and cohesive force of religious feeling had been a decisive factor in the eight-century struggle against the Muslim invaders of the peninsula. That struggle, which ended with the recapture of Granada in 1492, forged the Spanish national identity. Hence it is not surprising that no true Protestant tradition exists in Spain, such as that in France, for instance, which is none the less a country with a Catholic majority.

Only in the 19th century did Protestantism return to the Iberian peninsula. About 1830, Protestant presence in the peninsula began with the "hawkers," persons who distributed, and at times commented on, the Sacred Scriptures. Of these the best known is the Englishman George Borrow, who traveled through almost all Spain and recorded his experiences in a now famous book.

In this first phase, Protestant activity was entirely in the hands of foreigners. There was, however, one Spanish scholar, Luis Usoz y Río, who between 1848 and 1865 carried out the important task of publishing the works of Spanish Protestants of earlier centuries.

The revolution of 1868 began an era of religious freedom which continued into the troubled period culminating in the First Republic. Nevertheless, in 1873 the organ of the American Baptist Missionary Union had the following to say: "The work, like that of all denominations in the country, remains *in statu quo*. All expect that the separation of Church and State will redound to our benefit, but State decrees do not change hearts or excite interest in evangelical religion." What gives this comment added significance is that William Knapp, who was the first outstanding American Protestant to come to our country and who eventually became the principal leader of the Spanish Baptists, had been in Spain since 1870.

In 1876, after the restoration of the monarchy under Alfonso XII, a new Constitution was adopted. Article 11, which had been negotiated with the Holy See, laid the groundwork for the system of religious tolerance that is still in force in Spain and is now embodied in Article 6 of the Charter of the Spanish People (*Fuero de los Españoles*).

Until the great campaign of 1910, when a petition was submitted to the Cortes, there was no Protestant activity of any significance. But the interpretation of Article 11 of the Constitution given by Canalejas satisfied Protestants for the time being.

The Second Republic, which lasted from 1931 to 1936, and in some areas to 1939, proclaimed absolute freedom of religion, and during the Civil War directed a bloody persecution against Catholics alone.

On February 16, 1936, the Popular Front won the elections. The majority of Protestants, as John D. Hughey has written, "tended to look upon the Popular Front as the less dangerous of the two coalitions. . . . The country was clearly on the edge of a precipice. . . . Leftists and rightists were assassinated; churches and convents were burned; street fights took place; and strikes crippled industry and commerce. In a speech to the Cortes, Gil Robles indicted the government for leniency toward the doers of violence and stated, among other things, that 160 churches had been destroyed and 251 set on fire or otherwise attacked."

This situation—particularly after the assassination of José Calvo Sotelo, leader of the Parliamentary opposition, by the government police—led directly to the national uprising of July 18, 1936. Thus began the Civil War, the religious aspects of which were commented on by the same Protestant author as follows: "Leftist extremists took things into their own hands in Republican Spain during the first days following the outbreak of civil war; and prominent people were killed, churches and other religious buildings were destroyed, and priests and monks were murdered in large numbers. . . . No Catholic worship was permitted in most of Republican Spain till near the end of the war."

While these horrors were taking place in Spain, the Duke of Alba, who was the unofficial representative of Nationalist Spain in London, was instructed to make a statement, which was published in the *Times* of November 19, 1937: "Complete toleration now exists in Nationalist Spain for all Christian communions, and . . . complete toleration will continue to be the policy and practice of the National Spanish Government after the war." He added: "I make this statement on the authorization of General Franco himself."

In 1945, the Charter of the Spanish People, which is one of the Fundamental Laws that together make up our present Constitution, was promulgated. Article 6 of this Charter, which reproduces Article 11 of the Constitution of 1876, lays down the principle of religious tolerance.

The Charter was received by authoritative Protestant spokesmen with genuine satisfaction. It must be noted, however, that while Article 6 is a declaration of principles that has provided the dissenting communities with the protection needed to carry on their activities and to develop, the absence of supporting legislation has left to the discretion of regional and local authorities the specific application of this general norm.

Various incidents have occurred, of which the following may be cited:

On January 23, 1956, at the request of Church spokesmen, the civil authorities closed a Protestant theological seminary and school in Madrid.

On April 18, 1956, the Ministry of Information received another complaint from Church authorities to the effect that the British and Foreign Bible Society, which had run into difficulties in 1940, was violating the Press Law. The diplomatic representations and international outcry on this occasion attained extraordinary proportions. His Eminence Cardinal Frings, Archbishop of Cologne, publicly stated, in reply to a letter sent him by Pastor Dibelius, that these were measures taken by the Spanish government and that in no case could responsibility be laid at the door of the Spanish episcopate or a religious order or any Church authority. Evidently the Cardinal Archbishop of Cologne was misinformed, and though the truth did eventually prevail, the harm to the Spanish State cannot easily be undone.

The government nevertheless gave serious attention to this case. It determined to what extent the Press Law had been violated through the publication of pamphlets offensive to the Catholic religion, and it recognized, on the other hand, that the British and Foreign Bible Society had the right to publish or import the Sacred Scriptures, as necessary for the worship and religious practice of the dissenting communities. I can personally testify to the concern of the Spanish government to deal with this matter in a spirit of justice. In 1959, the Bible Society was awarded compensation for the illegal attachment of its property, and some weeks ago, with the approval of the Conference of Archbishops meeting in Madrid, it was authorized to resume its activities in Spain.

To sum up the present situation, there is in Spain no persecution of dissenting Christians nor any legal discrimination against them in any aspect of Spanish law. The only exception, and one that has its counterpart in other countries, is the requirement, under Article

9 of the Act of July 26, 1947, that the Head of State must profess the Catholic religion.

It will be apparent, however, from this objective examination of the facts that a Protestant problem does exist in Spain. Though Spanish law obviously does not sanction discrimination, it embodies nothing more positive than a general statement of tolerance (Article 6 of the Charter of the Spanish People), which has never been clarified through the enactment of subsidiary laws and regulations. This in turn leads to the question: Why does this situation continue in 1963?

The persistence of the non-Catholic problem in Spain has what is essentially a legal explanation. As a consequence, the Spanish State has no choice but to define the de facto situation in so far as relations between the various religious denominations in our country are concerned; to determine what are the interests of the Spanish State in terms of the common good; and to request of the Holy See that, taking into account these interests and those of the Universal Church, it should resolve this question and indicate how the general principles ought to be applied to our particular circumstances.

It would be added that in submitting the problem to the Church of Rome the Spanish State has acted not merely out of respect for the papal directives previously referred to, but also because it is legally so obligated.

The Spanish State must, in the first place, be consistent with its Catholic faith, as stated in constitutional form in the Principles of the National Movement (Act of May 17, 1958), the Charter of the Spanish People, and the Act Providing for Succession to the Office of Head of the State (July 26, 1947). It is also bound by the provisions of the concordat with the Holy See of August 27, 1953, except in so far as the two powers have agreed otherwise.

Of particular importance in the concordat is a statement in the Final Protocol relating to Article 1 of the concordat. This statement specifies tolerance of private worship for non-Catholics of peninsular Spain while permitting public worship for those in the Spanish territories of Africa, this being in accord with the actual practice there.

We must therefore conclude that the Spanish State is unable to hasten the process of promulgating some form of legal status for the non-Catholic denominations of its own accord, but can do so only with the express agreement of the Holy See. Any settlement of the problem will have to deal with two separate matters: the individual rights of non-Catholics, and the status of the various non-Catholic associations before the law.

In so far as the individual rights of non-Catholics are concerned, the State must guarantee the free profession and practice, both private and public, of all religious faiths within the limits imposed by the moral order and the common good. It is this general principle which His Holiness Pope John XXIII has unequivocally endorsed in *Pacem in Terris.*

Though some individual rights are recognized by law, others are not expressly recognized or have in practice given rise to controversy. Among these the most important and the most discussed is the marriage problem. The difficulty for non-Catholics arises from Canon 1099, under which all persons baptized in the Catholic Church are considered to be subject to its regulations.

A highly controversial issue is the attendance of non-Catholics in military service at religious ceremonies. Despite the existence of subsidiary regulations excusing them from such attendance, it cannot be denied that the enactment of provisions to deal with this matter in a comprehensive way would have prevented some of the incidents that were widely publicized in the world press.

Another matter that has frequently been a bone of contention is the burial of non-Catholics. This problem has usually been tactfully solved in the larger cities but not in the small towns.

Concerning the legal status of non-Catholic associations, it must be pointed out that the right to form and join associations is guaranteed to all Spaniards under Article 16 of the Charter of the Spanish People and the Act of June 30, 1887. It is revealing that during the many years the latter law has been in force, non-Catholics, and more specifically Protestants, have not availed themselves of its provisions. Instead they have taken advantage of the provisions of mercantile law to set themselves up as foreign corporations, and thus be entitled to the constant protection of their respective flags.

In any event, the only way in which this more or less justified mistrust can be dissipated is to restate the right of association in unmistakable terms and clearly specify that it may be exercised for religious purposes. Satisfactory solutions can be found, too, for most of the other problems that Protestants today encounter in Spain, such as the opening and functioning of churches, cemeteries, schools and seminaries.

As regards publications, it is noteworthy that the British and Foreign Bible Society was authorized several weeks ago to resume its activities in Spain—a step that could serve as a pattern for a final solution of the question.

We have not dealt, in this short article, with all the questions that have given rise to complaints and controversy on the part of non-Catholic denominations in Spain. We do believe, however, that we have treated all the main issues, or rather, all but one—the thorny subject of proselytism.

In this matter, we wish to affirm our will to defend our Catholic unity as a precious asset to the Spanish nation; our satisfaction at seeing the terms in which this matter is being considered by the World Council of Churches, in the distinction it makes between "proselytizing" and "testimony"; and our filial trust in the Church and particularly in our Holy Father Pope Paul VI, who will point out the road we must take in order that the teachings of *Pacem in Terris* may become a living reality in Spain.

But even though it may fall to the Church of Rome to have the last word in this matter, all of us—Catholics and non-Catholics, Spaniards and non-Spaniards—can work together and, through prayer, mutual understanding and a genuine ecumenical outlook, contribute to achieve religious concord in Spain.

ROBERT A. GRAHAM
"Civil Rights" in the Church

¶The unspoken issue at Vatican II: A charter for Catholic writers and thinkers

During the dramatic first session of the Vatican Council, last October and November, probably no outside group followed the course of events with more personal concern than the Catholic writers and intellectuals of Europe. For some years now, the morale of this tiny but important elite has been low. These men feel that their function

as writers and thinkers at the service of the Church is not adequately recognized, especially in Rome. They protest that conditions are imposed on them that render their work sterile and their
position stultifying. Remedies intended to cure diseased members
have adversely affected the sound organs as well. Though these intellectuals have submitted with admirable obedience to the measures taken against them—their books have been removed from sale
or relegated to the "reserved" section of Catholic libraries, their
manuscripts sidetracked, and even their professorships taken away
from them—the wounds have cut deep.

As the Council opened, therefore, the intellectuals hoped against
hope that the Fathers would lift this weight from their minds. Some
of the most pessimistic among them predicted a "slaughter of the
intellectuals." All agreed, however, that if the existing trend was
not arrested, the Catholic intellectual, whether lay or clerical,
stood in jeopardy of being eliminated as a meaningful force in the
life of the Church.

This is not to say that these writers do not in some cases thoroughly deserve the admonitions they receive or the suspicion their
ideas arouse. It would be a rash apologist who undertook a blanket
defense of everything written in the past two decades by professors
in Catholic institutions. Dilettantism is rampant on the fringes of
that world. What is more, many a professor has been poorly served
by his own disciples. These masters can aptly lament, adapting an
old saying: "As for my reviewers, I can take care of them myself;
but God protect me from my students."

The protest we are considering here, however, is raised not by
triflers or nobodies, but by top-notch scholars whose learning and
good sense are equaled only by their loyalty to the Holy See and
their proved respect for the voice of the teaching Church. While
they fully acknowledge the prerogatives of the Church and its organs in safeguarding correct doctrine in faith and morals, these
scholars protest that the existing procedures for implementing this
high purpose do violence to elementary justice and are conducted
in casual disregard for charity. The refrain is that Church decisions,
however justified they may be, are too often taken and transmitted
in ways that are harsh and even unfair. Terse and peremptory, they
leave the point of controversy unclarified, and the person concerned
in a state of doubt. These circumstances, the scholars say, weaken
their force and, supernatural considerations aside, throw doubt on

their correctness from the purely human point of view. In the end, the prestige not only of the Holy Office but also of the Holy See is diminished. Is this, they ask, the true face of the *magisterium* of Holy Church?

It is difficult to furnish a bill of particulars for these protests. Those who are involved are humbly sparing of details, when indeed they have not been enjoined to keep silent. The Holy Office operates under a secrecy almost as severe as that of the confessional, and it never publishes its own rules, which it changes without promulgation. But this writer, in the course of repeated visits to Europe in recent years, prior to the Council, has heard complaints that present a fairly consistent pattern.

The following procedural practices of the Holy Office have come under particular criticism:

Books or articles are judged without the author's being heard in his own defense. Teachers are ordered to be removed from their posts without having any specific charge made against them, much less being given a chance to defend themselves.

Notice of the condemnation of a book is sometimes made public before the author himself is informed.

The reputation of authors is not adequately safeguarded. Little effort is made to differentiate between a writer with a distinguished record of service to the Church and another who is a declared enemy of the faith. Calumnious accusations against authors are not punished when their falsehood is discovered.

Even the bishop whose imprimatur has been granted to the edition condemned or ordered to be withdrawn from sale, is not consulted or informed.

Grounds for the condemnation are not given, except perhaps in an unofficial and allusive form, without a shred of canonical force, in the *Osservatore Romano*.

In disputed areas, such as modern philosophy, which require specialized knowledge, the decision is taken without consulting experts in the field as to the exact meaning of the writing under examination.

Some would answer such criticisms of the Holy Office by saying that the writers have only themselves to blame, because they dared to touch controversial questions. They would do better, it is said, to limit themselves to "safe" issues. Often is it said, too, that the Holy

Office's so-called victims virtually and perhaps knowingly invite a strong reaction by their imprudent and arbitrary sorties into dangerous terrain, made in a spirit of intellectual adventurism. This sort of answer, however, is both unrealistic and unhistorical.

It is unrealistic because, for the Catholic intellectual as for every intellectual, writing and publishing are the very air he breathes. His cast of mind and the talents God gave him lead him willy-nilly to the threshold of these "dangerous" questions, which are almost by definition the real questions of the day. These writers do not create the problems they write about. They take cognizance of questions already raised by non-Catholic thinkers and already widely circulating, if not dominant, in the non-Catholic world. The Catholic intellectual is driven spontaneously to interpret them in the light of his own faith.

It is unhistorical because theological science has always grown through discussion and publication. Many great theologians whose status is now unchallenged were regarded in their own day as dangerous innovators. Theology, precisely because it is rational thought, cannot stand still. There is always need for new answers —to new problems and old problems alike. If the group of Catholic intellectuals who now protest their treatment do not try to find these answers, no one else will. For no one else is capable of finding them.

Another answer to criticisms of the Holy Office's methods is that current procedures, while they may offend Anglo-Saxon, common-law notions of justice, are nevertheless quite legitimate. Officials in Rome are reported to be surprised that their practice is questioned. These procedures, they argue, have been developed through many years' experience, in conformity with the principles of Roman and canon law and the exigencies of the Church's *magisterium;* hence there is no need for change, much less for a "reform" of the Holy Office.

A prestigious name and an important papal document, however, can be invoked in confutation of the cliché that Roman and canon law reflects no concern for individual or "civil" rights. The name is that of Pope Benedict XIV, whose bull or constitution *Sollicita et Provida*, issued as long ago as July 9, 1753, laid down norms for the administration of the Index of Prohibited Books. Its prescriptions were ratified by Leo XIII and were for years prefixed to successive editions of the Index, until 1925, when for some reason they were dropped.

During the Council last autumn, the principles of Pope Benedict XIV were unearthed and circulated among the bishops. It is highly instructive to read these wise directives today. Benedict, while still Prospero Lambertini, was one of the most brilliant canonists of his time. Having taken a special interest in procedural law all his life, for his master work he systematized the process of the canonization of saints.

Pope Benedict clearly grasped the need to safeguard the interests of the individual whose writings are under examination in Rome. In his *Sollicita et Provida,* these points deserve particular notice:

When a book is prohibited with the proviso "until corrected" (*donec corrigatur*), the decision should not be immediately published. Instead, it should be withheld so that the author may be informed as to what is to be deleted, changed or corrected.

The argument that what is being judged is not the person, but his doctrine and his works (and that therefore there is no need to consult the author or give him an opportunity for a defense), is not to be accepted without qualification. It is indeed the concern of the Church to warn the faithful against error. But it is nevertheless just and prudent for the body examining a work to hear the author in his own defense, or at least to appoint one of its consultors to defend him.

The objections made against a book should be communicated to the author or his representative, as the officials are authorized to do.

As for the qualifications of consultors whose advice is to be taken: "Those only should be admitted who possess, through long study, a knowledge of the matters with which the various denounced books deal." "*Decet enim de artibus solos artifices judicare*"—"For only craftsmen should judge the works of their craft."

Judgment should not be made on the basis of ambiguous passages and others taken out of context. Where a distinguished Catholic author is concerned, "equity itself" would seem to demand that the doubt be resolved in his favor.

The Catholic intellectuals of Europe with direct knowledge of the workings of the Holy Office claim that these sage prescriptions of a Pope dead two centuries are being honored more in the breach

than in the observance. Others will go farther and say they are not
being honored at all. It should be noted, however, that the late
Pope Pius XII, in his 1943 encyclical on Holy Scripture, *Divino
Afflante Spiritu,* warned that Scripture commentators must judge,
"not only with equity and justice but also with supreme charity,"
the efforts of those exegetes who are striving to unravel the most
difficult questions.

The crisis of today's Catholic intellectuals is more than the personal drama of a few individuals. At issue is the problem of finding
a workable relationship between true intellectualism, on the one
hand, and, on the other, a Church which, in virtue of its divine
constitution and mission, exercises the right to determine without
appeal what teachings its adherents may hold.

Traditionally, of course, the Church has contended that there is
no basis for conflict between the natural order and the supernatural.
For faith, though it completes reason, does not contradict it. This
basically sound position would be easier to demonstrate convinc-
ingly if the dedicated Catholic intellectual, pending definitive statements from the teaching authority, were able to go about his work
of criticism, reflection and exposition under conditions of relative
security and peace of mind.

It is evident that the Catholic intellectual, as a Catholic, does
acknowledge the high authority of the Church, the validity of
whose supernatural teaching, as Pope Pius XII stressed in one
of his messages, does not depend on purely human reasoning. He
therefore has a right to expect certain guarantees of equitable and
courteous treatment. It is to be hoped that these guarantees will be
provided for at the next session of the Council or in the forthcoming revision of canon law.

The unrest of the intellectuals appears, to certain influential
circles in Rome, and perhaps also to the average priest and the
faithful, as a wrongheaded impatience with restraint. This impatience, they remember, has in the past led some intellectuals to set
themselves above and against the Church's teaching authority.
They recall the Modernist crisis, a storm that rent the Catholic
community during the pontificate of Pope St. Pius X, in the first
decade of this century. The impact of that crisis is still felt in the
Church, and it is no wonder that the effervescence of *avant-garde*
writers causes worry.

One can almost hear a Roman veteran of the anti-Modernist war wearily saying to himself: "We have gone through all this before, and the phases are almost predictable. First you have a bright and apostolic-minded young Catholic scholar, often a priest, who wants to convert the intellectual world. But he is all sail and no anchor. Nothing suits him better, in his self-appointed mission, than to 'Christianize' Marx or Hegel, Darwin or Kant, Heidegger or Comte —or to 'Catholicize' Luther and Calvin, for that matter—on the grounds that this is the way modern man thinks and we must, for-sooth, 'speak his language.'

"His attempt to adapt Christian theology and culture to modern times and modern philosophy," our veteran commentator goes on, "turns out to involve a wholesale jettisoning of the basic tenets of our faith by emptying Christian revelation of its substance. While claiming a broad outlook, he tries to straitjacket theology into the very narrow framework of ideas currently in popular favor. How many, and what kind of, converts—intellectuals or others—are won by this capitulation all down the line? These self-styled intellectu-als, who claim to be true defenders of the Church in the modern world and to have the only prescription for salvation, prove in the end disobedient and irresponsible sons of Holy Church, tossed by every wind of intellectual fashion. Is the Church, custodian of Christ's salvific teaching and shepherd of the flock entrusted to it, to stand idly by while false prophets fill the air with their rantings? The sacred deposit of faith is not the plaything of dabblers or an intellectual kindergarten for angry young men in academic garb!"

Is this an authentic portrait of the present crop of top-flight intellectuals in Europe or elsewhere? Is it fair to link these Catholic writers of today with the Modernists of sixty years past? It is un-fortunately a matter of historical record that some prominent schol-ars in the early nineteen hundreds gravely compromised the faith with their poorly conceived attempts to adapt Catholic theology to modern thinking. The later apostasy of such intellectuals was a measure of their disbelief and pride, though they all posed to the bitter end as saviors of the Church. But today's writers have given, on the contrary, an exemplary display of humble devotion to the cause of the Church. Their very anguish is testimony to the con-flict caused within them by the actions of the organs of the Church they wish only to serve. By their nearly heroic submission under circumstances of which this article gives some slight hint, they have rendered dramatic proof of their respect, unknown among the Modernists, for the sacred teaching authority of the Church.

As it turned out, developments at the first session of Vatican II brought great reassurance to Catholic intellectuals. Although the work of the preparatory commissions seemed to bode ill, the bishops did not rally to the thesis that the Church today faces a revival of Modernism to be combated by redoubled vigilance and rigorous condemnations of suspect theses. As Pope John declared in his inaugural address to the Fathers in St. Peter's on October 11, a council would not have been necessary for such condemnations. The Council, in the now famous debate on the sources of revelation, declined to accept the draft proposal, which would have gone farther than the Council of Trent or Vatican I and seemed to be based on the theory that everything ambiguous had to be clarified and every loose plank in theology nailed down then and there.

The pastoral approach, rather than the doctrinal, will prevail in the forthcoming discussions when the Council convenes again. It is fair to suppose that the Fathers, without dreaming of discounting the importance of safeguarding correct doctrine, believe that, in the end, orthodoxy of opinion may be just as well defended through open and free discussion as through perhaps premature decisions motivated by an excess of caution. It is not too much to anticipate also, and for the same reasons, a review of the procedures by which the Roman authorities carry out their mission of vigilance.

This review, it is hardly necessary to repeat, should not simply embrace the reform of the Index. On the need for such a reform no real dispute seems to exist in Rome in any quarter. What is more important and necessary, in view of the experiences of recent years, is a review of the Holy Office's own conception of its function. Its role is essentially negative, that of vigilance over orthodoxy of doctrine; in practice, because of its all-pervasive authority, it has taken over in effect the direction of the progress of research. For such a positive task it is completely unqualified. Some balance needs to be established between the two exigencies of orthodoxy and scholarship. The Holy Office, duly conscious of its negative mission of vigilance, is not the proper agency for guaranteeing such a balance.

A charter for the intellectual apostolate, embodying both rights and duties, may emerge from Vatican II. In the search for ways and means of assuring fairness and equity, along with full recognition of the Church's *magisterium*, two suggestions occur to this writer as worthy of special attention. On the one hand, it is desirable to eliminate or reduce to a minimum the practice of anonymous denunciations, on which the Holy Office so often seems to rely. For this system opens the door too wide to calumnious charges by incompetent persons. Such denunciations only embitter and discourage the parties accused.

The other suggestion concerns a related failing on the part of the embattled intellectuals themselves. Have they perhaps unwittingly contributed to their own predicament? This writer strongly suspects, without being able to cite any clear-cut instances, that writers today suffer from an excess of loyalty to their class. In an instinctive but self-defeating tactic of defense, they close ranks and fail to criticize each other's writings with vigor and sharpness, though this is as much their duty as their right. By their comparative silence concerning dangerous trends among their colleagues, or their slowness in denouncing publicly the half-baked writings of amateurs, they seem to give tacit consent to them. In this way they only provide ammunition to those who suspect a conspiracy among intellectuals, and so they do their own cause great harm. The price of free discussion of their own personal scholarly work should be their willingness to give each other the merciless but fruitful criticism that marked theological debate in the best periods of the medieval university.

JOHN COURTNEY MURRAY
On Religious Liberty

¶Freedom is the most distinctively American issue before the Council

The issue of religious liberty is of the highest interest to me both as a theologian and as an American. It is, as it were, *the* American issue at the Council. The American episcopate is greatly pleased that the issue has finally appeared on the agenda of the Council, notwithstanding many efforts to block discussion of it. Through Cardinal Spellman the American bishops made a strong intervention, demanding that the issue be presented to the conciliar Fathers. And all of them are prepared strongly to support, and indeed to strengthen, the text that has been written by the Secretariat for Promoting Christian Unity.

Actually, two texts are to be presented. The first is the text of Chapter Five of the Decree on Ecumenism, entitled "On Religious Freedom." The second is the lengthy *relatio* of Bishop Emile De Smedt, of Bruges. This latter document is the more important, in a sense, since it develops at length the rationale of the decree. I shall therefore undertake to state briefly the tenor and scope of the decree in the light of the *relatio*.

The Secretariat for Promoting Christian Unity composed its text before Pope John XXIII published his encyclical *Pacem in Terris*. But the doctrine of the text is identical with the doctrine of the encyclical. The text represents the term of a lengthy development of theological thought in the matter, and the encyclical confirms the validity of this development.

There are, in general, two essential points of doctrine. First, it is asserted that every man by right of nature (*jure naturae*) has the right to the free exercise of religion in society according to the dictates of his personal conscience. This right belongs essentially to the dignity of the human person as such. Secondly, the juridical consequences of this right are asserted, namely, that an obligation falls on other men in society, and upon the state in particular, to acknowledge this personal right, to respect it in practice, and to promote its free exercise. This is, in a mode of general statement, the heart of the matter.

Four reasons are given for the proclamation of this doctrine. All of them derive from the concrete situation of the world today. First, it is necessary today to state the true doctrine of the Church with regard to religious freedom in society, as this doctrine has been clarified by theological reflection, and also by political experience, over the past few generations.

Secondly, it is necessary today for the Church to assume a universal patronage of the dignity of the human person and of man's essential freedoms, in an age in which totalitarian tyranny has imposed itself upon nearly half of the human race.

Third, we are living in the age of the religiously pluralist society, as it is called. Men of all religions and of no religion must live together in conditions of justice, peace and civic friendship, under

equitable laws that protect the whole range of human rights, notably including the right to religious freedom. It is therefore necessary for the Church to show the way to justice and peace in society,
by espousing the cause of human freedom, which is, as John XXIII
taught, both an essential end of organized society and also the
essential method and style of political life.

Fourthly and finally, we are living in an age in which a great
ecumenical hope has been born. The goal of Christian unity lies,
of course, beyond the horizons of our present vision. We do, however, know that the path to this far goal can lie only along the road
of freedom—social, civil, political and religious freedom. Hence
the Church must assist in the work of creating conditions of freedom in human society; this task is integral to the spiritual mission
of the Church, which is to be herself the spiritual unity of mankind
and to assist all men in finding this unity. These, in brief, are the
four reasons for the decree on religious freedom.

The *relatio* proceeds to clear up the confusions and misconcep-
tions with regard to the concept of religious freedom which remain
the heritage of the 19th-century conflict between the Church and
the laicist ideology that issued from the Enlightenment, so called,
and the French Revolution. Briefly, the Church today must still
reject a concept of religious freedom that would be based on the
ideology of the "outlaw conscience," which asserted that the human conscience is not bound by any divine laws, but only by such
norms as it individually creates for itself.

Again, the Church today must still reject a concept of religious
freedom that would be based on the ideology of religious indifferentism, that is, on the notion that all religions are equally true, or
equally false. Furthermore, the Church today must still reject a
concept of religious freedom that would be based on the ideology
of doctrinal relativism, that is, on the philosophical notion that there
is no objective criterion of truth.

These 19th-century ideologies, which still exist among us in one
or other way, falsified the notion of religious freedom, just as they
misconceived the dignity of man. Man is not God; he is only the
image of God. God alone is the Lord. And man's essential dignity
consists in his dependence on God alone; man's essential freedom
requires that he should be governed, in the end, only by the will
of God. From this point of view, the true notion of religious freedom begins to appear.

In consequence of his personal dignity, man, in his quest for God, has a right to be free from all manner of coercion or compulsion that might be brought to bear on him by other men, by social or political institutions, or by the power of human law. Man's quest for God, man's adhesion to the truth of God, must be free. This is itself a divine law, which is written in the nature of man, and written even more clearly in the gospel of Christ. True religious freedom therefore consists, negatively, in the immunity of the human person from all coercion in what concerns his personal relations with God, and, positively, in the free exercise of religion within civil society.

This is the conception of religious freedom that is contained in the conciliar text and developed in the *relatio*. I must confess immediately that I do not find it adequate, though I think it is true as far as it goes. One must have in mind that it will be the duty of the Council to establish the formula, "religious freedom," within the Christian vocabulary, to define or describe its full sense and meaning, and to do this in such a way that there may be at least general agreement among all Christians, Catholic and non-Catholic, with regard to the essential content of this formula. I hope therefore that in the course of the conciliar discussion the concept will be more fully elaborated. However, I shall not enter this subject here.

The intention of the decree is pastoral and ecumenical. Therefore it undertakes to define the attitude that Catholics ought to maintain and exhibit toward their fellow Christians and toward all men. This attitude is based on the Catholic doctrine with regard to the necessary freedom of the act of Christian faith. God our Father through Christ our Lord freely spoke to men His word of salvation, which is a word of truth and love, an invitation to an interpersonal relationship between man and the one God, living and true, who is Father, Son and Holy Spirit. God's word was freely spoken; it is for man to respond to it freely. The response, whether acceptance or rejection, is a matter of personal responsibility. No man may abdicate this responsibility. No man may assume this responsibility for another, but only for himself.

The decision, for God or against him, must be a personal decision. Hence no man, and certainly no Christian, may bring to bear any kind of coercion, physical or moral or legal, on another. This would be to contravene the essential law of the divine economy of salvation, which is that men must accept God's gift of grace freely, or not at all. Therefore the theology of the act of faith obliges Christians to an attitude of respect and reverence toward others who do not share their faith. This is not religious indifferentism. One does not affirm that truth and error are equal in the sight of God. One must, however, affirm the dignity of the human person and the freedom of the act of personal religious decision.

All this is quite clear. But the decree and the *relatio* enter another area, which is most difficult. Religious freedom is to be a right whose exercise takes place in society—in a civil society that is politically organized, that receives its structure from a juridical order, and that is governed by duly constituted political authority. Here the difficulty begins. Within organized society no human right, not even the right to religious freedom, is unlimited in its exercise. Hence the essential question is: what are the principles according to which the social exercise of the right to religious freedom may be justly and legitimately limited? Or, from another point of view, what is the competence of civil government in regard to the exercise of the right to religious freedom in society? Concretely, what are the canons of jurisprudence that must control the use of the coercive weapon of law in this most delicate and sensitive field? These questions are extremely difficult. But they cannot be avoided. Religious freedom is not simply an ethical or moral problem. It is also a constitutional problem. One meets the problem in its full concreteness in the order of law and government.

In my opinion the decree is not sufficiently clear and explicit in its dealing with this problem of social and legal limitation of the right to religious freedom. Rightly enough, it asserts the principle, which is also a fact, that the exercise of the right to religious freedom, since it takes place publicly and in society, is subject to some legitimate restrictions. These restrictions, it says, may be imposed in the name of the common good, or in the name of the rights of others. All this is true enough. But I find it too vague. An appeal to the common good, as the ground for legal restrictions on religious freedom, may be no more than the invocation of a *raison d'état*, which is dangerous doctrine. Moreover, the allegation of the rights of others, again as the ground for restricting religious freedom, may be no more than a veiled invocation of the rights of a majority, which again is dangerous doctrine.

The *relatio* is somewhat more satisfactory. It clearly adopts the juridical conception of the state which was developed by Pius XII, and even more sharply emphasized by John XXIII in *Pacem in Terris*. These Popes laid aside the more Aristotelian, ethical conception of the state that is to be found in Leo XIII. The *relatio* therefore makes clear that the primary element in the common good consists in the legal protection and promotion of the whole order of personal rights and freedoms which are proper to the human person as such. Therefore the *relatio* also makes clear that an infringement of the personal rights of man, including notably his right to religious freedom, cannot be justified by an appeal to the common good. Such an infringement of personal rights would be a violation of the common good itself. This is good political philosophy and jurisprudence.

I think, however, it is necessary to take one further step. And here I speak as an American, out of the Anglo-American tradition of politics, law and jurisprudence. The American constitutional system is based squarely on two fundamental principles: first, man is endowed by his Creator with certain inalienable rights; second, government and the order of law exist primarily for the protection and promotion of these rights. These principles were clearly affirmed by Pius XII and by John XXIII. However, the American system also enshrines another principle, namely, the incompetence of government as judge or arbiter in the field of religious truth, as also, for instance, in the field of art and science.

Government is a secular authority whose competence is limited to the temporal and terrestrial affairs of men who must live together in justice, peace and freedom. Government therefore would act *ultra vires* (beyond its scope) if it were to undertake to judge this religion to be true and that religion to be false. Government would be acting even more evidently *ultra vires* if it were to enforce upon citizens, by the medium of law, any kind of theological judgment; if, that is, it were to assert by law that a particular religion—say, the Catholic religion—ought to be the religion of the national community.

This principle, which asserts the incompetence of secular political authority in the field of religion, is deeply embedded in the true political tradition of the Christian West. It is also affirmed within the theological tradition of the Church. Leo XIII, for instance, made it quite clear that political authority has no part whatsoever in the care of souls (*cura animarum*) or in the control of the minds of men (*regimen animorum*). It is, of course, true that this political principle was obscured in Europe for centuries, largely in consequence of the rise of royal absolutism and the "Union of Throne and Altar." The true tradition was, however, preserved in the American constitutional system. Absolutism never set foot in America, much to the joy both of the Church and of the American people. Together with my fellow countrymen, both Catholic and non-Catholic, I should like to see this principle asserted in the final conciliar text on religious freedom. It is, I think, essential to the case for religious freedom in society. It completes the theological and ethical arguments by adding to them a sound political argument. And this political principle, namely, that political authority is incompetent in the field of religion, needs particularly to be invoked when there is question of legal limitations to be imposed on the free exercise of religion in society.

The *relatio* deals at length with another problem in the present matter. It is a theological problem. The fact is that, at first sight, the affirmations of *Pacem in Terris* with regard to the right of religious freedom and with regard to the juridical consequences of this right, seem at first sight to be directly contrary to certain utterances of the Church in the 19th century, which seem to have denied this right. The *relatio* deals with this problem in the only way in which it may legitimately be dealt with, that is, by regarding it as a problem of true and genuine development, both in the doctrine of the Church and in her pastoral solicitude for the dignity and freedom of man.

In conclusion, I might note that two essential questions face the Council. The first is pastoral and ecumenical. The Church has always fought for her own freedom and for the freedom of her children. The question today is, whether the Church should extend her pastoral solicitude beyond her own boundaries and assume an active patronage of the freedom of the human person, who was created by God as his image, who was redeemed by the blood of Christ, who stands today under a massive threat to everything that human dignity and personal freedom mean. The second question is doctrinal. Is the assumption of this universal pastoral solicitude warranted? Is it grounded in the doctrinal tradition of the Church with regard to human dignity and the rights of man? I think the answer must be affirmative, if only the tradition of the Church is understood to be what it is, namely, a tradition of growth in fuller understanding of the truth.

G. B. HARRISON
Words to Pray With?

¶Let's have good, modern English in the forthcoming translation of the liturgy

Of all English translations of sacred writing, the King James Bible is rightly regarded as supreme. Great care was taken to organize the teams of translators. Moreover, the King had commanded the bishops to communicate with all learned men in their dioceses and to collect their suggestions. Now that the liturgy is to be translated into English for public use, that example is worth following.

There are several popular missals in English, but in none of them is the translation up to the standard of the King James Bible or those earlier versions of the missal made by the ill-starred Cranmer, which are the glory of the Anglican Book of Common Prayer. In our eagerness to offer the Mass in English, there is some danger that we may settle for inadequate versions that will clog rather than intensify devotion. For immediate use, one of the existing versions in English can be temporarily adopted; but before a permanent version is authorized for all English-speaking Catholics, the aims, principles and methods of translation should be fully discussed and (so far as mortal frailty allows) agreed upon. It will take time.

It is obviously desirable that there should be one uniform version prescribed for all. Familiarity with the words aids devotion; unfamiliarity distracts. Most of us, when attending Mass away from home and joining in the final prayers at the foot of the altar, have been jarred by a different order of words for "Hail, Holy Queen" or "St. Michael the Archangel." It will be far worse if we meet new twists of language with every other prayer.

There are several problems, not always appreciated. The Canon of our Latin Mass goes back to at least the time of St. Gregory the Great—more than 1,350 years. If we are to abandon that Mass, the substitution should be durable, if not till 3000 A.D., at least for a couple of generations. It must—if the aims of those who promote it are to be realized—be in modern English, free from archaic phrases or (what is worse) sanctimonious verbosity. Such words as "vouch-safe," "beseech," "professor" (meaning believer), "bounden," "deign," "deem," "oblation," "handmaid"—all taken from current missals in English—are outmoded and have ceased to be part of the living language of those for whom the changes are to be made. Should such words be changed? Or retained? If retained, then the people will be asked to pray in words that are either hazy or meaningless. If we are to pray in words that come naturally to us, then modern words must be substituted—if they can be found.

There is no easy answer to this problem. Take, for instance, the two most sacred of all our prayers—the Our Father and the Hail Mary. Both prayers in the current version contain words that no one now uses in normal conversation. "Our Father, who art in heaven, hallowed be Thy Name." "Hallowed" is almost medieval. When used nowadays, it has a poetic and therefore slightly unnatural sound; it is no longer part of our common vocabulary. Small wonder that the little boy was overheard to murmur by his bedside: "Harold be thy name." "Trespass" also has only a narrow legal meaning today.

Should we retain "thou," "thee," "thine," "art"? Maybe we should, as a sign of adoration in prayer. But if so, we are preserving archaic and therefore artificial forms of speech; and all the masters of prayer urge us to talk to God naturally. Or again, "Hail Mary, full of grace." No one now uses "hail" as a greeting. Yet we rightly shudder to think of some of the possible substitutes.

Just before the Pater Noster in the Canon of the Mass occur the words *Praeceptis salutaribus moniti, et divina institutione formati, audemus dicere.* One version reads: "Taught by Thy saving precepts and guided by the divine institution." Another offers: "Directed by saving precepts and guided by the divine teaching." We ourselves would feel embarrassed if anyone were to address us with such stiff formality.

Nor is the difficulty confined to the prayers of the Mass. The right choice of words is as necessary in those popular devotions usually provided for private use before or after communion. Some missals include the Universal Prayer of Clement XI, which is a fine example of stark, balanced Latinity. It begins: *Credo, Domine, sed credam firmius; spero, sed sperem securius; amo, sed amem ardentius; doleo, sed doleam vehementius*. It is not easy to reproduce this in English, but perhaps the following could be pruned: "O my God, I believe in Thee; do Thou strengthen my faith. All my hopes are in Thee; do Thou secure them. I love Thee; teach me to love Thee more and more. I am sorry that I have offended Thee; do Thou increase my sorrow." There are thus 46 English words for 17 Latin ones. A little later, the prayer continues: *Studeam superioribus obedire, inferioribus subvenire*. This, in one version, is rendered: "May Thy grace help me to be submissive to my superiors, condescending to my inferiors." God forbid! That was the attitude of the Pharisee toward the publican. It is not what Clement XI meant at all.

Vocabulary and right use of words, however, are only one of the problems. For prayers offered aloud, either by the priest alone or by the people in unison, rhythm is as important. One of the advantages of the Anglican Book of Common Prayer is that its compilers had such a magnificent sense of rhythm. The prayers pray themselves: "Lighten our darkness, we beseech Thee, O Lord; and by thy great mercy defend us from all perils and dangers of this night; for the love of thy only Son, our Saviour, Jesus Christ." Or the version of the collect for the 19th Sunday after Trinity: "O God, forasmuch as without Thee we are not able to please thee: Mercifully grant, that thy Holy Spirit may in all things direct and rule our hearts; through Jesus Christ our Lord." Compared with this, the following Catholic version of the latter is drab and stilted: "Let the exercise of Thy mercy direct our hearts, we beg of Thee, O Lord, since without Thee, we are not able to please Thee."

One of the deservedly most popular of the bilingual missals is the "Knox," which gives the Knox translation for passages of Scripture and a new translation of the prayers. This version has a great advantage over most others, because the translators, abandoning the older English phraseology, have thought through the Latin to produce a rendering entirely new, unfamiliar and arresting; it forces its user to realize the real meaning of the prayers. Nevertheless, though I have never heard the English of this version prayed aloud, I doubt whether its rhythms would hold up to public recitation. Thus the Common Preface: "Right indeed it is and just, proper and for our welfare, that we should always and everywhere give thanks to thee, holy Lord, almighty Father, eternal God, through Christ our Lord. It is through him that thy majesty is praised by Angels, adored by Dominions, feared by Powers; through him that the heavens and the celestial Virtues join with the blessed Seraphim in one glad hymn of praise."

These examples show considerable difference between the various English versions. Before the perfect translation can be made, the translators must agree on just what the Latin words *mean*. That is not so simple as it sounds. Comparison of several popular English missals shows sometimes substantially different shades of meaning. In one, the last clause of the Nicene creed is rendered thus: "In the Church that is one, holy, Catholic, and founded upon the apostles, I put my trust. —I hold to only one baptism for effecting the remission of sins. —Hopefully I look forward to the resurrection of those who are dead and to a future life." Between this version and the more usual translation there is perceptible change of meaning: "And in one, holy, catholic and apostolic Church. I confess one baptism for the remission of sins. And I look for the resurrection of the dead. And the life of the world to come."

Latin hymns offer an even greater difficulty. Probably it is too much to expect that any English translation can ever reproduce the original meter, rhythm and dignity of the Latin because of the natural looseness of the English tongue, which often requires three or more English words for one Latin. The Knox missal, for instance, renders the "Tantum Ergo Sacramentum" thus:

> Down in adoration falling
> Lo, the sacred Host we hail;
> Lo, o'er ancient forms departing
> Newer rites of grace prevail;
> Faith for all defects supplying
> Where the feeble senses fail.

The translator into English is not only handicapped by having to find English words to match the Latin; he is forced also to fit his words into meter and to find rhymes. Few attempts to translate the Latin poetry succeed in avoiding poetic clichés and outworn sentiments. Very seldom does the writer succeed in producing a version that evokes the original devotional responses. Too many hymns just repel the sensitive reader.

This problem also needs much thought and discussion. Maybe the answer is that hymn writers should break altogether with conventional notions and look for new forms that will express the modernization of the Church. We shall lose more than we gain if we try to substitute the usual kind of tinkling ditty for the original hymns of St. Thomas Aquinas and the others.

For the final translation of the liturgy, then, much thought and infinite tact are needed. Decisions should doubtless rest with a small committee; but if so, it should include theologians to insure that the right doctrinal words are used, liturgists to look after the form, but also some with a delicate feeling for words and their sounds. These final arbiters of propriety and orthodoxy would be greatly aided if all who may be interested are invited to submit suggestions. Lay cooperation might indeed be helpful; for skill in the art of translating from the Latin is not confined to religious. Such an invitation might even reveal inspired hymnologists as yet unknown. Holy Church needs them at the present time.

But there is something further. Words affect us on more than one level. On the surface they affect us by their meanings, in the subsoil by their sounds, especially when combined into rhythms, and in the depths through the fusion of meaning, rhythm and association. And it is in the depths that the spirit communes with spirit. Nothing but perfect expression can suffice for the union of God and man in the Mass.

SECTION VIII

FOR SOCIAL JUSTICE

JOHN W. CLARK
Is Business Socially Responsible?

¶The "inexorable laws of the market place" must yield to justice
for neighbor

The middle 1960's mark a time of crisis and decision for American
business. Businessmen are beginning to understand, perhaps as
never before, their role in American society. Many are becoming
keenly aware of the social character of their decisions and are calling on the whole business community to commit itself to a doctrine
of social responsibility. At the same time, a hard-core revolt is developing against these advocates of a new business conscience. This
revolt is not just a minor skirmish on the fringes of our economic
system. It represents an ideological battle that is one of the most
important developments of our time. The stakes are extremely
high—higher than most businessmen realize. For the future course
of American capitalism will in all likelihood follow the route
charted by whoever wins out.

The concept of social responsibility is, of course, not new.
Neither is its application to the business area. Msgr. John A. Ryan,
Bishop Francis J. Haas and Fr. John F. Cronin are among those
who have in the past urged its acceptance as an operational creed.
But never before have so many businessmen and so many scholars
of leading universities supported it. The last five years have wit-
nessed such a widespread acceptance of obligations above and
beyond the immediate goal of maximum profits, or "profit maximization," that they may be truly characterized as the beginning
years of social responsibility.

At first sight, resistance to the doctrine of social responsibility is
difficult to understand. Like motherhood, the new creed is something that is hard to oppose. Its apostles plead for a sense of responsibility toward interests beyond those of the stockholder: a
concern for the welfare of employees, suppliers and customers of
the corporation, and for the community as a whole, as well. Open

hostility to such a philosophy carries with it a stigma of selfishness, materialism, greed and sometimes even inhumanity.

Yet the opposition grows. More and more business leaders are speaking out against the new creed, arguing the case against the corporate conscience, urging a return to faith in "free enterprise" as a provider of the social good. Indeed, so strong has the dissent grown that it is beginning to challenge the new creed itself. These attacks on the doctrine of social responsibility are not unreasoned, emotional arguments. Quite the contrary. They are the result of mature and carefully worked-out thinking. They are expressed articulately and forcefully.

Why does such strong opposition arise to what appears no more than a humane mitigation of a relentless price mechanism? Among many charges, the advocates of revolt have leveled three theoretical objections to the concept of social responsibility.

The new creed, they hold, does not simply mitigate the more inhumane aspects of the price mechanism, as the advocates of social responsibility suggest. Rather, it undermines and weakens the market mechanism itself. By introducing into the business unit a variety of non-economic goals, the singleness of purpose of the free-enterprise system is so diverted that the one goal that best recommends the capitalist system—the efficient production of goods—is likely to be lost. As Theodore Levitt, a Chicago business consultant, puts it in his article, "The Dangers of Social Responsibility" (*Harvard Business Review*, Sept.-Oct., 1958): "The power which the corporation gains as a sort of demichurch it will lose as an agency of profit-motive capitalism. Indeed, as the profit motive becomes increasingly sublimated, capitalism will become only a shadow—the torpid remains of a creative dynamism which was and might have been."

And having cast aside the market mechanism, what does the new creed offer in its place? What means does it provide for measuring economic performance? Here too, the dissenters hold, the new creed seems to fail. For as Gerhard Andlinger, a management consultant, observes, in place of the single concrete criterion of profit maximization, what is now proposed is that each independent manager should follow the inner light of his own conscience. But, he asks, in an article entitled "The Crucible of Our Business Creeds" (*Business Horizons*, Fall, 1959): "What about the rather frightening prospect of thousands of thoroughly professional managers all ad-

ministering their individual companies by following their individual
social consciences in living up to antithetic and contradictory responsibilities? How this can result in the greatest common good
. . . is difficult to rationalize."

Serious as this first objection is, it does not tell the full story of
the evil consequences that those in revolt against the doctrine of
social responsibility foresee as its result. Even more serious, they
contend, is the effect the new creed will have on democracy itself.
For we must remember what this doctrine implies. It implies that
the corporation, an essentially materialistic organization, should
extend its influence over the widest possible range of human endeavor—over education, religion, politics, art, leisure and all else
that can fall under the influence of corporate decision-making. For
the new corporation is concerned with the whole gamut of human
values. Nothing that is of concern to man himself can be a matter
of indifference to a socially responsible business. To be sure, the
business will have nothing but the highest motives in this activity;
it will encourage only what it sincerely believes to be best for society. But this can be a dangerous thing. As Mr. Levitt observes in
his article: "We are against the all-embracing welfare state not because we are against welfare, but because we are against centralized
power and the harsh social discipline it so ineluctably produces.
We do not want a pervasive welfare state in government, and we
do not want it in unions. And for the same reason we should not
want it in corporations."

The corporation should strictly confine its role in society to its
economic function for still another reason. For the corporation is
not a democratic society; quite the contrary, it is built upon the
authoritarian concept of private property. It is hardly desirable that
such an institution should extend its influence, and with it the influence of a powerful few, to the non-economic values of modern
life. For democracy to flourish, then, the corporation should scru-
pulously restrict its activity to its economic objectives.

The third objection of the advocates of revolt is related to the
defense that some offer on behalf of social responsibility. The corporate conscience has been described as not unlike the conscience
of a feudal nobility. In the 11th century, to use an example of A. A.
Berle (*The 20th Century Capitalist Revolution*), Duke Rollo meted
out justice to all who had been wronged. As the Duke went from
place to place throughout Normandy, any aggrieved person could

cry: "Ha! Rollo!" and the Duke would then and there stop and hear his grievance, "deciding it according to the law of God and good conscience."

According to Walter Adams, professor of economics at Michigan State University ("Corporate Giantism, Ethics and the Public Interest," *Review of Social Economy*, March, 1963), one deficiency in the new creed is that there is no way of assuring that corporations will be headed by Duke Rollos. But even with Rollo, he adds, the system of social responsibility provides no compulsive control, no servo-mechanism that necessarily sanctions those who fail to heed its precepts. And even if such a system of sanctions could be worked out, the doctrine of the corporate conscience is so obscure and unstructured that it is grossly inadequate to provide a guide for action. The system of social responsibility is so much a collection of generalities that it is inoperable even under a leader with the maximum of good will.

These three objections by no means exhaust the list of charges leveled against the new creed. But they represent the most cogent arguments mustered by the advocates of revolt, and they point to the major theoretical problems of the concept of social responsibility.

The first objection is both serious and fundamental. If the doctrine of social responsibility destroys our capitalist system, it is indeed worthy of mistrust. But does it? Just how completely does the new philosophy undermine the traditional faith in the market mechanism? To determine this we need to look at the market mechanism as it exists today.

The picture is not an altogether reassuring one. As a matter of fact, the realities of the market place seem to have little in common with the descriptive models furnished by traditional theorists. Free competition, the prerequisite for a properly functioning price mechanism, seems to be in very short supply. Various terms have been used to define the market structure of some of the most important industries in today's economy: oligopoly, monopolistic or imperfect competition, countervailing power. But what it all adds up to is that producers today often possess a market power that renders the model of the market mechanism somewhat less effective as an arbiter of trade. Top executives of many of our largest corporations unquestionably exercise a certain discretion in regard to price, quality and other market factors; and this is enough to make us wonder just how much it means to adhere abolutely to the market mechanism as the ultimate rationale of the modern capitalist economy.

The simple fact is that the market mechanism, important as it is, is not working smoothly enough to provide adequate control in and of itself. It is operative, of course, and in a very real way; but its operation does not extend perfectly to all times and all places. To propose such a system as the alternative to the doctrine of social responsibility may be logically consistent. Unfortunately, it is not sufficiently relevant to conditions as they are.

But what about those industries that still remain competitive? Would not the concept of social responsibility, in these cases at least, substitute private ethical judgments for an efficient and automatic control mechanism? The question is a difficult one. It goes to the very core of the extreme philosophy of free enterprise proposed by a few of its ardent defenders. What we are asking is this: Can any system of production be fully automatic? Can ethical judgment be completely removed from the parameters of human conduct? And if it can, is such a condition desirable?

Those who propose an automatic mechanism to substitute for ethical judgment may be coming dangerously close to destroying the autonomy of the individual. If a man loses his responsibility for his acts, he loses that quality which has made his activity worthy of a man. We ought to examine seriously the far-reaching implications of a theory that replaces personal responsibility with an automatic control mechanism.

The second objection to the concept of social responsibility likewise needs thoughtful consideration. Do these relationships of social responsibility arise simply because businessmen choose to acknowledge them? Or are they, rather, actual parameters of executive decision-making, whether managers acknowledge them or not? Such decision-making may profoundly influence the social system of which business is a part. Simply to ignore certain harsh consequences of economic decisions does not change the fact that the consequences are there. On the contrary, it invites other institutions of society to step in and grapple with the problems that managers have chosen to ignore. Indeed the advocates of revolt against social responsibility need to ask themselves this very pertinent question: By advocating that the corporation ignore noneconomic parameters, are we not putting the corporation in a position where it will force the government to step in and take away certain prerogatives that now remain in private hands? Will the abdication of responsibility bring freedom or restriction to business? Certainly the long-run welfare of the business enterprise cannot be ignored even by a profit-centered management. And it may be that such a long-range perspective demands that profit maximization be subordinated to higher human values.

The third objection seems to suggest that there was something wrong with good Duke Rollo, that the world would be better off without his kind. Many modern social philosophers feel that the truth is just the opposite of this. In a free society every man is called to be a Duke Rollo, to render justice to his fellow men to the best of his ability. It is true that men do not always live up to this ideal. And society needs to protect itself against excessive power wielded arbitrarily. It needs to propose a rule of law instead of a rule of men. But it need not despise the individual who acknowledges responsibility beyond the law. Social responsibility may be only a partial solution to the economic injustices of our day; for collective social control is needed too. But as we modify our social institutions to conform more fully to our ideal of justice, we should not condemn or prohibit the efforts of individuals, be they businessmen or others. The progress of social justice is everybody's business.

The creed of social responsibility does not provide the clear and precise measure of performance that profit maximization does. Net income in a financial statement can be expressed in very concrete terms. By contrast, the quantity or extent of the values of social responsibility to a large extent cannot be so expressed. But is this a weakness of the new creed or a strength? As students of business come to know the dimensions of their discipline more thoroughly, they become less sure that every aspect of corporate life can be reduced to a statistical or financial measurement. In making day-to-day decisions, the modern executive is constantly grappling with imponderables. As Richard Eells has said (*The Meaning of Modern Business*), "corporate intelligence requires a high degree of judgment in addition to the collection of 'hard information.'" A system that takes such judgment into account is an advanced and sophisticated one. By ignoring such imponderables we obtain, no doubt, a clean-cut, exact and universally comparable measure of business success. But such a measure, many executives affirm today, is far removed from the total reality of the business world.

It is disconcerting to find that this reality is more complicated than the market-mechanism theory had led us to believe. The doctrine of social responsibility, now in the early stages of its formulation, may well provide us with a theory closer to the real-world situations with which the modern businessman must live.

JEANNE RIHA
The Triple Revolution

¶A warning about the technological problems facing us draws increasing attention

The vigorous brain child of 32 intellectuals was born into our complacent society in March, 1964—and neither its parents nor the society has been quite the same since.

"The Triple Revolution" was a 29-page statement addressed to President Johnson and Congressional leaders by a group of distinguished citizens. They called attention to momentous changes taking place in methods of production, concepts of human rights, and in weaponry. Urgently they called for planning and action to direct these revolutionary forces before they should overwhelm society in mass joblessness or destruction.

The somber tone of the document broke on a nation enjoying unprecedented, if uneven, prosperity. It stirred shock waves that few publications could ignore. Its provocative warnings made their way in the first half-year into some 500 editorials and three dozen newspaper and magazine columns. The document itself was reprinted in whole or in part by nearly a score of magazines and newspapers. The eminence of most of the 32 signers gave it added weight.

Organized as the "Ad Hoc Committee on the Triple Revolution," the signers included historians H. Stuart Hughes of Harvard and John William Ward of Princeton; economists Robert Theobald and Robert L. Heilbroner; labor leader Ralph L. Helstein, president of the United Packinghouse, Food and Allied Workers; journalist Gerald W. Johnson; Gerard Piel, publisher of *Scientific American;* W. H. Ferry, a vice president of the Fund for the Republic's Center for the Study of Democratic Institutions; Linus Pauling, Nobel Peace Prize recipient; Michael Harrington, author of *The Other America,* and others.

Only the first of the upheavals, cybernation (the alliance of computers and automated machines), was explored in depth. The other two will be discussed in later papers. While cybernation was recognized to have a hopeful side in its promise of wealth and leisure, the Ad Hoc Committee chose to emphasize its bleaker aspects. It considered these more likely to manifest themselves if society simply drifts. Spreading unemployment, deepening poverty in the midst of plenty, hostility between classes, alienation, the human slag heap: these were the prices of drift.

Chronic unemployment will expand as machines take over men's jobs. From the blue-collar and agricultural areas, unemployment will spread into clerical and service jobs and even into middle management. The traditional link between jobs and income will be severed. New arrangements, other than jobs, will be needed to distribute the abundance that automation makes possible.

In recent months, critics have argued that the prospects of automation are not actually as gloomy as "The Triple Revolution" makes them out to be. Taking note of these claims, one of the authors has conceded that "the statistics about unemployment and underemployment can be read to arrive at many different conclusions about their scope and points of impact." Yet he remains convinced that the Ad Hoc Committee was correct in its original forecast.

How do the three revolutions mesh? The new technology will intensify the problem of the Negro in finding a job, said the committee, while defense cutbacks deepen the dilemma of finding new work for many of the millions now in military activities. Hence the human rights revolution and the growing awareness of the obsolescence of war are closely tied to economic concerns.

In one of its most quoted sections, "The Triple Revolution" warned that new job creation in the private sector, except for service industries, has almost ceased. New jobs will come henceforth from the public sector, and even there, some pessimists feel, they will not be enough to provide full employment.

"Major changes must be made in our attitudes and institutions in the foreseeable future," declared the committee in its keynote plea. "In the absence of real understanding of any of these phenomena, especially of technology, we may be allowing an efficient and de-humanized community to emerge by default. Gaining control of our future requires the conscious formation of the society we wish to have."

In its two principal recommendations, the Ad Hoc Committee proposed a government-guaranteed income to go to all who need it, as a matter of right, and advocated, as a transition measure, a vast program of public works.

The guaranteed income would provide a minimum living if an automated society could not offer jobs. Drawn out of an anticipated pool of plenty, the guaranteed income would keep up a decent minimum living standard and would provide purchasing power to keep cybernated industry whirring. The public works would in-clude both traditional programs and a few novelties: a public power system based on the abundant coal of distressed areas; rapid transit systems; community use of obsolete military bases.

Ever since the TR statement hit the President's desk and the headlines, requests have poured in for copies. More than 18,000 reprints have been sent out. The requests have come from every-where in the world: Switzerland, South Africa, Finland, Holland, Canada, Britain, Tasmania. Most important, they come in floods from America, the nation that is the "stage on which the machines-and-man drama will first be played for the world to witness."

The public's interest is reflected in an information service and a discussion program that are being organized on problems of peace, human rights and technological change, at the Center for the Study of Democratic Institutions in Santa Barbara, Calif. The new programs, financed by the Irving Laucks Fund, are not associated with the Ad Hoc Committee's activity but deal with these problem areas without taking positions on solutions.

A bulging correspondence file on the Triple Revolution has been accumulated by Ad Hoc Committee members. The file will soon be transferred to the Princeton Library to be added to the latter's collection of contemporary Americana.

Scores of letters have been received from teachers and college professors who were intending to discuss the Triple Revolution in class; from members of computer firms whose products are helping to displace men; from social science students writing papers on leisure or "the ultimate goals of economic activity"; from welfare workers concerned about the displaced, and from the unemployed themselves.

Another Laucks Fund project involves a questionnaire presently being circulated among those who ordered the TR pamphlet. More than 60 per cent of the occupations represented are from college or university faculties. Results so far indicate that 40 persons used the TR in teaching, 39 in discussion groups, 31 used it for speeches and sermons, 12 for writing papers and books, and five institutions and organizations reprinted it for hundreds of members and students.

Comments, both critical and appreciative, included these: "One of those few tracts in a generation with the force to effect significant change" (from a businessman); "Provocative, even though not free of 'howlers' . . . I intend to use it in a book"; "Excellent intentions, good inside, very poor policies" (a professor of economics); "Positive and Christian approach" (Catholic seminarian); "Excellent opening up of the kind of debates this country needs" (religious leader); "Tremendous—should be the 'big news' of the decade"; "Too intellectual, needs to be restated for man in the street" (history professor); "Best analysis I've seen."

W. H. Ferry, who became one of the prime movers of the Triple Revolution, on his own initiative and without the agreement of a number of his Center colleagues, points out: "None of us expected the remarkable reception of this statement. . . . We hoped merely to go a little way toward clarifying some situations and connections that appeared to us to contain seeds of catastrophe. We ended up not with a mild pop but with a big boom."

The most jarring note in that boom came from editorial writers who took exception to the proposal for a guaranteed income and to the idea that work was becoming outmoded as a means of distributing income. Arguments on the purely economic factors undoubtedly will continue far into the future, till the facts of life clarify them and determine whose reading of the statistics has been correct. But meantime, discussion of human aspects of the statement —both public and professional—has been vigorous.

This discussion prompted some healthy analysis among the authors as well as the critics of TR.

Ferry, who has spoken widely on the statement in recent months, has come away from Triple Revolution audiences "deeply impressed by the almost universal anguish aroused by the proposal for a guaranteed income." "This anguish I at first interpreted as the normal abhorrence of an unusual idea," he said recently, "but I now see it as genuine fear of demoralization of the community."

Intent on presenting its economic diagnosis, the Ad Hoc Committee did not attempt a detailed prescription for a wholesome cybernated society. For this they have been taken to task by friends and foes alike. But this shortcoming may actually have been a blessing, for it has encouraged others to try to fill the gap. As a result, the debate on these human aspects has intensified on all sides.

The human factors are the province of all men, not only of the experts. Everyone can discuss with equal authority the values he wants to see in tomorrow's world. If machines take over men's work, will we have a lazy society? Need we have a lazy society when so much work remains to be done? What are the new types of work ahead as the grimy chores are taken over by machines? How can we give higher purpose to lives that now revolve around the twin poles of making and spending money? All these questions are being discussed not only in public statements by many of the TR signers, but also in the mail that pours onto the Ad Hoc Committee's desks.

Robert Theobald, New York economists and an important contributor to TR, has fought doggedly against outraged conservatives for his principle of the guaranteed income. This position is a well-known one. Less well known is his insistence that he was not advocating indolence. He was fighting to give people the "chance to do things with their lives that are worth doing. That is what 'work' will become. Each person ought to be given the opportunity to make something of himself."

Michael Harrington distinguishes between a society of abundance in which "people do nothing" and a society in which they vigorously involve themselves in useful, absorbing activities. "The first is a terrible place; I wouldn't want to go there," exclaims this furiously energetic young man.

Harrington describes the "new definitions of work" that become practicable as machines take over the "sweaty, routine, miserable" jobs of industrial life. Most important will be "the human care of human beings." This will consist in bridging the chasm of indifference that now separates the lonely aged from the rest of society. It will involve wiping out the slums, psychologically and physically. It may include providing warm-hearted aides to take over the teacher's "mothering" duties, thus permitting her to teach.

W. H. Ferry has been reminding audiences that cybernation is only eight years old. It requires a new ethic and new patterns of life, just as did the Industrial Revolution. These will not be produced in a moment; but—man willing—they can be worked out. And they can offer a far nobler pattern of life than the physical drudgery and niggardly spirit that have existed under the industrial system. But the awful responsibility of creating this life pattern and ethic is man's. That is both the glory and the terror of cybernation.

The men and the two women who signed the document are not self-satisfied viewers of their own creation. Some of the sharpest comments on its shortcomings have come from them.

Norman Thomas, in a memorable "farewell address" in May, 1964, endorsed TR tenets but warned:

"I do not think it will be good for great numbers of able-bodied adults to live on what marvelous machines have made, without personally contributing to the material and cultural wealth that is shared." He suggested another problem, one rarely touched upon as yet by the heralds of cybernation: "It will not be easy to maintain a true democracy if economic power is vested in the hands of the comparatively few who make and program the machines."

Dr. Frances W. Herring, of the Institute for Governmental Studies of the University of California, partly echoed Norman Thomas, recently, as she declared the need for every "able-bodied person" to contribute to society in return for an income from the government. Work must not be downgraded, she insisted. She warned also that "not every means of keeping production wheels whirring is equally good." If cybernated industry concentrates only on producing abundant goods, with no thought of what it is producing, we may have a "permanent overdraft on nature." Both she and Mr. Thomas signed "The Triple Revolution."

These are issues very much in the minds of the informed public: the psychological value of work, conservation of resources, the quality—not just the quantity—of production. It is important that

Ad Hoc Committee members should take them up to insure a wide public consensus.

Will this national explosion of concern continue to gain strength, or will it fade away as other promises of an American renaissance have faded over the last generation? It is too early to tell. At the end of last September, 1,000 to 2,500 copies were being mailed out weekly in response to requests, and this continuing flow of mail indicates unflagging public interest. Can the public's attention be directed into a search for a new vision of life as well as new economic and social schemes? That is the great question, as leading TR intellectuals see it.

JAMES L. VIZZARD
The Agricultural Revolution

¶Those who have made a new abundance possible are suffering as a result of it

The overwhelming fact of American agriculture today is the agricultural revolution. After having stagnated technologically for countless centuries, agriculture is now undergoing a revolution of a scope and depth comparable to the Industrial Revolution of the 18th and 19th centuries.

This agricultural phenomenon began in the United States with the widespread substitution of the gasoline engine for horse and mule power during and after World War I, and continued with the development and the now almost universal availability of electrical power. It was greatly accelerated by the rapid application to agricultural production of improved farming and conservation practices, the scientific breeding and feeding of livestock, the development of highly productive and disease-resistant crop varieties, and the introduction of much more effective insecticides, pesticides and fertilizers.

The most obvious result of the agricultural revolution has been a spectacular increase in productivity per acre and an even more spectacular increase in output per man-hour of farm work. In

1963, one hour of farm labor produced five times as much food and other crops as it did in 1919–1921. In the same period, crop production per acre increased by 75 per cent, and output per breeding animal by 92 per cent. In the decade of the 1950's, productivity of the American farm worker increased by 5.4 per cent a year, while in non-agricultural industry the increase was only 2.1 per cent a year. Today, one farm worker produces food, fiber and other farm commodities for himself and 28 others. There is every reason to believe that these trends will continue into the indefinite future. It is equally certain that eventually the phenomenon will become world-wide.

In the United States, this peaceful revolution has already led to the first era of true agricultural abundance ever achieved by any major nation. It enables our consumers to obtain a high-quality and varied diet for a good deal less than what a poorer diet costs even in other technologically advanced countries. In 1963, food costs represented only 18.8 per cent of the average U.S. family's income after taxes. By contrast, consumers in the United Kingdom spent 29.5 per cent of their income for food; in France, 30.6 per cent; in Italy, 34.7 per cent; in Japan, 46.9 per cent; and in Russia, 53 per cent. In the less developed areas of the world, virtually all personal income is spent on food.

By releasing many millions of persons from the necessity of tilling the soil, the agricultural revolution has enabled the rest of our economy and society to grow to its present developed status. If farmers today produced at the productivity level of 1910, in order to feed our population, which now approaches 200 million, we would need to have kept about 20 million more persons in our farm labor force and would have that many fewer for manufacturing, trades, services, professions and the arts.

It is evident, then, that the agricultural revolution has already made important and beneficent contributions to the welfare of our country. But what has it meant to those most directly involved in it—to farmers and rural communities? Has it been an unmixed blessing? The answer, unfortunately, is no.

Instead of being the chief beneficiary, the farmer has been the chief victim of this revolution. Because he did not recognize and control soon enough the forces for change, the farmer now finds himself in a desperate struggle for survival. He and his government have found no adequate answer to the three chief problems that result from the agricultural revolution: 1) the seemingly uncontrollable tendency of production to outrun effective demand; 2) an inexorable cost-price squeeze, which leads to bankruptcy; and 3) the accelerated exodus from farms and rural communities to cities, often with disastrous results to both. Let us consider each of these problems in order.

It is obvious that we have not yet learned how to control the exuberant flood of products flowing from our farms and ranches. The production pipeline that supplies consumers with food and fiber, and that once flowed with grudging slowness, now pours out abundance that threatens to swamp us. Markets and concepts geared to scarcity must now be revised to cope with abundance. For the first time in the history of the world, a nation's concern is focused not on shortages but on surpluses.

Nor is this a passing phenomenon. Great as is our present productivity, if effective demand existed, our farms, simply by applying more intensively and more widely the already available knowledge and techniques, could easily double production. Moreover, science and technology show no signs of a slowdown in the discovery and development of new means of increasing productivity. We are not at the end but rather still at the beginning of the agricultural revolution.

Almost everyone recognizes that such abundance and the productivity that makes it possible are a blessing of unprecedented proportions. It makes it at least theoretically possible to guarantee that no American citizen need go hungry. Even more, it makes it possible for our nation to provide urgently needed foods to the countless millions of the world's peoples who previously have never said any prayer with more desperate urgency than "Give us this day our daily bread."

But for the farmer who produces this abundance, things have not been so favorable. Operating within the one major part of our economy still characterized by free competition, in which the law of supply and demand still holds considerable sway, the farmer finds that as the volume of production goes up, the price he receives in the market place goes down. In the process of becoming ever more efficient and productive, the farmer is in danger of bankruptcy.

Other industries that have increased productivity have found ways to control both production and prices. When signs appear that the market can absorb no more steel or autos at a predetermined price, U. S. Steel shuts down its furnaces and General Motors its production lines. They create their surpluses not in products but in idle plants and unemployed workers.

Farmers, however, are too many and have been too lacking in organization to be able to act thus. Moreover, their productive plant cannot be shut down overnight. They cannot stop pigs from fattening or corn from growing. And even if the individual farmer should respond to oversupply and low prices by cutting back his operations where possible, too many other farmers at the same time will be expanding production to the utmost to make up in volume what they cannot secure through adequate prices.

This kind of problem, of course, did not exist when productivity was low, demand was generally high and farmers found a profitable outlet for whatever they could produce. But in this new age of abundance, the inability of farmers to limit supply and in some degree to control prices has become a major national crisis.

Most people would agree that, if it were possible, control of supply and prices would best be left in the hands of the farmers themselves. All experience indicates, however, that except for relatively minor and geographically limited crops, farmers have not been able to organize so as to achieve this end. To be sure, one of the most encouraging developments of recent years has been the growth of the co-operative bargaining approach, by which farmers unite to contract with processors for specific volumes of products at mutually agreed-upon prices. Should this movement reach sufficient size and power, it could well solve one of the farmer's most pressing problems. It is not yet clear, however, whether this approach will be able to provide an adequate answer, in the near future, to the productivity and price problems of the agricultural revolution.

If farmer-sponsored and farmer-controlled efforts do not succeed, the size and nature of the problem demand and justify government intervention. For three decades and more, a great variety of farm programs have been proposed, and some adopted, by which the government was committed to help farmers control overproduction and achieve satisfactory prices and income. Most of these programs have been based on voluntary co-operation of the individual farmer. Each farmer could choose to come in or stay out. Various kinds of government supports and subsidies have encouraged him to participate, but if he judged he could do better on his own, he was free not to participate.

Repeated and varied experiences, however, prove that voluntary programs simply have not worked with much success. Witness the billions of dollars of taxpayers' money that the government spent in vain efforts to harness run-away productivity. Farmers acting individually in their own interest have frustrated every effort at control.

From an ethical standpoint, moreover, it is becoming increasingly clear that if farmers are to receive the government assistance and support that they need and deserve, in justice they must be willing to accept such limitations and controls as are necessary. Important though farmers are, their needs are not the only ones that government must consider. It is doubtful that the common good, which is the central concern of the state, allows farmers, or any other group, to make unreasonable and unlimited demands on the public treasury. Taxpayers have no right to begrudge such expenditures as may be necessary to solve the critical problems of disadvantaged groups, but they surely have a right to expect that such expenditures should ultimately lead to a solution.

It should be evident to all, by now, that voluntary controls are expensive and inefficient. To retain them in the face of accelerating productivity-increases is both an imposition on taxpayers and an invitation to disaster. Without yielding to an inferiority complex, farmers must recognize that they now represent a small and decreasing proportion of the U.S. population. Their importance in the economy is not diminished, but their power at the polls and in Congress is a thing of the past. Unless non-farm voters can soon see that their tax money is being spent for a constructive solution to the farm problem, inevitably and not without justice they will rebel and put an end to the whole attempt.

A word should perhaps be said here about the opinion held by some that controls themselves are morally wrong, a violation of the purported God-given law of supply and demand. One can only answer that if they are so, every manufacturer who limits production and administers prices, every profession that limits the entrance of new candidates, every union that negotiates for wages not freely granted by the "market," in other words every other major segment of our economy, stands indicted of violating this presumed law. Even the most ardent advocates of free enterprise admit in practice, if not also in theory, that cut-throat competition is and should be dead.

It is generally agreed, as previously observed, that, where possible, controls should be voluntary. But as is proved by innumerable laws at every level of government, where voluntary controls are inadequate, mandatory controls must be imposed. This world is no Utopia where every individual citizen on his own initiative and responsibility modifies his personal aims and actions to conform to the requirements of the common good. One of the most basic purposes of a civil society is to impose and enforce precisely such limitations on the individual in the interest of the general welfare. The no-control school of thought can find no support either in theory or in practice.

The second major problem that follows in the wake of the agricultural revolution is the cost-price squeeze that has ruined and continues to ruin so many farmers. In the simpler days of agriculture, almost any farmer with an adequate piece of land could at least get by on hard work and frugality. Even though his production was small and the prices he received were low, his expenses and his need for cash were low, too, and he could be sure of eating well on home-grown food.

In today's agriculture, however, the farmer is entirely caught up in the market and money economy. He has to buy his factors of production at inflated prices and, as previously indicated, must sell his products in the largely unregulated free market. In effect, he buys at retail and sells at wholesale.

As a result, the farmer finds his costs constantly increasing while the prices he receives for his products fail to keep pace. This cost-price squeeze can perhaps be best illustrated by comparing the year 1947, the historical high point in farm income, with 1963. Between these two years, while realized *gross* farm income *increased* from (in round numbers) $34 billion to $41 billion, realized *net* income *decreased* from $17 billion to $12 billion. This discrepancy is explained by the increase of production expenses from $17 billion to $29 billion.

This vast and crucial increase in production expenses is the price that farmers must pay for modern, efficient farming. Almost all the increase goes for products that did not exist before the agricultural revolution. Each year, for instance, the farmer has been spending an average of $3.1 billion on new tractors and other motor vehicles, machinery and equipment; $3.3 billion for fuel, lubricants and maintenance of machinery and motor vehicles; and $1.6 billion for fertilizer and lime. Moreover, each year he purchases products containing enough rubber to put tires on 6 million automobiles, uses enough electricity to supply the annual needs of Baltimore, Chicago, Boston, Detroit, Houston and Washington, D.C.

Concealed in over-all figures on declining farm income is the fact that, in 1963, farm people received $1,480 of personal annual income per capita, of which $510 was from non-farm sources; whereas per capita annual personal income of non-farm people was $2,515 from all sources. Again, the average hourly return for farm work was $1.01, while, by contrast, one hour's work in a factory averaged $2.46.

Almost any statistical index illustrates the deteriorating position of the farmer. For instance, the average worker's family paid 15 per cent more but farmers received 15 per cent less in 1963 for the same kinds and quantities of foods purchased in the years 1947–1949. Items in this "market basket" include bakery products, of which the farm value of all ingredients declined 12 per cent from 1947–1949 to 1963 and the retail cost increased 42 per cent. The farm value of a fixed quantity of dairy products dropped 5 per cent in this period, while the retail price of these products increased 18 per cent.

These data are cold and abstract, but to farm families the cost-price squeeze is something very real and personal. For hundreds of thousands of them it means decreased income, increased debts and a constant, precarious battle against bankruptcy. Indeed, since 1945, two and a half million farmers have lost that battle and their farms have disappeared.

This last statistic indicates why the third major problem created by the agricultural revolution has been an accelerated exodus from farms and rural communities. It is true that surplus farm population has always migrated to the city, but in recent decades the trickle has turned into a flood. The U.S. farm population has decreased from 24 million in 1945 to 13 million in 1963, and this, of course, was during a period when the total U.S. population was growing by the tens of millions.

Most, but by no means all, of the farm people who have left the land have been from smaller farms, particularly in the deep South. In 1959, some two and a quarter million of these smaller farms were still operating farms with total annual sales of less than $5,000 (*net* income, of course, averaged a great deal less than that). But each year before and since 1959, hundreds of thousands of these farmers fell victims to the agricultural revolution, pulled up such roots as they had, and, with their families, headed for the cities to look for work.

This exodus, forced by stark economic hardship and often accompanied by racial pressures, has only rarely led to improved conditions for those who moved. Most of them, in fact, only fled from a rural slum to an even more distressing urban slum. Whether white or colored, their assimilation into the urban environment has been slowed by their poverty and lack of education and their total lack of preparation for urban living. Without any economically valued skills, they find open to them only the lowest paid jobs, if they find any jobs at all. They are the last to be hired and the first to be fired. Hope for those families seems to lie only in the next generation or two, when their children will have acquired an adequate education and a more secure place in the community. Thus some of the most distressing and urgent city problems have their origin back in the depressed, rural areas of America. This fact is one that city people and their representatives often tend to overlook.

Meanwhile the rural communities that the cityward migrants have abandoned, poor and deteriorating as they already were, disintegrate still further. Without enough business to be economically viable, they gradually turn into ghost towns. The side roads of major parts of rural America already present a sorry spectacle of abandoned homes, ruined barns and decaying towns.

This process, however, is not inevitable or irreversible. There still are economically valuable resources in most of these distressed areas, which, if mobilized, if given new directions and incentives, can revitalize local economies.

The chief of these resources, of course, is the people themselves. Given better education, job training and local opportunity, they will easily recognize that they can do far better for themselves as well as for their communities in at-home jobs than by fleeing to heartless and jobless city slums. It is precisely to achieve these constructive purposes that the Area Development Program and the Rural Areas Development Program have been undertaken in recent years. If these programs work as planned, one can look forward to a reversal or at least a significant slowing down of the rural exodus, a new and more vigorous life for rural communities and an easing of the already overwhelming problems of city slums.

But it is not only the small inefficient, subsistence farms that are disappearing. Many a farm that only a few years ago was considered adequate and even substantial, is now succumbing to the pressure of the cost-price squeeze. Perhaps because of inadequate capital and credit, or perhaps because of limited education or managerial ability, the farmer just can't make it. He gets tired of the struggle and sells out.

When the farmer finally sells out, the land rarely goes out of use. Rather, it is incorporated into another larger and probably more efficient operation. Thus, despite the loss of two and a half million farmers in 20 years, agricultural production, as we have seen, has continued to increase. In the meantime, though, farms become larger and fewer. In a generation, the average size of farms in this country has increased from 150 acres to well over 250 acres. It is not easy to see how far this trend will continue, but it seems clear that it will go on indefinitely unless checked by conscious and effective national policy.

RAYMOND BAUMHART and
GEORGE D. FITZPATRICK
Inertia in Business Ethics

¶Why can't businessmen and theologians get together on these tangled problems?

The recent, internationally publicized decision of an American woman to go to Sweden for an abortion was met in the Catholic press by a thorough, firm explanation of the moral issues involved in that decision. Catholic thinking was clearly stated; restated really, for on this subject it is as traditional as it is unequivocal. Thanks to the writing and teaching of moral theologians, and to the sermons of countless pastors, the informed Catholic need have no doubts concerning the moral aspects of abortion. The same may be said of euthanasia and artificial contraception. In the areas of medical ethics and sexual morality, the Church's teaching is lucid and well developed, indeed.

In clearly marked contrast to the ubiquity and unanimity of Catholic opinion on the Finkbine abortion has been the absence of authoritative Catholic writing on the 1961 price-fixing conspiracy in the electrical manufacturing industry. Missing from the comments which followed the price-fixing scandal was that scholarly analysis which the professional moralist might have supplied. And missing from the national discussion on business ethics which has been growing since the 1959 television travesty is a developing Catholic exposition of the ethical problems which are of much interest to the business community.

One result of Catholic taciturnity is confusion among businessmen of good will about the moral issues and the norms by which men may cope with these issues. This note of confusion is sounded by a Washington stockbroker: "'Ethical' means accepted standards in terms of your personal and social welfare, that is, what you believe is right. But what confuses me, partly as a result of discussions on the electrical industry price-fixing, is the possibility that I have been misguided, or that somebody else has been poorly educated. Maybe each of us thinks he knows what is ethical, but we differ. How can you tell who is right, then?"

Although many men have written recently about business morality, the majority have neither the training nor the esteem to exercise significant influence on the mores of the business community. This area of business ethics should be part of the bailiwick of the professional moralist. And yet, two compilations of current writings—totaling more than 500 entries—in the field of business ethics reveal only a handful composed by Catholic theologians. It seems that they are content to leave the discussions of business ethics in the hands of laymen. The businessman's problems are seldom deemed worthy of the science of moral theology. In fact, if attendance at university-sponsored seminars is used as a criterion, not many theologians are interested in business ethics.

Why this apparent neglect of businessmen by theologians? A well-educated, high-ranking executive gives this caustic answer: "Theologians are the laziest men in the world. Fortunately, they don't have to worry about eating. They are the only group of professional men who have not knuckled under to the tremendous changes of our era, the only profession which has not kept up with the times. Many of them are still living in the Middle Ages and teaching ideas from them."

This is the view of a man facing one side of the problem. From the other side come the words of a Jesuit moralist who has written competently about business ethics, Fr. John J. Lynch: ". . . it should not be forgotten that many of the 'problems' which might be submitted as characteristic of the modern market place are reductively as old as the Decalogue itself, and that for an answer these require only a thoughtful reference to that definitive norm. . . . Sometimes when this type of problem is submitted for moral appraisal, there is reason to believe that what the consulting party really wants explained is how to succeed in business while avoiding implication in practices which conscience has already instinctively and correctly judged to be patently wrong. Counsel of this sort does not seem to be the proper function of the moral theologian."

Father Lynch's point is well made. It does not, however, apply to the matter of price collusion in the electrical-manufacturing industry. In that thorny situation, as the *Wall Street Journal* observed, "there evidently developed in wide segments [of the industry] the philosophy that collusive activity was ethical, illegal though it be." Comment on such a philosophy in a situation of national concern certainly is the proper function of the moral theologian. Unless we are mistaken, no scholarly comment on the electrical-industry scandal has come from the pen of Catholic moralists. And we think this is typical of their reaction to complex problems in business.

The reluctance of moralists to write or lecture about business ethics has an unfortunate chain reaction. Pastors, having learned little about business problems, are ill-prepared to preach or offer counsel about them. Gradually some lay Catholics acquire an attitude like that of a New England marketing executive: "During the war I was close to a chaplain; now religion is less accessible. It's a long way from the pulpit to my office, and there seems to be little direct association between the two. I've always thought of personal matters as close to God; for example, anything to do with my family. But I guess that all along I've been assuming that business is less directly associated with God, and with reward and punishment. Business was 'the other eight hours' of the day."

Perhaps we expect too much of moral theologians. Every single human action has a moral dimension, so these men are asked questions from all sides. Specialists press the moralists for opinions on matters as diverse as prize fighting, the use of nuclear bombs, segregation, censorship, Church-State relations. To be competent in every area of specialization is practically impossible. In the future, priests who have done advanced study in business administration and economics will have to qualify themselves as moralists for businessmen.

Before theologians can comment meaningfully on business problems, there must be improved communication between managers and clergymen. In part, at least, the current lack of communication is due to the laymen. A vociferous minority still clings to the Neanderthal notion that the priest is meddling when he comments on business and social problems. But, as we learned by surveying 228 Catholic businessmen, the majority want more guidance from their priests. (See *Ethics and the Catholic Businessman*, a pamphlet, America Press, 50¢.) Only one in every four of these managers thought that the Church and clergy had provided adequate assistance for the businessman's ethical problems in the last five years.

Many Catholic businessmen desire assistance in this area, and there are moralists and pastors willing to help these men. What is preventing rapport? Misapprehensions on both sides, we think. One such misapprehension results in the businessman's ambivalence about seeking clergy counsel. He fears that he will not be understood: he is afraid that the priest will not comprehend the economics of the problem, or will not appreciate the competitive pressures under which he operates.

It is true, in the words of a New York stockbroker, that "the average clergyman has scant understanding of the U.S. economy." But it does not necessarily follow that the average clergyman cannot be helpful in the solution of some ethical problems in business. Many of these problems require no more than a new application of a well-established moral principle. For example, the traditional teaching on rights and obligations with respect to secret information can be applied more or less directly to today's industrial problems of industrial espionage and pirating competitors' employees. From conversations with managers, we are convinced that many of them underestimate the breadth of understanding of moral problems and principles possessed by the average priest.

Another way of saying the same thing is that many businessmen overestimate the uniqueness of their problems. As a consequence, they hesitate to discuss the problems with a priest. This is unfortunate, because they have much to gain, including peace of conscience. (We think that most businessmen are honestly interested in doing what is right, even when it is financially costly. Unless this is so, their talk about ethics is a sadly misguided attempt at winning public support, which will backfire in the long run.)

Businessmen possessing a spiritual outlook have little to lose by discussing their problems with a priest. After all, no one is obliged to follow counsel that is unreasonable. Apparently, however, some good men who know that they have no obligation to follow unreasonable advice feel that their ignorance of moral theology leaves them in a poor position to evaluate the quality of priestly advice. So, unless they thoroughly respect a priest's knowledge of business as well as his judgment, they don't broach their problems. Basically, they are reluctant to expose themselves to advice which may complicate an already difficult situation.

Assuming that they are willing to discuss their problems, businessmen must practice patience in explaining them. Like every other specialist, the businessman has developed technical terminology to facilitate communication with his associates. But this jargon mystifies the uninitiated. How many nonbusinessmen know the meaning of everyday terms like capital gains, price-earnings ratio, and vertical integration? If the businessman wants counsel, he must first translate the problem, which he sees in technical terms, into language that is easily intelligible to the clergyman. He may find solace in the thought that priests face the same problem every Sunday morning when they try to make theology understandable to their parishioners.

Another block to communication between managers and clergy is the attitude on the part of some theologians that, in the words of a student of theology at a recent workshop, businessmen should phrase their questions in a way that makes it easy for moralists to apply appropriate principles. Problems rarely are presented on a platter. Scholarly work necessarily includes the grubby digging out of relevant facts and the state of the question. Even those who study theology, the queen of the sciences, are not exempt from this toil.

There are a few bright spots in the big picture of Catholic interest in business ethics. Effective action in highlighting the moral aspects of industrial problems has been taken by Fr. Henry Wirtenberger, S.J., and Professor Herbert Johnston. These two academicians (the former from Loyola University, Chicago, the latter from the University of Notre Dame) have produced eminently suitable books for collegiate courses and businessmen's seminars. [Notably Father Wirtenberger's *Morality and Business*, Loyola University Press, 1962, and Mr. Johnston's *Business Ethics* (second edit.), Pitman, 1961.—ED.] Prof. William F. Kennedy of the University of California has recently contributed a perceptive analysis of some ethical aspects of the electrical industry scandal, in "The Ethics of Conspiracy," in the *Atlanta Economic Review*, August, 1962.

Perhaps the most promising activity initiated by laymen in this area is the National Conference of Catholic Employers and Managers. Led by an able and articulate Chicago industrialist, Edward S. Jamieson, NCCEM has small groups in eight cities studying ethical problems in business. In August, NCCEM published an *Operating Guide*, containing a suggested program for a series of twelve meetings. This booklet will prove a boon to Catholic businessmen who want to start a discussion group but lack the material for discussion. Each NCCEM group comprises from fifteen to twenty managers and a chaplain, and meets at least monthly. Mr. Jamieson's analysis of the over-all problem of business ethics reveals: "What we need further is more concerted effort (closer co-operation between businessmen, moralists and Catholic social scientists) to formulate, grasp and refine our guiding principles; and much wider and more intensive studies of factual situations so that the principles may be applied prudently and intelligently to changing situations."

The challenge to business and theologians is an exciting one, somewhat like the challenge that moralists and Catholic physicians took up years ago in the field of medical ethics. Today the priest and the Catholic doctor have a comfortable dialogue, each complementing the other as they work toward the solution of difficulties which once seemed so formidable.

There are, evidently, problems worthy of joint study by priest and businessmen, problems of pricing, taxation, discrimination, competition, etc. Currently there is much Catholic inertia concerning these problems. There need not be. On the one hand, many managers say that they seek guidance for their ethical problems.

On the other hand, Catholic moralists are competent to discuss the application of moral principles to these problems; so are a number of other priests who are specially trained in business administration or economics.

Counseling situations are generally regarded as most promising when the meetings are initiated by the client, rather than by the counselor or some third party. For this reason we think that Catholic businessmen should demand greater involvement by the clergy, especially moral theologians, in the ethical problems of business. Reinforcing our contention is the recent statement of Dutch Bishop Jan van Dodewaard: "Laymen should stimulate, even press, professional theologians to give their full attention to those questions which urgently call for solution."

Catholic businessmen of America, speak up! Until you do, many clergymen will not appreciate the complexity of your moral problems nor the good will which prompts your desire to solve them.

BENJAMIN L. MASSE
Poverty, U.S.A.

¶Ours is a land of incredible prosperity, but the poor we have always with us

Not long ago, two middle-aged and balding gentlemen, one lay, the other clerical, were discussing the son of a mutual friend.

"The young man is getting along very well," observed the cleric. "He has four healthy kids and recently he got another raise. He must be making close to $10,000 by now."

"I'm mighty glad to hear that," the layman said. "Jim's a fine boy and always did have a lot on the ball. But let me tell you something, Padre, in case you don't know it. With four kids and $10,000 a year, he's scrambling all the time just to make ends meet."

That observation came back to the cleric not long ago as he sat reading a blistering rebuttal to John Kenneth Galbraith's *The Affluent Society*. "Affluent, my eye," was the author's theme, though expressed in more scholarly terms, of course. "The poor aren't a small hard core in the United States. Poverty is a mass phenomenon among us, however invisible it may be to the myopic well-to-do. Let the lyricists of affluence take note that in this year of our Lord over 40 million Americans are languishing in dull-eyed poverty."

Is this angry critic making a valid point? Surely, if a family of six cannot live comfortably on $10,000 a year, it would seem that he is. After all, the vast majority of the nation's families have to manage on less than $10,000, many of them on considerably less. How many Americans these days are poor? How poor are they? Are imbalances between rich and poor, against which our late great-souled Pope warned so vigorously in *Mater et Magistra*, increasing or decreasing in the United States?

Questions like these are hard to answer, partly because it is much easier to know poverty from experience than it is to define it. One of the difficulties is, as the philosophers would say, that proverty is relative, in fact as well as concept, just as much as it's absolute. Anyone who has ever seen the slums of the Orient, or of Africa or Latin America, knows that many people considered to be poor in this country would be regarded as fairly well off by the tattered homeless folk in Calcutta or by the shack-dwellers on the barren hills of Hong Kong.

In a recent article in the New York *Times Magazine*, Herman P. Miller, of the Bureau of Census, emphasized this point in describing poverty in stricken Harlan County, Ky. Two-thirds of the houses, he wrote, are substandard. Half don't have baths or inside toilets. A quarter even lack running water. Yet 88 per cent of the families in those run-down houses have a washing machine, 67 per cent have TV, 45 per cent have a telephone, and 59 per cent have a car. Are these people poor? Of course, they are. By our cultural standards, not many Americans are much poorer. Yet the trappings of an affluent society which they possess—even when water for the washing machine must be drawn from a well, and the car is a sputtering jalopy—place these people much higher on the totem pole than their counterparts anywhere else in the world.

What is poverty? Most people would agree that poverty is the lack of those goods and services—housing, food, clothing, health services, education and recreation—which are considered by the community generally as necessary for a decent human life. For anyone concerned about his neighbor next door, or in the next city or State, it makes no difference that this lack of goods and services differs from country to country, and even within the same country at different periods of its history. (Many poor Americans today have necessities which people a century ago would have considered comforts and even luxuries.) It is enough for him to know that his neighbor is ill-fed, ill-clad, ill-housed, insecure—that he is, in a word, poor.

In a money economy, the most practical way to define poverty is in terms of income. Pope Leo XIII did this for workers when, in 1891, he taught the doctrine of the living wage. Any worker earning less than a living wage is poor. The Pope did not define a living wage in dollars and cents, but described it as a wage adequate "to support a worker who is thrifty and upright." Later on, Pope Pius XI made it clear that the doctrine of the living wage went beyond the individual worker and extended to his family. He also described it in greater detail: "But social justice cannot be said to have been satisfied as long as working men are denied a salary that will enable them to secure proper sustenance for themselves and for their families; as long as they are denied the opportunity of acquiring a modest fortune and forestalling the plague of universal pauperism, as long as they cannot make suitable provision through public or private insurance for old age, for periods of illness and unemployment." (*Atheistic Communism,* §52)

In translating this moral concept of a minimum living wage into monetary terms, it is scarcely possible to avoid controversy.

In a study published by the Congressional Joint Economic Committee in 1959, *The Low Income Population and Economic Growth,* Prof. Robert J. Lampman considered a four-person family to be in the "low-income" category if its total *money* income was not more than $2,500 in 1957 dollars. The corresponding figure for unattached individuals was $1,157. If we equate low income with poverty, there were 32.2 million poor Americans in 1957.

The widely discussed analysis by the Conference on Economic Progress, *Poverty and Deprivation in the United States,* which was published last year under the direction of Leon H. Keyserling, assumes that multiperson families with less than $4,000 in 1960 were living in poverty. Mr. Keyserling's cut-off figure for individuals was $2,000. Even after allowance is made for price changes since 1957, as well as for such nonmonetary income as food raised and consumed on farms, which Prof. Lampman excluded, the CEP figures are considerably higher than those in the Joint Economic Committee study. Mr. Keyserling puts the poor in the United States at 38 million.

Michael Harrington, in his scorching *The Other America: Poverty in the United States,* also uses the $4,000 figure for families and the $2,000 figure for individuals as the poverty dividing line. His estimate of the number of poor, though, is higher than Mr. Keyserling's. Between 40 and 50 million Americans are poor, he claims.

Then there is a scholarly, multi-authored book out of the University of Michigan, *Income and Welfare in the United States,* which sets the poverty level at $4,330 and goes on to conclude, somewhat disconcertingly, that only a fifth of the nation's families, or about 35 million people, are poor.

Finally, in any discussion of poverty in this country, or of the monetary equivalent of a minimum living wage, reference must be made to the U. S. Department of Labor's "modest but adequate budget for city workers' families." Compiled by the Bureau of Labor Statistics, this budget is certainly "modest." Some might consider it Spartan. It allows the father of a family of four, for instance, a heavy wool suit every two years, a light suit every three years. The mother can buy a suit every ten years and a skirt every five years. The family takes a vacation away from home every three or four years. It is permitted a new car every 12 to 18 years. The provision for recreation is limited—a movie, for example, every two or three weeks.

A study made by BLS in 1959, but translated into 1960 dollars by the CEP staff, reveals that in twenty cities, ranging in size from Scranton to New York, a four-person family needed an average of $6,142 a year for a "modest but adequate" standard of living. The budgets varied from a high of $6,629 for Chicago to a low of $5,421 for Houston. A breakdown of the Chicago budget on broad lines shows $709 for taxes, $1,768 for food and beverages, $1,399 for rent, heat and other utilities, $2,493 for goods and services, and $260 for other costs (life insurance, Social Security tax, union dues). The budget-minded reader will know better than this writer how realistic this breakdown is.

In any study of poverty, other considerations besides income are pertinent, of course. Place of residence is important: one can live more cheaply in small rural communities than in big cities; in the South than in the North. The size of the family is highly significant, as is the age of its members. For the twenty cities studied, BLS estimates, for example, that the average budget for a family of six or more persons ranges between $6,080 and $9,357, depending on "the age of the head of the family, age of the children and other family composition factors." The budget for a four-person family ranges from a low of $5,036 to a high of $7,678. The budget for an unattached individual, from $2,273 to $3,071. And in all cases, how prudently a family conducts its affairs has great significance, as everybody knows. So has the incidence of sickness and accidents.

Where does this leave us?

For the sake of argument, I would accept the CEP figure of under $4,000 for multiperson families and below $2,000 for unattached individuals as indicative of the poverty level in this country. (There has been a rise in the consumer price level since 1960 but not big enough to change the picture notably.) Selecting a standard of this kind does not mean, of course, that all families with less than $4,000 are poverty-stricken, or that all families with more than $4,000 may not be poor. Some families in some parts of the country can live decently on less than $4,000, and on the other hand some large families are poor even though they have more than $4,000.

It follows from this that as a general rule any wage below $4,000 is certainly less than a minimum living wage for an American worker and his family.

In addition to the poverty level, the CEP study explores what it calls the "deprivation" level, a level that "means genuine denial of many of the goods and services which most Americans have come to regard as 'essentials,' and in most cases imposes a continuing sense of insecurity." Families with more than $4,000 but less than $6,000 are said to be living in deprivation. So are individuals with more than $2,000 but less than $3,000. No doubt, some moralists would equate the minimum living wage with the deprivation rather than the poverty level.

The following table, adapted from studies of the U. S. Commerce Department's Office of Business Economics, as are the other tables in this article, shows the number of families and individuals on the lower rungs of the income ladder in 1960:

TABLE I

Personal Income Before Taxes	Families (in thousands)	Individuals (in thousands)
Under $2,000	3,370	3,943
$2,000–$2,999	3,088	2,090
$3,000–$3,999	4,170	
$4,000–$4,999	4,943	
$5,000–$5,999	5,315	

Thus a total of 10,628,000 families and 3,943,000 unattached individuals were in the poverty-income group. Since there were 45,370,000 family units and 10,680,000 unattached individuals in the country in 1960, this means that 23 per cent of all families and 37 per cent of all individuals were living in poverty. An additional 10,268,000 families and 2,090,000 individuals, though not poor, were living on the deprivation level. According to the Conference on Economic Progress, there were 77 million Americans in these low-income categories in 1960. Although some change for the better has taken place since then, it doesn't amount to much. For instance, the number of family units and unattached individuals with less than $2,000 a year declined by only 200,000 between 1960 and 1962.

This is not a pretty picture of an affluent society, especially when one bears in mind that a sizable number of low-income families and individuals belong to minority groups which are victims of racial discrimination. Over the years, however, as is illustrated in Table II, considerable progress in reducing poverty has been made. For the purpose of comparison, all the income figures in the table below are based on 1962 dollars:

TABLE II

Family Income (before taxes)	Families and Unattached Individuals (in millions)		
	1929	1947	1962
Under $2,000	11.2	7.2	7.2
$2,000–$3,999	13.9	12.6	10.9
$4,000–$5,999	5.6	11.7	12.2
$6,000–$7,999	2.4	6.0	10.8
$8,000–$9,999	1.1	3.1	6.7
$10,000 and over	1.9	4.1	10.9
Total	36.1	44.7	58.7

Because of New Deal reforms, full employment and high farm income during World War II, the number of poor fell sharply between 1929 and 1947. Families and unattached individuals with incomes below $4,000 declined from 70 per cent of all families and individuals to 46 per cent. Since 1947, the number of families and individuals with less than $2,000 has remained stable absolutely, but has fallen relatively from 16 per cent of all families and individuals to 12 per cent. On the other hand, there has been a large growth in the income brackets between $4,000 and $10,000. Half of all American families are in those brackets today. Only a quarter were there in 1929. The increase of the comfortable and well-to-do, however, has been even more remarkable. Those with incomes of $10,000 and over jumped from 5 per cent of all families in 1929, to 9 per cent in 1947, and to 19 per cent today.

In a rich country, imbalances in income distribution are less noticeable, and certainly less productive of social disorders, than they are in poor countries. But they are relevant in a rich country, too, for moral as well as economic reasons. During World War II and through 1953, there was a noticeable improvement in the pattern of income distribution in the United States. In recent years, though, that trend has been halted, and even slightly reversed. If we divide all consumer units into five numerically equal groups, it will be seen that the shares of the national income received by the three low quintiles have declined, whereas the shares of the two top quintiles have increased. This is true whether income is considered before or after taxes. In Table III, the income is considered after taxes:

TABLE III

| Quintile | Percentage of Total Income | |
	1955	1961
Lowest	5.2	5.0
Second	11.9	11.5
Third	17.0	16.9
Fourth	22.7	23.0
Highest	43.2	43.6

The top fifth of U.S. consumer units have a considerably bigger share of the national income than the three lower fifths have together. One can easily doubt that this highly unequal distribution of income satisfies the canons of social justice. Some economists believe that it is at least partly responsible for the periodic recessions that have marred the postwar years and for the failure of the economy to grow at a faster rate. That is the logic behind much of the current agitation to concentrate tax reduction in the lower income brackets.

No doubt, the United States is an affluent society, as Prof. Galbraith says. But it is well to remind ourselves that millions of Americans live on the fringes of this society, or even outside it. Their immediate goal in life is not the acquisition of luxuries but the age-old struggle for necessities—for food, clothing and decent lodging. The poor we shall always have with us, to serve and to cherish, but there are many more of them in the United States than there need be or should be. Despite all our progress, the elimination of poverty remains unfinished American business.

SECTION IX

OPEN WINDOWS

JOHN COGLEY
American Catholic Panorama

Some day you would like to write a book about Catholicism in America as you have known it. You keep putting it off, and the relentless years keep passing. The book will probably never be written. But as time goes by, experience broadens, understanding is enriched, complexity becomes more evident. The result is that this year's unwritten book is better than last year's, and next year's promises to be the best yet. Thinking about it, though, is like paging through an album of yellowed snapshots, watching yourself age while the perennial youth of the Church becomes ever more verdant.

The first impressions begin in the parochial school. You can evoke certain sights, sounds and smells from the past and take satisfaction in the knowledge that they are part of the present life of your children: ". . . with liberty and justice for all, goodmorning-sister"; the clink of heavy rosary beads and rustle of black veiling; the exultant swell (combined frequently with a sense of deliverance from captivity) of "Holy God, We Praise Thy Name"; the sudden spring of a May altar; the clinging sweetness of funeral incense hanging on in a church, like the presence of death, after the mourners have left; the special shouts of schoolboy encouragement when one of the Sisters takes a turn at bat; the pastoral eloquence of a report-card compliment; the shattering realization that there is disorder in the universe when ink is spilled on a nun's immaculate white bib.

(You recall such things and realize, all these years later, that because the school was attached to a parish church, with its baptisms, weddings, funerals and liturgical markings of the Christian year, life, love and death seemed as natural as breath; you were steadily exposed to their claim on man—and you even knew, if only in a dim way, that the manifestations of the liturgical cycle taking place at the altar were tied in with the life around you because they celebrated a greater birth, a more inclusive love, a more terrible death, and yet held out the assurance of resurrection.)

You remember, you remember:

A small boy having his first doubts about the power of prayer, and the power of the American idea as well, when the Sister, bitterly resigned, said that the defeat of Mr. Smith proved that none of you should ever hope to be President of the United States—and so soon after her announcement that the Pope is always an Italian. . . .

The Servite high-school teacher, freshly returned from ordination in Rome, speaking with astounding familiarity of such storied places as Saint Peter's Square, the galleries of Florence, the village of Assisi, the processions of Lourdes, even repeating the gossip of the College of Cardinals. The young priest's conversation was full of *ecco's and arrivederci's,* though he was as native to Chicago as the rest of you. You got the impression that, like him, you too "belonged" wherever Catholicism flourished. Though he did not know he was teaching the lesson, through him you first learned that the Thing you knew best in its big-city American manifestation wore a thousand different expressions and yet somehow transcended them all. . . .

A few years later the scholarly Jesuit, taking a satisfaction that was just this side of smugness in the knowledge that the Thomistic wonders being discovered at the campus on the Midway, the cause of a nationwide academic uproar, had been a Catholic possession all along. . . .

Still later, another clerical scholar, this one a Dominican of international reputation, telling your class in Fribourg that there are no theologians in the American Church but only teachers of theology, a young Jesuit named John Murray being perhaps an exception. . . .

Remember the stain of tears on Jacques Maritain's cheek when he said, with infinite sadness, that the fiery chaplain at Princeton simply did not see what harm he was doing, so blinding was his zeal, nor did he realize how long it would take to undo it. . . .

Then—where, oh where is that Sister who blasted your boyhood hopes?—recall a plane landing in Houston, Texas, in September, 1960. The Senator is saving a voice badly bruised by the unrelenting schedule of his campaign. He has been scribbling notes to you. This one reads: "It is rather hard for a Harvard man to answer questions in theology. I am sure my answers will cause a good deal of heartburn at Fordham and B.C." Later, your heart goes out to him, caught in the clerical squeeze-play, when he walks up to the platform and faces his inquisitors. One on the campaign staff, a non-Catholic, whispers to you as the Senator steps to the mike: "Who are those nuns who pray that Notre Dame wins? We need them now."

Remember, remember. . . . The little girls all raising their hands when the curate asks how many intend to be nuns. . . . Rumors that the prettiest nun had once been offered a Hollywood contract, and the perennial fiction that Father gave up a big-league career to enter the seminary. . . . The high-school metaphysician triumphantly demanding to know whether God can make a stone so big He cannot lift it. How does Father get around that one? . . . The shock passing through the room like an electric current when the first one in your class announces boldly that he has lost the faith. There will be others later. . . . The big retreat and one of those worldly-wise, too-traveled missionaries ("At a boys high school in Phoenix last month . . .") letting it be well understood that he knows a great deal more about the Facts of Life than his adolescent congregation, for whom the same Facts seem to be making all the difference between a Catholicity worn easily throughout childhood and a Catholicity become a sudden burden. . . . The common agreement, rarely a complaint, that religion courses are the easiest to pass, require the least work, are taught by the least proficient professors, and seem to have nothing to do with anything else in the course of studies.

The boy grows older. *Remember, remember.* . . . .

The breadline stretched along Mott Street and wound around Canal Street, little fires blazing along the curb in the pre-dawn. You are going to early Mass with Dorothy Day. A few men stop the two of you to complain about the way life has treated them; most are busy keeping warm.

The Catholic Worker house in Chicago closes at the beginning of the war, but what is to happen to the old men, unemployable even in the wartime boom? You bring one of them to the Little Sisters of the Poor. Questions. The nun sits there writing notes. "Any income at all?" "No." "Any insurance?" "None." "Anyone who might be willing to take care of him?" "No one." Your blood pressure goes up with each new social-worker quiz. It subsides abruptly when at last she smiles: "Then he is the most welcome of all. . . ."

The crowd is gathered around a home said to be the scene of heavenly visitations. Reporters have pulled out the Ethelbert Nevin stops, describing the simple faith of the expectant people, their shameless prayers, their thrilling conviction that mountains can be moved. The actual crowd you smell is not the devout assemblage of Breton peasants described in the news columns. This is a gang and it wants action (in the Las Vegas sense). They won't be back tomorrow if there is no performance tonight. Nothing happens. The "miracle" disappears from the headlines. . . .

The parish church near the big Army installation in the South. The Catholic magazines on the rack have been dutifully censored. Articles about the race question have been clipped, like an unnecessary growth on the body of Catholic thought. That way, the pastor reasons, his parishioners will not suffer doubts and will still be given the benefits of Catholic reading. . . .

So many different kinds of parishes you have been involved in, but not really, because somewhere along the line you discovered, at first to your dismay, that though you were to get your name in the *American Catholic Who's Who*, you were destined to remain always an Outsider. . . .

Remember, remember. . . . The big church near the Catholic Worker house, once the pride of the Chicago Irish. When you are going there, the Irish have already moved on. The church is almost empty even at ten o'clock Sunday morning. . . . The suburban crowd fulfilling their Sunday obligation in a barn-like hall, with no "consolation" but only the stark religious reality that a Carthusian might seek (as the Poor Clares break their nocturnal rest, like young mothers arising for an early feeding). But the parishioners are not Carthusians, they are Long Islanders and the magazines are beginning to be full of their desire for comfort, their need for sense-satisfaction. Yet they keep coming to the dreary hall in ever greater number—and isn't that a kind of wonder? . . . The church in Beverly Hills. One of the nation's Our Lady of the Cadillacs. Here and there a movie star in the pews, but the congregation is well behaved or at least blasé—there is no gawking, no special distraction. . . . The transient parish near the railroad station, with its odd impermanence, priests and people like ships passing in the night. . . . The little frame churches in rural America, gifts of the Extension Society. You leave them with a feeling that Catholicism belongs to the cities, Protestantism to the countryside, for there is always a sense of a "Protestant" atmosphere. Obviously a silly idea when you think of wayside shrines, rogation days, etc. But why do you have it? . . . The Broome Street chapel on the lower East Side of Manhattan. When you knew it, the parish took in a single block. You cannot forget the priest, a white-haired Italian who looked like a holy-picture saint. "Be a good man or woman as the case may be," he tells you in the confessional. . . . The sheer perfection of Fr. Ford's Corpus Christi on Morningside Heights and the startling realization that the priest preaching is Martin D'Arcy, S.J. . . . A particular Sunday, the Feast of Christ the King, at the Mission in Santa Barbara. The Franciscans are singing with the kind of free-spirited sweetness that only Franciscans should be encouraged to indulge in, the sermon is excellent, and it seems that Paul Blanshard himself would see the Point were he here. . . . The overdressed church where novena devotions are carried on, over a mike throughout the Mass, and the ushers keep running up and down the aisles to take up third and fourth collections, while the congregation drones "Mother, Dear, O Pray for Me." Do, Mother, do. . . . The Negro parish where the only pale face in the church, were you not there, would be that of the priest. . . .

So many memories, places, different kinds of work, modes of worship, different manifestations of the Thing that makes them all one. . . . Priests—priests in the rectory, the classroom, the gym, lecturing to Newman clubs, scurrying with briefcases into chancery offices, chanting the office in choir, delivering scholarly papers to academic societies, walking the last mile with convicts, orienting GI's to their new life, playing *salon abbé* at fashionable cocktail parties, correcting proofs for diocesan papers. How would you account for them all in the book?

Or nuns. Nuns in the schoolroom, the hospital, the laboratory, the orphanage, the poor family's kitchen, outside Gimbels waiting for alms, moving silently behind cloistered walls, managing retreat houses, taking up parish censuses, writing poetry, administering colleges and social-work projects, washing the bodies of forgotten old women, scrubbing a bishop's floor—and don't forget the one you knew who lobbied for an FEPC law in Washington. It is not true that they all look alike—though, on a subway, when they cast their eyes down that way, it might be so. . . . Don't forget the monks. The hermits of the Big Sur as well as the much-publicized Trappists, the sophisticates of Portsmouth and Saint Anselm's as well as the gnarled lay brothers of a hundred monasteries—Salesian, Premonstratensian, Capuchin, Carmelite, Augustinian, Jesuit, Redemptorist, black-, brown-, white-habited men of God. You will have to account for them all.

Remember, remember. . . . The Holy Name Societies you have known, Catholic Action groups, Third Orders, Vincent de Paul Societies, Catholic War Veterans, the Serra Club meeting you spoke at, the Catholic Poetry Society, the National Catholic Educational Association convention you attended in Atlantic City, where the nuns looked like an invasion of sea-birds along the boardwalk. And why has no one ever asked you to join the Knights of Columbus?

Don't forget. Don't forget. . . . The press: *America*, the *Sign*, the *Catholic World*, *Cross Currents*, *Spiritual Life*, *Our Sunday Visitor*, *Jubilee*, *Novena Notes*, all those Franciscan publications (why are they lined up on the "conservative" side so often?), *Worship*, the diocesan papers, including such different cups of tea as the Brooklyn *Tablet* and the Indianapolis *Criterion*.

Get it all in. Put it all down.

Remember, remember. . . . The boys hawking Father Coughlin's *Social Justice* outside the churches; and Bishop Sheil wiping away the spittle of a woman who contemptuously spat out "Rabbi!". . . . The editors at the Catholic Press Association convention dutifully going up to the head table to get their copies of the "documents" the junior Senator from Wisconsin had waved like a flag throughout the talk; and the Catholic conscientious objectors, who refused to take cover during an alert, being hauled away in a police van. . . . The ever so proper tea dance at the nuns' college; and the harassed young curate trying desperately to keep order at the parish youth center in the slums. . . . The rosy monsignor sopping up the ladies' flattery like a sponge; and Msgr. Higgins challenging Paul Blanshard at the seminar on religion and the free society. . . . The sprightly military hymn to Christ the King enthralling the mammoth youth rally; and the silver laughter of that twisted girl in Yonkers who found her apostolate in pain and suffering. . . . The

retreat preached by an awesomely intellectual priest to a handful of
writers, artists, critics and aesthetes; and the time you wandered
into Saint Francis Church on 31st Street and heard a visiting Pas-
sionist tell his congregation of middle-aged women that were Mary
filling out a passport application, she would surely list her occupa-
tion as Priest's Housekeeper. . . . The Park Avenue matron wring-
ing her hands over Bishop Sheen's latest stellar convert. "Of course,
I am glad to see her in the Church, but I wish she were more like
that Dorothy Day. Miss Day knows her place and stays in it"; and
the earnest young radical suggesting a new order of beatnik friars.
. . . The nervous politician enquiring about how he could "reach"
the bishop; and the busy Washington office-holder studiously leading a discussion of *De Regimine Principum*. . . . Cardinal Spellman
standing on the steps of the cathedral as the St. Patrick's Day
parade swings up Fifth Avenue; and the lonely pastor in South
Dakota taking his evening meal at the town's one diner. . . . The
policemen guarding the home of an unwanted Negro in Cicero,
Illinois; and the burning zeal of Friendship House workers in neighboring Chicago. . . . The Maria Monk pamphlets that poured into
Kennedy's campaign headquarters; and Msgr. Murray patiently explaining a knotty theological problem at a meeting of the National
Conference of Christians and Jews. . . . The fiery anticommunism
of a dozen Communion-breakfast orators; and the low-key recital
of their prison ordeal by two Maryknoll nuns returned from Red
China. . . . A conversation about Catholicism with James T. Farrell
that stretched far into the night; another conversation, same subject, almost as long, with a Jewish convert from the University of
Chicago. . . .

Remember, remember, remember people. . . . J. F. Powers
stoutly resisting invitations to address the next meeting of the
Francis Thompson Literary Society; Clare Booth Luce passionately
defending Richard Nixon's Checkers speech; Sen. Eugene Mc-
Carthy replying to the nun who asked if it wouldn't be better for a
nice young man like Senator Kennedy to lose the nomination so he
would not be forced to make "compromises"; Peter Maurin pre-
dicting that the Vincentian Fathers would find their true identity
by opening houses of hospitality for the unemployed graduates of
Jesuit colleges; William F. Buckley, fifteen years later, reporting
on the burgeoning of campus conservatism at a Catholic forum; Fr.

Gustave Weigel disputing amiably with Paul Tillich before a delighted Catholic-Protestant-Jewish-humanist audience; Mike Quill, on television, telling Mike Wallace that yes, he is indeed a Catholic but religious opinions have no place on a "peep-show"; Anne Fremantle announcing the discovery of the best young Catholic writer yet—can't recall his name; the youthful Ed Marciniak hurrying from the stockyards (where he handed out leaflets quoting *Quadragesimo Anno*) to make his first class at Loyola; Jane Wyatt admitting that when Fr. Peyton came to her with his idea that movie stars could be rounded up to say the rosary over the air, she thought the dear man was incredibly naïve; Fr. Godfrey Diekmann, happy as a child, explaining the symbolism of the new Saint John's Abbey Church; Jean Kerr, even in a serious discussion of parochial schools, lighting one witticism on the butt of the last; William Clancy, on the "Open End" program, tapping Bishop Pike gently on the shoulder: "Don't worry, Bishop, *I* think you are invincibly ignorant"; Ed Willock—an unsung giant, too soon dead—explaining to a group of young matrons that he did not believe there was anything *intrinsically* wrong with washing machines.

So much to cover, so wide the world—Notre Dame; the *Commonweal;* Gethsemane, Kentucky; the American Cardinals; the Christian Brothers; "No Irish Need Apply"; Barclay Street; Emmett McLoughlin; the *American Ecclesiastical Review;* the CYO; the "powerhouse"; the Mindszenty Society; the Laetare Medal; the National Catholic Welfare Conference; the Alexian Brothers; Louis Budenz; birth control law; Fr. Reinhold; the North American College; the *Linacre Quarterly;* Saint Benedict's Center; Eastern rites; the Glenmary Missionaries; the Christian Family Movement; Necedah, Wisconsin; the Military Ordinariate; the Pink Sisters; Fr. Keller; *Liturgical Arts;* the Grail; Senator McCarran; the Paulist choir; Harry Sylvester; Sister-Formation; the Joseph P. Kennedy Foundation; Thomas Merton; the Legion of Decency; the *Messenger of the Sacred Heart;* Msgr. John Tracy Ellis; Ade Bethune; Sheed & Ward; Fr. Ginder; the Catholic Hour; the Association of Catholic Trade Unionists; etc., etc., etc., etc.

It will have to be two or three books. If it can be put off until the year after next, or the one after that, it might be monumental.

JAMES J. HENNESEY
The Church in America

¶New dimensions for the universal Church evolve from our unique
history

One of the facts noticed by observers of the Second Vatican
Council has been the emergence of the American bishops as an
influential voice in the conciliar deliberations. The fact itself is not
surprising. American Catholics *are* different. The Church in the
United States *is* different. No American can live very long in
Europe, or anywhere else in the world, without having that fact
brought home to him. Catholics of other lands, too, have long been
struck by the peculiar phenomenon that is the American Church.
It is precisely in the explanation of this phenomenon—through a
study of Church history—that the contribution American Catholicism can and must make to the universal Church is to be found.

American Catholics frequently regard themselves, their accomplishments and those of their fathers before them with diffidence.
Whether the American Catholic stands on the left or the right or
on dead center, he is all too often affected by a lack of confidence
in himself and in the specifically American characteristics of the
Church as he knows it. For some, the temptation is to identify the
terms "Roman" and "Catholic," to confuse unity with uniformity.
Others feel that for intellectual and spiritual inspiration they must
turn to transalpine Europe. It is there that Catholic thinkers are
really grappling with modern problems.

Ours is a bricks-and-mortar Church, the argument runs, its bishops and pastors are administrators, it has lived in a ghetto, it has
produced no theologians or philosophers worthy of attention. It has
been, at least until the present generation, the Church of an embattled immigrant minority, turned in upon itself, exhibiting all
the characteristics of a minority group. In its zeal to be American,
it has been super-American. In its zeal to be Roman, it has been

super-Roman. Uncomfortable in Protestant America, it has with-drawn into itself.

The argument is a familiar one. I do not suggest that it is completely fallacious. It contains a great deal of truth. It helps to explain the phenomenon of the American Church. The "immigrant minority" theme has been a constant one in American Catholic history. It is a theme that has been explored in any number of books, monographs and articles that have enriched our knowledge of the American Catholic past and therefore of ourselves.

But is the picture quite so one-dimensional? Is there not another side to American Catholic history? In fact, are there not many other sides? In the three-hundred-odd years since the *Ark* and the *Dove* deposited the first substantial contingent of Catholic settlers in English America, has there not evolved a more positive Catholic contribution to American life? And has not America made a more positive contribution to Catholic life that American Catholics can proudly share with the rest of the Church?

Catholicism in the United States, for all its faults, is certainly more generally vital than it is in many countries of the Old World. This phenomenon alone should encourage consideration of how it came to be.

The "minority" theme should not blind us to other, equally im-portant, developments that fill out the picture. Some slight research uncovers a well-nigh infinite variety of attitudes and reactions on the part of U. S. Catholics to the cultural milieu in which they found themselves. What follows is not meant to contradict previous analyses of American Catholicism, but to supplement them.

The first point to be made is that considerable confusion is caused by univocal use of terms that have a special meaning rooted deep in the history of Europe.

"Separation of Church and State" is an obvious example. The separation of the two in mutual respect that grew out of the Ameri-can revolutionary experience and subsequent constitutional de-velopment has little but the name in common with the separation in hostility inherited from the French Revolution that has colored so much European thinking on questions of Church and State.

"Ultramontanism" is another example. In Europe, the word con-jures up memories of men like Count Joseph de Maistre, and the crusading French editor Louis Veuillot, and William George Ward with his papal bull at breakfast each morning. Nineteenth-century

European ultramontanism meant a political as well as a religious devotion to the papacy. In the United States, the situation was quite different, as some examples will show. The American Church has always been ultramontane, but not exactly in the European sense of the word.

When the young Sir John Acton was visiting the United States in 1853, Orestes Brownson remarked to him that "all the American bishops were ultramontanes." In the American understanding of the word, an understanding in which ultramontanism had as its object the spiritual supremacy of the Pope, Brownson was right. But no self-respecting European ultramontane could have, or would have wanted to, accept the declaration made by many of those same American bishops in 1837 at the Third Provincial Council of Baltimore, when they stated unequivocally that they acknowledged no "civil or political supremacy, or power over us, in any foreign potentate or power, though that potentate might be the chief pastor of our Church."

Again, in the decrees of the Second Plenary Council of Baltimore in 1866, the American bishops accepted the argument that, "given the circumstances of the times," maintenance of papal temporal power was "in some sense necessary" for the free exercise of the Pope's spiritual functions, but two years later, in 1868, the Archbishops of Baltimore, Cincinnati and New York did not hesitate to issue a joint condemnation of efforts to recruit an American battalion for the defense of the Papal States against the aggression of the new Kingdom of Italy.

Undoubtedly, the archbishops were influenced by the adverse reaction they knew the project would arouse among American Protestants. But it is too simple an explanation to attribute their stand solely to a defensive "minority" posture. The "thesis-hypothesis" approach in such matters was not, and is not, something natively congenial to American Catholic thinking. In other words, the three archbishops were not shrinking, because of fear of unpleasant consequences, from an obligation they honestly felt was theirs. In the European ultramontanist context, the recruiting of troops for the defense of papal political sovereignty was intelligible. In the American ultramontanist context, where loyalty to the papacy was a religious loyalty, it was not intelligible.

The same American mentality accounts for the fact that the great weight of American Catholic opinion has historically been opposed to the establishment of formal diplomatic relations between the United States and the Holy See. The existence of such relations is intelligible in the context of European diplomatic practice, and in the practice of those non-European nations formed in the European tradition. It is alien to the concept of Church-State relations evolved in the American experience.

Not surprisingly, the peculiarly American approach to 19th-century ecclesiastical problems caused some confusion in European circles, just as it does today. The story of the American bishops in the First Vatican Council provides some illustrations. On the eve of the Council in 1869, Isaac Hecker, founder of the Paulists, discussed the American scene with John Acton's collaborator, Richard Simpson, in London. Simpson reported their conversation to Acton and commented of the American bishops' attitude toward the Holy See: "They have the art of hiding an uncompromising resistance under the show of most hearty loyalty." Simpson misunderstood the Americans because he interpreted them in European terms. They were not hypocritical or Machiavellian. Their loyalty to the head of the Church was uncompromising, but so was their determination to keep that loyalty a religious loyalty, uninvolved in European politics.

The German church historian Ignaz Döllinger, who also met Hecker at about this time, came closer to the truth in his evaluation of the Americans, although the first part of his judgment needs distinguishing. He wrote to Acton that the Americans were "all opponents of the dogma of infallibility, but at the same time very devoted to the Pope personally."

The facts are that most of the American bishops in 1870 were very devoted to the Pope and to his spiritual supremacy, but that most of them would have preferred that papal infallibility not be defined. Of these, the majority acknowledged the fact of the doctrine, but thought its definition inexpedient. They felt, quite simply, that the definition would arouse unnecessary hostility to the Church and that it would hinder the possibility of conversions among non-Catholics. Infallibility was not for them a political as well as a religious question. In Europe, on the other hand, political considerations played a large part in influencing those, including Pope Pius IX, who felt that a clear definition of papal authority was needed in the face of contemporary challenge to that authority, both spiritual and temporal.

In the First Vatican Council, what might be called the "purely religious approach" was typical of most of the American interventions. Even before the sessions began, Archbishop Spalding of Baltimore had expressed his apprehensions that the European experience of Church-State relations might provide the basis for the universal decree of the subject, and that the European-oriented *Syllabus of Errors* of 1864 might be similarly universalized in conciliar definitions. With regard to infallibility, he realized that it would be a major problem to fix the limits of doctrinal definitions. He had no difficulties with formal definition of the Immaculate Conception, but he was concerned with the status of such papal pronouncements as encyclicals and allocutions.

Other American interventions struck a similarly practical note. Bishops from the United States, a predominantly Protestant country, urged full and accurate use of scriptural and patristic foundations in the writing of constitutions, and they insisted on both fullness and accuracy. They were particularly strong in their opposition to too wide a use of accommodated senses of Scripture and the Fathers. A decade previously, the same emphases had been found in the suggestions of Bishop Michael O'Connor of Pittsburgh and Archbishop Francis Kenrick of Baltimore when they were consulted regarding the 1854 definition of the Immaculate Conception. Apologetic reasons were important in the argumentation of the bishops of 1854 and of 1870, just as they were important in the related area of American opposition on both occasions to multiplication of condemnations, but American apologetics in the mid-19th century were not exclusively the defensive kind usually associated with minority groups.

As Archbishop Purcell of Cincinnati, one of the many bishops of the time who was not afraid to engage in public debates on religious issues, remarked: "All we want is a free field and no favor. Truth is mighty and will prevail; and as we are here side by side with every sect and denomination of Christian, it is for the people to judge which of us is right, which of us teaches that which is most conformable to the Holy Scriptures."

Similar examples of a positive approach to religious problems abound in the history of the American Church. There is an authentic American tradition in such matters as use of the vernacular, episcopal collegiality, seminary and university education, the handling of social problems and involvement with the great issues of the day.

In 1787, John Carroll, who three years later became first Bishop of Baltimore, wrote that introduction of a vernacular liturgy was "essential to the service of God and the benefit of mankind." In the early American Church, English was widely used in the administration of the sacraments.

The doctrine of episcopal collegiality found one of its clearest expressions in an 1839 work of Bishop Francis Kenrick, and was reaffirmed in 1854 by Bishop O'Connor, who proposed that it be made clear that the dogma of the Immaculate Conception was defined "with the consent of the bishops." At the First Vatican Council in 1870, Archbishop Spalding was responsible for inclusion of a statement that papal ordinary jurisdiction in no way conflicted with the ordinary and immediate jurisdiction of a residential bishop in his diocese. Uncertainty as to the respective roles of Pope and bishops kept Bishop McQuaid of Rochester from voting for the definition of papal infallibility. The questions raised by Spalding and McQuaid are among those that face the Fathers of Vatican II.

There were other areas in which the American Church was not afraid to insist on values proved by its own experience. Seminary education was one such area. In 1883, the bishops who went to Rome to prepare the agenda for the Third Plenary Council of Baltimore rejected the proposal that summer villas for seminarians be introduced. The American priest did not live in seclusion from the world; the bishops did not want their seminarians educated in seclusion.

McQuaid and Archbishop John Ireland, men who on other issues differed greatly, were one in demanding the highest standards in their seminaries. McQuaid's ideas on seminary formation were quite advanced. He wanted in St. Bernard's none of the "time-consecrated miseries and needless sufferings" found in other institutions. The seminary, to his way of thinking, was not to be confused with a reformatory. "There is no justifiable reason," he declared, "why Church authorities in America should be hampered by the customs and usages of older countries, where innovations are looked on in the light of sacrilege."

In the field of university education, the story of the foundation and purposes of the Catholic University of America deserves attention. It was projected by Bishop John Lancaster Spalding, the

educational theorist of the American Church, as the keystone of a
great Catholic intellectual effort, and men like the first Rector,
Bishop John Keane, worked hard to realize that dream. The growth
of other American Catholic universities, colleges and schools represents a unique contribution to the history and tradition of the
Church.

Other aspects of man's life were not neglected. In an age when
the Church in other countries was becoming alienated from the
working classes, the Church in America exercised effective influence in integrating its largely immigrant constituency into the
mainstream of American democratic life. Cardinal Gibbons' famous
1887 memorandum in defense of the Knights of Labor is one of the
landmarks in the history of the American labor movement. No
segment of the life of its people was foreign to the Church in the
United States.

Another authentically American tradition is that the Church has
not been afraid to involve itself with the issues of the day. John
Carroll accompanied Benjamin Franklin to Canada in a vain effort
to enlist Canadian support for the American rebels. During the
Civil War, Archbishop Hughes of New York undertook a diplomatic mission to Europe on behalf of President Lincoln, as did
Bishop Lynch of Charleston on behalf of President Davis. Hughes
was also largely responsible for putting an end to the Civil War
"Draft Riots" in New York City. At a later date, Archbishop Ireland did his desperate best with President McKinley to prevent
the outbreak of the Spanish-American War.

It is interesting to note that among the men who projected a
positive vision of the Church in America were descendants of the
First Families of Maryland (Kentucky branch) like the two Spal-
dings, and immigrants or the sons of immigrants like Hughes, Ireland
and Gibbons. They were joined by converts from American Protestantism like Orestes Brownson and Isaac Hecker. The only common denominator was that they were all Catholics and Americans,
and the net result of the amalgam was a synthesis that incorporated
Catholicism and Americanism without diluting either. There was,
no doubt, a very extensive and deep foreign influence in the shap-
ing of American Catholicism, but it does not tell the whole tale.

What then is the new dimension for which American Catholic
history provides the materials? It would take the form, I suggest,

of the development of theological and philosophical positions that
make use, within the ample framework of orthodox Catholic
thought, of the American experience. This is not a "Fortress
America" approach. It is simply based on the confidence that American Catholics have something to say that is worth hearing, just as
do European, Asian, African and Australasian Catholics.

American Catholic history has long since passed the stage where
it had to count noses in the Irish regiments of the Continental Army
and hopefully pretend that all the Timothy Murphys were Practicing Papists. There is a new role for it to play. The situation has
come to pass that John Lancaster Spalding foresaw 64 years ago
when he told an audience in the Roman Church of the Gesù:
"There is everywhere freedom to write, to publish, to discuss, to
organize; and there is no subject of thought, no sphere of action,
no interest which it is possible to fence about and shut in from the
all-searching breath of liberty. This condition of things exists;
every influence maintains and strengthens it; and so far as we are
able to see, it does not appear that any earthly power can change or
destroy it."

American Catholicism has lived and developed within just such
a context. As a result, American Catholics *are* different, the Church
in America *is* different, yet American Catholic variety has not dam-
aged its unity with the See of Peter. In the United States the Pope
is, more than in many other places in the world, very much the
Pope. The American Catholic experience is not an absolute, not an
ideal, but is a valid experience, with something to contribute. No
one will suggest that our approach today should be that of a Carroll, a Hughes, an Ireland or a Gibbons. They spoke in their own
idiom, for their own time. But their attitudes and approaches can
and should provide us with confidence and inspiration to do in our
generation what they did in theirs.

As an Italian priest remarked at the beginning of the Thomistic
revival in the last century, Aquinas' genuine heirs should be more
concerned with doing what he did than with memorizing what he
said. It is good advice with regard to American Catholic history.
We need reflection on our collective experience, so as to formulate
conclusions from it. Before that, we need knowledge of that experience. But finally, we must learn to apply our experience to the
needs of the contemporary world, of the contemporary Church.

The tariff barriers have long been down on the importation of foreign insights into American Catholicism. They should stay that way. But American Catholics owe it to the Church to know and to express their own experience, to share it with the Church. The bishops at the Second Vatican Council have the opportunity to do this. So do the rest of us, once we are conscious of, and informed about, our heritage.

EUGENE C. BIANCHI
Protestant Sanctity

¶Is it rooted in the sanctity of the Churches or is it an individual phenomenon?

The ecclesial nature of Protestant communities has been a lively topic of discussion at Vatican II. Various Fathers have urged the Council to refer to Protestant groups as "churches" in the schema on ecumenism. But although official Catholic documents refer to Orthodox communions as churches, this use has not been extended to the Protestants. The ecclesiological character of Protestant and Orthodox institutions such as the World Council of Churches was also a subject of much concern at the Faith and Order Conference in Montreal last year, and again at the WCC meeting in Rochester.

In the Catholic Church's re-examination of her own nature, the relationship to dissident groups unavoidably arises. For the ecumenical surge of our time calls for a confrontation of Christian communities, not simply of Christian individuals. A renewed theology of baptism has made all Christians more acutely aware of their common fellowship in the one Mystical Body of Christ.

But since the "how" of this belonging is not very clear, fresh theological perspectives are needed. I think that a closer look at the experience of sanctity, as it exists in Protestant communions, may provide a fruitful theological angle for exploring the problem of church status in separated Christian bodies.

In Catholic circles, the conversation about the ecclesiological nature of Protestant groups usually revolves around an accepted set of questions. What about their union with Rome? Have they rejected essential doctrines? What is their stand on sacraments? Are their orders valid and what kind of ministry do they have? Such questions are surely important for our Catholic understanding of separated communities. But perhaps we have overlooked a very crucial question: To what extent do these Christian families show the mark of holiness? This query opens an interesting, and as yet rather uninspected, horizon on the ecclesial aspects of Protestant communions.

From one point of view, holiness can be seen as the culmination of the other traditional marks of the Church. In this sense, the Church's unity, apostolicity and catholicity are ultimately directed toward holiness. The qualities of oneness, apostolic origin and universality are oriented to the building up of a fellowship of love in a chosen race, a holy priesthood, to paraphrase St. Peter's first Epistle. That Epistle (1:15–16) exhorts: "As he who called you is holy, be holy yourselves in all your conduct; since it is written, 'You shall be holy, for I am holy.'" J. A. Moehler, the famous Tübingen theologian of the last century and forerunner of today's renewed Catholic ecclesiology, envisioned all ecclesiastical laws and hierarchy as directed to fostering a communion of love in God's holy people. It is mainly in this light that canonical ordinances make Christian sense.

But four hundred years of polemic and religious isolation separate Protestants and Catholics. This long divorce has somewhat dimmed our insight into the deeds of sanctity inspired by the Spirit in separated communities. Pope John, at the beatification of Mother Elizabeth Seton in 1963, reminded us that she had been prepared "by the whole course of her former life"—a life of study, prayer and charity in the Episcopal communion—to become a "wonder of heavenly grace." A similar point was made by Pope Paul, in his opening address to the second session of the Council, when he spoke of the "treasures of truth and genuine spirituality" among other Christian communities.

Now let us take a closer look at the meaning of holiness. God alone abides in ineffable and incomprehensible holiness. But the Father reveals His sanctity to men in Jesus; and it was in Him, especially as the risen Saviour, that "the fullness (pleroma) of God was pleased to dwell" (Colossians 1:19). The risen Lord sends the Pentecostal Spirit into the Christian community, the Church, as the constant source of her essential beliefs, sacraments, ministry of the Word and hierarchical structure. Thus, from our point of view, the Church herself, inasmuch as she inherits Christ's pleroma, is holy in the first and foremost sense. This in no way denies the faults and miseries of the Church as also made up of fallible humanity. Fr. Yves Congar, O.P., speaks of holiness in that which is "from above," and sinfulness in that which is "from below." Without essentially tainting what is from God, these elements from above and below live in an earthly symbiosis.

Now, all the faithful, though sinners and constantly falling away from grace, share in and witness to Christ's sanctity in the Church. Yet prior to any individual holiness, there is the primordial sanctity of the corporate Church, as the Body of Christ. This is a key point. Holiness is first an ontological "givenness" from the Father through Christ and the Spirit to the Church community. Only secondarily do Christians as individuals participate in the Church's holiness either through Word and sacrament, or through a moral life of co-operation with grace.

When, however, we turn to consider the sanctity of separated Christians, we find a tendency among Catholics to view Protestant holiness solely as an individual phenomenon. We admire the selfless zeal of Protestant missionaries, leading them at times to martyrdom. We respect their charitable dedication to the poor and the sick. Their thirst for social and racial justice assumes at times heroic proportions. We are inclined, nevertheless, to see them as so many generous individuals, responding to the Spirit, speaking outside the body of the Catholic Church. We are accustomed to viewing their mystics, as does Anne Fremantle in *The Protestant Mystics* (Little, Brown, 1964), in a Plotinian flight of the alone to the Alone.

But how adequate is this view? Individual holiness, in the sense of union with God's will in a brotherhood of love, flowers from a prior, ontological rooting in the given sanctity of the communion of saints, a corporate reality. Even the holiness of a hermit is never isolated from a Church community that bore him to faith and sustains him in grace. It seems to me that we have not paid sufficient attention to an important communal and ecclesiastical element in Protestant sanctity.

Lest I be accused of well-intentioned naïveté, a word is in order about the objections of some Protestants to being called "holy." Their difficulty stems not only from abuses in the cult of saints nor from a dislike of canonization processes. But rather, attributing holiness to a man seems to derogate from the sovereign holiness of God, who is, especially in the Calvinist tradition, "wholly other." The Catholic view of participation and the Orthodox concept of "deification," while rejecting pantheism and admitting sinfulness, are more optimistic about man's possibilities for holiness. But ideas of sanctification and perfection are also well known in Protestant bodies. Suffice it, then, to say that I intend the word "saint" in the Pauline sense of those gathered by the Spirit into the churchly community of new life: "Greet every saint in Christ Jesus" (Philippians, 4:21).

The Protestant saint was baptized into the corporate Christ. His faith was nourished by the Word preached in a worshiping community, and often sustained by the sacramental bread received in a Eucharistic assembly. (It is significant that today more Protestant communities stress a real presence of Christ in the Eucharist, however they may doctrinally explain it.) He grew up in a family of believers who enjoyed some form of Christian ministry. Fr. Avery Dulles, S.J., writing in *Theological Studies* in 1960, has illuminated the prophetic and spiritually fruitful character of Protestant preaching, which is fostered by "the institutional structure of the Protestant church." And finally, the Protestant's life of Christian self-giving is fostered in a community of fellowship and service.

Holiness, therefore, in separated Christian communities cannot be understood as merely an isolated, individual and purely charismatic event. This is not said to inculcate a false sense of religious indifferentism. Cardinal Newman, whom we would hardly charge with being indifferent in matters of faith, could say in his *Apologia* of the Anglican communion in which he was formed as a Christian: "The Church of England has been the instrument of Providence in conferring great benefits on me. . . . And as I have received so much good from the Anglican Establishment itself, can I have the heart, or rather the want of charity, considering that it does for so many others what it has done for me, to wish to see it overthrown?" Thus, it is not a question of glossing over religious differences, but of recognizing and exploring spiritual depths.

The words of Pope John and Pope Paul, already referred to, invite us to ponder a new vein of theological thought that they and other leading thinkers have opened. Cardinal Ritter, for example, said of the newly beatified Mother Elizabeth Seton that she "was undoubtedly a saint long before she became a Catholic." This does not denigrate the full flowering of her Catholicism, but it makes us brush aside some of the smoke of Reformation polemic and gain a more integral view of separated Christian families.

An ecumenical era has brought Christians together not simply as individuals, but as members of believing communities. From this fact, a question naturally arises: What does it mean to grow in holiness through a given Christian community? What does this tell us about the ecclesial structure of separated communions? The purpose of this article is not to give definite answers to these queries. I doubt whether such answers yet exist. But I believe that the problem is worthy of much more theological exploration than it has thus far received.

Just before the Council began, Cardinal Bea remarked in AMERICA (8/11/62): "Those who, in all sincerity, accept and live the faith in which they were born and educated, receive—in virtue of their baptism—the necessary aids for a truly Christian life." As the Council approaches the long awaited statement on ecumenism in the next session, it seems imperative that we reflect earnestly on the ecclesial character of the "truly Christian life" of Protestant holiness.

ARCHBISHOP LAWRENCE J. SHEHAN
The Parochial School

¶The Archbishop of Baltimore says there is no reason for panic or pessimism

Recent vigorous criticism of the parochial school, voiced by a number of Catholics, forces all of us to re-examine the true worth of what has long been considered the most distinctive and valuable asset of the Church in the United States. Since the time when the Third Plenary Council of Baltimore wrote into our Church law the famous statute on Catholic education, the parish school has been commonly regarded as the necessary instrument for the preservation and development of the Catholic faith among our people. Every phase of our Catholic life has been profoundly affected by it. Few can doubt that the true strength of the Church in the United States has in large measure been the product of the parochial school system.

That this system, grown so rapidly from humble beginnings, has been far from perfect, we have all known very well. The great efforts made by religious teaching communities and diocesan agencies of supervision to improve and strengthen our schools bear witness to our consciousness of their shortcomings. What concerns us, then, is not that the defects of these schools should be criticized; for that, if accompanied by constructive proposals for improvement, could be helpful. What causes us apprehension is that some of our own people should attack the very existence of the parochial schools as if they had become an unbearable burden, dragging the Church down, impeding her progress and preventing her from fulfilling her mission to the people of this country.

It is being said, for instance, that the quality of education in the parochial school is poor and that there is little or no hope of its improvement; that the supply of religious vocations within the teaching communities is dwindling to such an extent that religious teachers, who have made the schools possible and have given them their special character, will soon be greatly outnumbered by lay teachers; that the payment of a just wage to the latter and other rising costs of education are creating an unbearable financial burden for the Church generally and particularly for Catholic parents. It is, we are told, no longer necessary to bear this burden, since the once hostile attitude of American non-Catholics and the sectarian atmosphere of the public schools, which formerly made Catholic schools necessary, now no longer exist. With neutral public schools, recognition of full parental responsibility and its exercise, together with development of strong parochial units of the Confraternity of Christian Doctrine, are proposed as a substitute for the parochial school that, under present conditions, is in every way preferable. Finally, since the parochial school has been the product of the "state of siege" and "defense mentality"—clichés dear to our critics—and since they perpetuate the "Catholic ghetto," they are contrary to the new spirit of Catholic ecumenism. Hence their time is up, and they must go. This, I believe, is a fair statement of the opinion of present-day Catholic critics of our schools.

The point of criticism that first demands our attention is that which is directed at the quality of parochial school education. If, indeed, the level of education given in Catholic schools were notably inferior to that offered in public schools, with little or no hope of improvement, then it would be difficult to justify the continued existence of the parochial school; for we could be quite sure that the quality of religious instruction would be no better than that maintained in other subjects.

Admittedly, it is difficult to make a fair comparison of two systems of education that vary so greatly from community to community. One study, however, with a relatively wide base, giving the comparative results of public and parochial school education, was recently made by Robert H. Bauernfeind and Warren S. Blumfield and published in the Summer 1963 number of *Education and Psychological Measurement.*

This study gave the comparative performance of eighth-grade public and Catholic school students who took the Science Research Associates high school placement tests in 1959 and 1960. The 1959 tests, administered to 80,000 children of public schools and 60,000 of parochial schools, showed that the group from parochial schools scored a mean Grade Equivalent one year higher than the other sample. The 1960 tests, administered to 120,000 public school students and 100,000 from parochial schools, showed that the Catholic school students scored about one-half a year higher (0.45 to be exact) on their achievement tests in Language Arts, Arithmetic and Reading. The authors of the study conclude with the observation that it is important to note that these broad findings will not necessarily apply to any given local group of parochial school and public school children. "But *on a national basis,* circa 1960, *Catholic school eighth-grade groups showed significantly higher levels of achievement* in three curriculum areas than did public school eighth-grade groups." (Emphasis mine) I have not seen references to this study in any of the recent criticism of the parochial school. This, it seems to me, is indicative of the level of competence of the critics if they did not know of such a study, or of their bias and prejudice if, knowing of it, they did not use it.

It may be argued that no matter what the quality of parochial school education may be, still the price that must be paid for it is beyond what our Catholic people are able to bear; or at least the anticipated results cannot possibly warrant the sacrifices required and the disadvantages entailed. The sacrifices and disadvantages are rightly attributed in large measure to the great disparity between the number of teaching sisters available and the needs of Catholic schools.

From the beginning, the development of the parochial school has depended above all on the communities of teaching sisters. Without them, the Catholic primary school program, as we have known it, would have been impossible. They still remain the key factor of the whole operation. It is well known, however, that in every diocese of the country there is a serious shortage of sisters, and that this dearth has been felt particularly in the past few years. One popular magazine has thus "ominously" stated the case: "During the year 1962 there was a decline of religious teachers in Catholic schools in the number of 1,643, or 1.31 per cent." Put thus baldly, the prospect does indeed seem alarming. But the author of the article failed to mention some important factors that have brought about the present apparent decline.

Within the past few years, many religious communities—all the larger ones—have pledged themselves to send up to 10 per cent of their active sisters into the missions, especially to South America, where their services are needed even more than in the United States. Furthermore, up until the recent past, it was customary in many religious communities for young sisters to be assigned to classroom work while pursuing their higher studies in summer schools and in afterschool classes. Now, however, it has everywhere been agreed that this was an unwise policy, dictated by the pressures of the moment. Not only have religious communities abandoned this procedure, but they have also withdrawn a considerable number of their sisters from teaching posts to permit them to advance their education and acquire postgraduate degrees as full-time students.

This new policy has caused certain gaps in existing staffs and a temporary interruption of the regular flow of teachers into classrooms. When this period of special stress has passed, we can expect a filling of the gaps and a resumption of the normal flow. Meanwhile, many communities are providing increased facilities for religious formation and teacher training, clearly indicating that they have no doubt about future growth. With good programs of vocation recruitment, there is no reason to doubt that the future will see an increase in the number of teaching sisters. I do not mean that the supply will meet the demand in the foreseeable future; but the picture, I believe, is not nearly so dark as some have thought it necessary to paint it.

But though increase in religious vocations meets our highest expectations, still the parochial school will continue to be faced with grave financial problems. Catholic parents are seriously burdened with the double cost of education. One of our most important tasks is to see to it that they are relieved of this injustice. Perhaps relief in the form of tax credits or some kind of direct public aid to Catholic elementary and secondary education may not be so far away as it seemed a few years ago. The recent proposals regarding Federal aid to education and the prospect of yet another tax burden being imposed upon Catholic parents for exercising their natural and constitutionally guaranteed rights have alerted many to this injustice. As is well known, there has been a notable shift in the polls of opinion on this question. A growing number of those who had formerly expressed opposition to or doubt about the advisability of including Catholic schools in a program of Federal aid to education are becoming convinced that some just measure of help is due parents of children in these schools. An increasing number of authorities on constitutional law openly affirm that there are no insuperable constitutional difficulties in the way of implementing these rights by tax credits or other means. There is, I believe, no reason why such a system of help as has been practiced for some time in England, Holland, Ireland, France and Canada, should not eventually be put into effect in the United States.

Such public help to the cause of parochial school education, however, may still be in the distant future. Meanwhile the burden remains. But it is scarcely so great as to warrant either panic or pessimism. When we recall that our forefathers in their straitened circumstances brought into existence, developed and maintained the parochial school system, we can hardly believe that, in the greater affluence of the present, Catholic parents will be unwilling to make the sacrifices needed for their children's religious education.

But are these sacrifices really necessary? It is indeed true that the conditions that brought about the development of the parochial schools in the 19th century have greatly changed. We do not find the old anti-Catholic spirit, at least not in its intense bitterness, in our present-day American society. The once dominant influence of sectarianism has disappeared from the public school. But can it be said that Catholic children can best receive their secular education in the public school, and that parental responsibility and the Confraternity of Christian Doctrine can be counted on to give them religious instruction and training?

All who are concerned in any way with religious education will readily admit that, with or without parochial schools, the fulfillment of parental responsibility is an essential factor in the religious development of the child. Without it very little can be accomplished. In individual cases, where for some reason Catholic schools have not been available, some parents, with the help they have received from the Church, have succeeded very well in the religious instruction and training of their children. But no one who has reflected on the subject will say that parents generally, without help, can be expected to fulfill this task.

Nor can it be said that the Confraternity of Christian Doctrine is an adequate substitute for the parochial school. Although its program, particularly as developed in this country, has proved remarkably effective in some places, yet in the nature of things it suffers from certain very serious limitations. In passing this judgment I speak from long personal experience. In the parish in which I was pastor for many years and in the two dioceses in which I have carried the over-all responsibility, there was present in this field leadership—clerical, religious and lay—of a very high order. The program in each case was as strong, active and effective as circumstances seemed to permit. The results, all things considered, were, I believe, as good as could be expected. But in no case did the Confraternity prove an adequate substitute for Catholic education. It simply seemed impossible to reach and to hold many of the young people once they had arrived at the period of adolescence. And this seemed especially true in the larger centers of population. Nor was the program, with its hour or hour-and-a-half of religious instruction per week, truly adequate.

I would not have it inferred that I am belittling the importance of the Confraternity. On the contrary, with more than half our children in public schools, I consider it just as important as the parochial school and the Catholic high school—more important in the sense that it attempts to reach those who have most need of religious instruction, guidance and training. I am simply saying that the Confraternity is not an adequate substitute for religious education.

Our belief in the need for religious education, and hence for the Catholic school, derives from the very nature of education and from the impossibility of eliminating religious instruction and values from the school system without doing great harm to education itself. For the object of education is truth—the whole truth, in which religious truth occupies a pre-eminent place and exercises an integrating force. Christian education is just as deeply concerned with other aspects of truth as is any other educational system; but it has a deep and special concern for the religious teaching of the Christian revelation, part of which is contained in the Old Testament, handed down by Israel, God's chosen people of the Ancient Covenant.

To exclude religious truth, the truth about man's origin in God and his ultimate destiny, is to truncate education. Our conviction that religious truths and values are an essential part of education will cause us to make the utmost effort to hold on to and develop Catholic education at all levels. It will never permit us to exclude those formative years of the elementary school, whatever may be the adjustments required to meet the special circumstances in certain localities.

The need for religious education, and hence for the parochial school, is every bit as acute now as it was in the past. For while the primary responsibility for the complete education of the child, including religious instruction and training, remains with the parents and with the Church, yet modern social conditions make the task increasingly difficult for both. They need the help of the school. When, either voluntarily or under compulsion, the school eliminates religion from the curriculum, it actually impedes the task of both home and Church; for it all but marks religion as a subject that is unnecessary and even irrelevant. It leaves with students, parents and others the impression that religion is of little importance—even a detriment to the development of good citizenship and alert social consciousness. Indeed, countless Catholic parents, together with their fellow citizens of other religious faiths, are deeply concerned over the secularism and practical materialism that, in effect, is being forced upon public schools by recent court decisions. It is interesting to note that the rate of growth in non-Catholic religious schools in the past two decades has been greater than that in Catholic schools.

One main defect of education emptied of religious content arises from the fact that religion forms the necessary foundation for morality. The great central truths of religion give the principles of morality their validity as moral law and their binding force in conscience. The elimination of religion from education is bound, in the long run, to contribute to the weakening and even the undermining of those moral principles and standards which not only are imperative in the life of the individual but are also the foundation, the indispensable underpinning, of our country, our civilization and indeed of society itself. For this, history is our witness. In the words of George Washington: "Reason and experience both forbid us to expect that national morality can prevail in exclusion of religious principle."

If education by its very nature requires that religion form part of, and be integrated into, the curriculum of the schools, and if religious truth is the very foundation of morality, it is scarcely necessary to dwell at length on the argument that the Catholic school by its nature is contrary to the modern spirit of ecumenism. Both Pope John XXIII and Pope Paul VI have given the answer to such an argument in insisting that the movement for Christian unity can never be fostered at the expense of Christian truth, and that true ecumenism must be carefully distinguished from a false irenicism. Having said this, however, we hasten to add that our schools must be suffused by that renewed spirit of charity which has been the first fruit of the Second Vatican Council. In the past these schools have undoubtedly been affected by the unfriendly atmosphere in which they were born and through which they lived. They can continue to serve as effective instruments of the Church only if they are animated by the Pentecostal spirit of the Council.

Other changes must take place in our schools if they are to remain a valuable tool of Catholic education. Already they enjoy one considerable advantage: while for the most part they have incorporated sound developments in educational psychology, they have not fallen victims to the so-called progressivism that has played so much havoc in modern elementary education. But now more than ever it is necessary that they keep abreast of every true ad-

296 ARCHBISHOP LAWRENCE J. SHEHAN

vance in the field of pedagogy, particularly in training in the basic skills and in the presentation of the fundamentals of mathematics and the natural sciences. Especially they must be alert to important developments in the field of religious education. The liturgical reform, so dramatically inaugurated in the Second Vatican Council, undoubtedly calls for a new approach to religious instruction. Modern Catholic scripture scholarship and new theological insights are destined not to remain in the rarefied atmosphere of biblical criticism and theological speculation. They have profound implications for the whole field of religious education at every level. They offer unmeasured riches, interest and vitality for the presentation of the unchanging truths of Christian faith and Catholic teaching.

This new leaven of liturgical renewal, of scriptural study and of theological insight, together with our efforts to perfect both curriculum and teaching, should bring substantial improvement to parochial schools. These will not, however, solve all our problems. For some time, no doubt, we shall have to suffer patiently the barbs of criticism.

Some of our critics speak as if all problems and defects are found in the parochial school, passing over in silence the shortcomings of its public counterpart. It is true that, with the public treasury to draw upon, state schools do not face financial problems as serious as those that we have to meet. There are, however, some difficulties that they share with us. Others affect them in a special way. In some parts of the country there is said to be a shortage of public school teachers and a serious problem of keeping good teachers within particular systems. One great public school system of this country has been plagued with teachers' strikes and threats of strike. Boycotts by students and picketing by irate parents have threatened the peace and orderliness necessary to the schools. Problems of discipline and even instances of violence have received more than their share of publicity. And the problems arising from programs of integration can hardly be said to belong particularly to Catholic schools or to be confined to the schools of any one area.

Both the Catholic and the public schools are faced with serious problems in the performance of the essential task of giving their students the best education of which they are capable. They ought not to be looked on as rivals—certainly not as enemies. They are both here to stay. They will both continue to expand and develop. They should be friends and partners. In meeting their problems, each needs the co-operation and support of the other. It is only as friendly partners that they can enable the great system of American education to maintain its traditional diversity, to attain its greatest efficiency and to produce its best results. Criticism, on the part of some Catholics, aimed at the elimination of the parochial school may cause us additional problems. It will serve a good purpose, however, if it spurs us to remove as soon as possible every cause of justifiable complaint.

ROBERT PELL

An Appeal for Christian Unity

That distinguished lawyer and businessman, Myron C. Taylor, who dedicated his latter years to diplomacy in the highest sense of the term, has quietly "set sail," as he was wont to say, "for that other shore." He has left behind with those who knew him and worked with him memories of unflagging loyalty to principles and men, of tireless devotion to what he conceived to be his duty and his unquenchable Christian faith. I had the privilege of working with Ambassador Taylor from 1938, when I was assigned by President Roosevelt as his Assistant at the Evian Conference on Political Refugees, until he left public life in 1950 upon resigning as the Personal Representative of the President of the United States to His Holiness the Pope. I can think of many episodes which would illustrate his high qualities, but none more poignant than his conversations in 1948 with leading churchmen to promote unity—among Christians and others who believe in God—in the face of the mounting threat of international atheism and materialism, and in the interest of peace.

Early in 1948 President Harry S. Truman decided that the time had come to appeal for the cooperation of the religious forces of the world to resist communism and turn the influence of all those who believed in God toward the positive preservation of peace. The President had held informal preparatory exchanges to this end with Pope Pius XII through the mediation of Mr. Taylor. He had discussed this "thought," as it was regularly described, with Protestant leaders, notably Bishop G. Bromley Oxnam and Dr. Samuel McCrea Cavert. He had consulted outstanding Jewish personalities and was in communication with Muslim leaders.

By March of 1948, the President decided that the time had come to translate his "thought" into action. Accordingly, he called Ambassador Taylor to the White House in the week of March 20 for talks about his plan. This review of the possibilities led to the President's decision to send Mr. Taylor on a "voyage of exploration," in which the Ambassador would discuss the President's "thought" with the outstanding churchmen of the Christian world. Then, if agreement could be reached among Christians on a simple, positive formula, others who believed in God would be brought into the conversations. Accordingly, on March 23, President Truman gave Mr. Taylor a commission appointing him as his Personal Representative, with the rank of Ambassador, for these exploratory conversations. At Mr. Taylor's request, the President designated me to accompany Mr. Taylor, with the rank of Minister.

At once, Mr. Taylor set off for his post at Rome, as his point of departure, by way of Lisbon and Madrid.

In Lisbon, Mr. Taylor conferred at length with the Catholic Patriarch of Lisbon, Cardinal Emanuel Gonçalves Cerejeira, to whom were confided the revelations of the three children who had the vision at Fatima. On the basis of these revelations, the Cardinal was confident that the tide of godless communism would recede when faith was restored in the Christian world. Mr. Taylor, fortified by the Cardinal's confidence, then flew to Madrid where, at the suggestion of highly situated persons in the Vatican, he had an appointment to meet Cardinal Pedro Segura y Saenz, Archbishop of Seville, who was reported to be unbending with regard to any contact between the Catholic Church and the Protestants.

Ambassador Taylor met Cardinal Segura in the Episcopal Palace in Madrid, with Cardinal Pla y Deniel, Archbishop of Toledo and Primate of Spain, acting as host. The ensuing conversations between Ambassador Taylor and the Cardinal were on a high plane of objectivity, although it was clear that Cardinal Segura had serious doubts about the feasibility of joint action by Catholics and Protestants. Nevertheless, he seemed to be won to sympathize with Mr. Taylor's moving message in behalf of President Truman.

Those of us who were present concluded that, at the very least, the Cardinal would not raise his voice in opposition to the President's appeal to the conscience of the world.

Thereupon, Mr. Taylor continued his flight to Rome, which he reached on April 4. The next day he visited the Vatican for a protracted review of the President's "thought" with Pope Pius. Mr. Taylor carried a brief, courteous letter from the President, but the main body of the message was oral, developed at some length by Mr. Taylor in a series of meetings with His Holiness, which took place on the balcony outside Pope Pius' private apartments.

Pope Pius XII was not only favorable to President Truman's "thought," but was prepared to support it in a letter to the President. This letter His Holiness handed to Mr. Taylor some days later, and it was considered by experts with a broad knowledge of Vatican practice and history as unusually liberal. Moreover, His Holiness gave Mr. Taylor permission to show a copy of the letter to other Christian leaders in the course of his exploratory tour.

President Truman thereupon directed the Commander-in-Chief in Germany to place his "Potsdam plane" at the disposal of Mr. Taylor. The Ambassador took off from Rome in the second week in April—I was with him and so was Miss Bushwaller, his confidential secretary—with Geneva as the first stop.

PROTESTANT REACTIONS

The object of Ambassador Taylor's visit to Geneva was to confer with the Provisional Executive Committee of the World Council of [Protestant] Churches, notably with Mr. Visser 't Hooft, its secretary. Immediately upon our arrival in Geneva Mr. Taylor sent me to notify Mr. 't Hooft that he wished to confer with the members of the executive committee on a matter of grave importance affecting the Christian world, and an appointment was arranged for the same afternoon. The American Consul General had advised the committee previously that Mr. Taylor would come to Geneva on a special mission, so that the Ambassador's arrival was not altogether unexpected. At all events, Mr. 't Hooft stressed to me that the committee was committed irrevocably to the principle of the separation of Church and State. For that reason it could not receive Mr. Taylor as the representative of a temporal sovereign. The members of the committee, as a courtesy, would talk with him, however, as a prominent Episcopalian layman who had important things to say.

At the appointed hour, Mr. Taylor and I presented ourselves at the headquarters of the executive committee. At the gate we were met by a spokesman for that austere body who repeated once more that the committee would not receive Mr. Taylor as the representative of a temporal sovereign. However, the members would be pleased to talk with Mr. Taylor in his capacity as a prominent Anglican, or Episcopal, layman. Mr. Taylor agreed to these terms and was ushered into the Council Chamber, where he was received coldly but with dignity and seated in a stiff-backed chair—I beside him.

Ambassador Taylor then outlined his mission, stressing the vital importance of union among Christians in the cause of world peace, threatened as they were by international atheism and materialism, and urging agreement on a positive statement of their intention of standing together under the banner of Christ. The members of the committee who were present heard Mr. Taylor through politely but without comment. However, they declined to read his Commission from the President or the copy of the letter which he carried from Pope Pius. Indeed, Secretary 't Hooft suggested that a wiser approach would be for the Protestant Churches to come together in the first instance with the President's "thought" in mind. Then, when they had agreed on a formula, approaches might be made to the Orthodox and Roman Catholic Churches. The secretary of the executive committee observed, moreover, that the Protestant Churches were planning to meet in the near future in Ecumenical Conference at Amsterdam. This would be the appropriate place and time to give further consideration to the possibilities of cooperation of the religious and moral forces of the world. He stressed, however, that this meeting would be held completely free from all governmental pressures. There would be no place at Amsterdam for Ambassadors or Personal Representatives of Heads of State. Mr. 't Hooft added that the World Council embraced over 150 Protestant communions in five continents. The Council, and as a consequence its proposed re-union at Amsterdam, was as inclusive as it had been possible to make it by several years of constant endeavor. There did not seem to be any possibility of widening its membership and scope at that late hour, despite Mr. Taylor's appeal to make the meeting inclusive of all Christianity.

I should like to take this opportunity to underscore that Mr. Taylor did not propose on this occasion, as some publications suggested later, that he should go to Amsterdam. Nor did he try to complicate "with the apparatus of diplomacy" what had already been accomplished. He confined his presentation to a solemn and very fervent appeal for contact between *all* Christian leaders, and those who believed in God, in the interest of peace and in defense against the inroads of international godlessness. He urged that this action be taken before it was too late.

From Geneva Mr. Taylor flew to London for a conversation with the Archbishop of Canterbury, Dr. Geoffrey Fisher, in his capacity as head, under the sovereign, of the English State Church. The Archbishop, accompanied by a Coadjutor and an Under Secretary of State at the Foreign Office, joined Mr. Taylor at luncheon in a private dining room at Claridge's Hotel. Dr. Fisher was most cordial but at the same time most cautious. He read President Truman's Commission without comment and expressed pleasure with Pope Pius' letter, which he read over twice. He indicated that the President's initiative was worthy of careful consideration, but indicated that there might be obstacles. However, they could be overcome, and he gave Mr. Taylor his full blessing and expressed the hope that his mission would lead to a concrete result. He would give much earnest consideration and prayer to President Truman's "thought" and would remain in contact with Mr. Taylor through diplomatic channels.

Paris was Mr. Taylor's next destination, where the ground had been prepared for conversations with Pastor Boegner, speaking for the French Protestant, or Huguenot, Church. Mr. Taylor sent me to sound out the Pastor preparatory to a meeting, and I found him far from conciliatory. Indeed, at first he was not sure that it would be possible for him to meet Mr. Taylor at all. Finally, with marked reluctance, he agreed to lunch with Mr. Taylor in a private dining room at the Ritz Hotel. However, he said over and over again that he could not see his way to coming to agreement with the Vatican and that the only form of cooperation which was conceivable, or desirable, was that based on a reaffirmation of their faith by the Protestant Churches, with which the Orthodox Churches might be associated, including the Patriarch of Moscow.

In any event, Pastor Boegner kept his luncheon date with Mr. Taylor, but merely reiterated his previous position. He was uncompromising with regard to cooperation with the Catholic Church, and those who were present could not help recalling the stand taken some weeks previously in Madrid by the Archbishop of Seville. They hoped, moreover, that the Pastor would unbend as far as the Archbishop had.

Finally, Mr. Taylor asked the Pastor point blank if he was to regard the statement of his views as closing the door to any form of further conversation with regard to President Truman's "thought." The Pastor replied that Mr. Taylor might consider his statement in that light. Mr. Taylor, a final time, asked Pastor Boegner to hold the door open at least a cranny while he continued further explorations, but the Pastor replied that he could not in all conscience do this. At least he would interpose no obstacle during the early stages of the talks and would be interested to hear how they progressed. The following day Mr. Taylor wrote Pastor Boegner, renewing his appeal. The Pastor replied with a letter firmly closing the door to further exchanges.

Thereafter, Mr. Taylor met in Paris with representatives of the German and Scandinavian Lutheran Churches. They were less obdurate than Pastor Boegner, but cannot be said to have been encouraging. The Ambassador also talked with the new Patriarch of Constantinople, Athenagoras I, an American citizen who had been obliged to assume Turkish nationality in order to take possession of his see. He was on his way to Constantinople and was most gracious in his meeting with Mr. Taylor. He expressed profound interest in the conversations initiated by President Truman, although he stressed most honestly that he foresaw that many obstacles would have to be overcome. For instance, he must not break irrevocably with the Patriarch of Moscow.

REPORTING TO WASHINGTON

It was now June, and Mr. Taylor believed that he should make a full report to President Truman before entering upon a further phase of the conversations. Above all, Mr. Taylor wished to avoid anything which might appear to be a break. Accordingly, he suggested to the President that it might be wise to have a breathing spell, while emotions cooled. The groundwork had been laid. The

Amsterdam Conference of the Protestant Church would be opening shortly. It might be well to wait and see what transpired there.
Later, when the atmosphere was more propitious and there was a
greater possibility of reaching a concrete accord, the conversations
might be resumed and further considerations given to President
Truman's "thought."

Mr. Taylor thereupon prepared a lengthy report for the President, to which he joined the memoranda of all his conversations
and such documents as might be useful as background. Mr. Taylor
instructed me to fly to Washington with this report and place it
directly in the hands of the President. He would return to Rome,
the seat of his Embassy, from where he could piece together the
various skeins and threads of his preliminary talks. Moreover, Mr.
Taylor directed me to go to Washington via London, where I was
to send word to the Archbishop of Canterbury through the Foreign Office of what had transpired.

I reached Washington, after completing my mission in London,
on June 13. On the 15th I went through what was then called
"the State Department passage" to the White House and placed
Mr. Taylor's report in President Truman's hands. Three days of
deliberation followed, and on June 18 the President handed me a
letter which he instructed me to deliver personally to Mr. Taylor
in Rome. In his letter, Mr. Truman, after congratulating Mr.
Taylor on the manner in which he had conducted his delicate
mission, agreed that the conversations should be suspended for a
time. He said it was deplorable that the Amsterdam Conference
would embrace only a section of Christendom and reaffirmed that
both State and Church had a solemn obligation to man the parapets
of Christian civilization.

In the meantime, plans for the Conference of the Protestant
Churches at Amsterdam had been completed. It had been announced, moreover, that invitations had been extended to leaders
of the Orthodox Churches. Indeed, it has been especially stressed
that these invitations had included one to the Patriarch of Moscow,
who had accepted. Finally, the Congregation of the Holy Office
on June 5 had warned Catholics that they would not be permitted
to attend the meeting. Every day the prospects of agreement
among the leaders of Christendom seemed to be more remote.
Nevertheless, in the thinking of Mr. Taylor, with which I understand President Truman agreed, the conversations were merely

suspended. At some time in the future they would be carried forward from the point where Mr. Taylor, to his profound disappointment and undying regret, left off.

In conclusion, it is my duty to stress that Ambassador Myron C. Taylor's negotiation in the spring of 1948, seeking unity among Christians in the interest of the preservation of peace, was conceived in the highest idealism and carried out step by step with profound sincerity. Mr. Taylor spoke as one modest, faithful Christian to other Christians, in moving, simple language straight from his heart. He tried earnestly to lift the conversations from the slough of politics. He offered modestly to serve as a simple workman in building even one bridge to cross the ravines which separated the churches. He strove mightily to help them find together a few positive words to express their unity in the interest of peace and in their rejection of international godlessness. He may have seemed to falter at one split second in the eternal course of history. But surely Mr. Truman's message, and Mr. Taylor's, still and small though it may seem amid the thunder of jets and missiles, lives on. It is not yet too late to heed it. But it may be, very soon.